Taku Osoegawa is Research Associate at the Institute for Languages and Cultures of Asia and Africa, which is part of Tokyo University of Foreign Studies. He holds a PhD in International Relations from the University of St Andrews.

Taku Osoegawa

Syria and Lebanon

International Relations and Diplomacy in the Middle East

I.B. TAURIS
LONDON · NEW YORK

New paperback edition published in 2015 by
I.B.Tauris & Co Ltd
London • New York
www.ibtauris.com

First published in hardback in 2013 by I.B.Tauris & Co Ltd

ISBN: 978 1 78453 233 8
eISBN: 978 0 85773 434 1

A full CIP record for this book is available from the British Library
A full CIP record is available from the Library of Congress

Library of Congress Catalog Card Number: available

Typeset by Newgen Publishers, Chennai
Printed and bound by CPI Group (UK) Ltd, Croydon, CR0 4YY

CONTENTS

ACKNOWLEDGEMENTS

This book arises from many arguments and debates that were developed whilst I undertook doctoral research at the University of St Andrews, Scotland. During my preparation of the original thesis, Professor Raymond Hinnebusch extended me invaluable academic support by sparing his precious time for discussing international relations theory and contemporary politics in the Levant region. Even after my graduation, he has consistently encouraged me to update the original study for publication and kindly given me shrewd comments on my draft. Thus, I would like to express my sincere appreciation to him for his proper guidance and warm support.

Although this study is owed to broad support that I have received in Japan, Lebanon and the United Kingdom, I would like to express my deep appreciation for the following academics and researchers in particular. Following Mr Koichiro Tanaka's special permit to dispatch me to Beirut, Professor Hilal Khashan offered me a research post at the American University of Beirut from May to October 2009. Professor Hidemitsu Kuroki and Professor Masato Iizuka have afforded me an opportunity to live and research in Beirut since November 2010. Professor Kazuo Takahashi, Professor Tomoko Yamagishi and Professor Toru Tachibana granted me opportunities to teach at several universities in Japan: these experiences have stimulated my thought about this book. In addition, special thanks are due to Dr Henrietta Wilkins and Mr Robert Flahive, with whom I have enjoyed friendly discussions in Beirut.

Regarding the process of publication, Ms Maria Marsh, editor of I.B.Tauris Publishers, has warmly supported my writing and quickly answered editorial questions. As my wife, Yoko, has patiently supported me during the process, I dedicate this book to her. My parents, grandmother and aunts and my wife's parents have always encouraged this project.

ABBREVIATIONS

ADF	Arab Deterrent Force
ASR	Arab Security Force
CDR	Council for Development and Reconstruction
CIA	Central Intelligence Agency
DFLP	Democratic Front for the Liberation of Palestine
FNC	Free National Current
Future TV	Future Television
GCC	Gulf Cooperation Council
GLC	General Labour Confederation
IAEA	International Atomic Energy Agency
IIIC	International Independent Investigation Commission
LBCI	Lebanese Broadcasting Corporation International
LF	Lebanese Forces
LMN	Lebanese National Movement
MNF	Multi-National Force
MTV	Murr Television
NBN	National Broadcasting Network
NDC	National Dialogue Committee
NLP	National Liberal Party
NSF	National Salvation Front
PFLP	Popular Front for the Liberation of Palestine
PFLP–GC	Popular Front for the Liberation of Palestine–General Command
PLA	Palestine Liberation Army

PLO	Palestine Liberation Organization
PNSF	Palestine National Salvation Front
PSP	Progressive Socialist Party
SALSRA	Syria Accountability and Lebanese Sovereign Restoration Act
SLA	South Lebanese Army
SNC	Syrian National Council
STL	Special Tribunal for Lebanon
UNIFIL	United Nations Interim Force in Lebanon
WMD	weapons of mass destruction

CHAPTER 1

INTRODUCTION: THE ANALYTICAL FRAMEWORK

By investigating Lebanon's own reasons for aligning with Syria, this book aims to answer the following question: Which theories of international relations are most relevant, or are best-suited, to explain Lebanon's relations – particularly its bandwagoning – with Syria from 1970 (when the Asad regime was established) to the present day? To achieve this aim, the actions and attitudes taken by Lebanon's political leadership, specifically the presidents and prime ministers, towards the Syrian regime are primarily focused on, although this study explores Syrian policy towards Lebanon. The aim of this introductory chapter is to lay out the broad perspective considered in this book by providing an overview of the literature on contemporary Lebanese–Syrian relations and the focal point of this study, by situating it within the field of international relations theory and by presenting the plan of this book.

A Brief Survey of Previous Works and the Focal Point of this Study

There is a vast amount of literature on Lebanese and Syrian affairs, specifically a dramatic increase in the number of studies on Lebanese–Syrian relations following the outbreak of the Lebanese Civil War in 1975, when Syria's deep involvement in Lebanon started. Most of the literature on relations between the two countries focuses on Syrian motivations and behaviour towards Lebanon, and numerous interpretations are put forward by a variety of academics and journalists. Their analyses fall mainly into one of the two schools, according to whether external or internal factors surrounding the Syrian regime have affected its Lebanese policy.

Works emphasizing the external factors include those of Avi-Ran (1991), Chalala (1985), Dawisha (1980 and 1984), Deeb (1989), Faksh (1992), Harris (1985), Hinnebusch (1986 and 1998) and Seale (1988). Their interpretations are that the civil war in Lebanon provided Syria with both opportunities and reasons for intervening in Lebanon, thus allowing Damascus to help its Lebanese allies whenever they faced difficult situations and to act as a mediator among the feuding Lebanese. More importantly, however, the turmoil also gave Israel an excuse to intervene militarily in Lebanon. On the basis of the recognition of Lebanon – especially the Biqa' region in the eastern part of the country – as Syria's 'soft underbelly', its policy was determined by the extent to which the civil war threatened its national security. Moreover, the conflict potentially meant the partitioning of Lebanon, which could have acted as an opening for Israel to intervene, something which greatly worried Syria, thus influencing its policy-making.

As a result, it is the general interpretation that Syria intervened to save Lebanon from being partitioned and to stop the conflict, even though Damascus would sometimes support the fighting to its own advantage. As Harik (1997), Hinnebusch (1998) and Perthes (2001) suggest, this school also presumes that even after the end of the civil war in 1990 the Israeli threat has continued to be a key factor determining Syrian policy towards Lebanon.

Works focusing on internal factors include those of Abukhalil (1994), Lawson (1996), Ma'oz (1988) and Pipes (1990). Among these is a sectarian explanation arguing that Syria's 'Alawi-dominated regime led by President Hafiz al-Asad feared that the Muslim, especially Sunni, power and success in Lebanon would affect the Sunni community in Syria and ultimately lead to a Sunni domestic rebellion against the Ba'th regime. According to this view, Syrian policy towards Lebanon was supposed to have been shaped by the internal security situation of the Asad regime. On the other hand, an economic explanation, such as that offered by Lawson (1996), argues that Syria's depressed economy, such as its capital shortages, had led the regime to seek to exploit Lebanon's economic assets as a means of maintaining the loyalty of the regime's supporters by permitting them to be involved in Lebanese businesses.

There are a number of weaknesses in the arguments of the latter school. First, Hafiz's reign (1970–2000) had been fairly stable except for a few occasions such as the Hama revolt in 1982 and the period of his illness between 1983 and 1984. By subordinating non-governmental actors in Syria and thus freeing the regime from domestic pressure, he was able to adopt a foreign policy based on the most important national interest for Syria, i.e. its protection from Israel. In fact, Syrian concern about an Israeli intervention in Lebanon prompted it to align itself with Lebanon's Christian-Maronites against the Muslim groups and the Palestine Liberation Organization (PLO) in 1976, in order to prevent the possibility of a decisive victory by the Muslim–PLO coalition, which would have raised the chances of an Israeli penetration into Lebanon. The succeeding regime led by Bashar al-Asad, one of Hafiz's sons, has generally managed to spare Syrian foreign policy from domestic pressure, although the fierce domestic opposition to the regime since the spring of 2011 might influence its foreign behaviour in the near future.

The second weakness, which was especially found in Lawson's argument, is that despite the existence of a certain measure of Lebanese–Syrian economic interdependency – with Syrian elites profiting from it mainly through smuggling – their economic interests do not seem to offer a sufficient explanation for Syrian motivations and behaviour towards the neighbouring country. Indeed, during the civil war in Lebanon, 'the [Syrian] intervention antagoni[z]ed his [Hafiz's] Soviet patron and even when – in the 1980s – the Syrian economy was actually in crisis, he continued policies in Lebanon which jeopardi[z]ed aid from Saudi Arabia and the Arab Gulf states (drives against the PLO and Maronites) and then from Iran (conflict with [Hizbullah])'.[1] Since the end of the civil war in Lebanon, Syria has continuously supported Hizbullah's military presence in southern Lebanon, although it has occasionally restrained the group, lest Israel intervene militarily. If Syria were to cooperate with Western countries to stop all political and military support to Hizbullah, it could gain more economic support in the form of both greater US and European aid and investment.

In general, it seems that Syrian policy towards Lebanon has been mainly shaped by the former state's security concern with regard to Israel. In this context, since Syria has tended to favour maintaining the status quo in Lebanon and stabilizing the country, its principal leaders have overall viewed Syrian involvement in their state positively, which could reinforce Lebanon's general tendency to align itself with Syria.

A number of works focus on Lebanon's political and economic dynamics during the civil war, as represented by Abul-Husn (1998), Deeb (1980), Dessouki (1988), Hamdan (1997), Hanf (1993), Kassir (1994), Koury (1976), Petran (1987), Rabinovich (1984) and Sirreiyeh (1989). These works naturally refer to Syrian policy towards Lebanon, since Syria was the main protagonist among the states that had intervened in the Lebanese conflict.

Later, after the end of the civil war in 1990, Syria's position in Lebanon was further strengthened and 'legalized' by the conclusion of the Lebanese–Syrian Treaty of Brotherhood, Cooperation and Coordination on 22 May 1991. Indeed, among those works that studied Lebanon's political and economic dynamics during the post-civil war period, Ellis (2002), Hudson (1999), Khazen (2001), Najem (2000), Nizameddin (2006) and Norton (1999) focus on the impacts of the Syrian position on the dynamics.

Syrian policy towards Lebanon could be characterized by the use of its trans-state ties with Lebanon's groups and figures more than its official ties with the Lebanese government. This has made an interplay between Lebanon's domestic and external factors decisive in shaping the country's political, economic and social situations; both factors have been indeed so interconnected as to be scarcely distinguishable. In addition to Syria's continuous penetration, its enormous influence wielded in Lebanon until 2005, when its hegemony was terminated by the forced withdrawal of the army and intelligence from Lebanon, has generally prompted researchers to shift their focus away from studying the Lebanese government and its foreign policy behaviour as a unitary actor. This is because, unlike countries 'where foreign policy remains insulated from the influence of domestic politics and well guarded by the regime in power, the demarcation line between foreign and domestic politics [has been] blurred in Lebanon'.[2] It is indeed very difficult to trace the foreign policy of the divided and penetrated Lebanese state. Salem (1994) also suggests the difficulties in separating foreign policy from domestic politics in a state such as Lebanon under foreign control.[3]

However, since most previous works tended to emphasize the dominance of external powers over Lebanon, especially that of Syria, they fall short of studying Lebanon's – at least the government leaders' – ability to influence or react to dominant Syrians. This study thus aims to fill this gap in the literature and, in particular, challenge the commonly-held claim that Lebanon and its leaders were simple puppets of the Syrian regime from 1975 to 2005, the period characterized as Lebanon under Syrian hegemony.

On the other hand, it seems that there are no existing English and French books with explicit theory-based explanations of Lebanon's contemporary relations with Syria. In order to explain the relationship theoretically, this study considers the applicability of the following theories of international relations: *simple realism*, *complex realism*, *constructivism* and *complex interdependence*. Regarding this point, as Lebanon has been largely penetrated by Syria and thus Lebanese domestic developments have been mostly inseparable from the influence exerted by the strong neighbouring country, this research focuses on the developments where Lebanese presidents' and prime ministers' relations with the Syrian regime, explained by the above-mentioned theories, have been observable. While admitting that international relations theory does not intend to explain domestic developments, it is different in the case of a penetrated state like Lebanon and this study could demonstrate that the theory is quite useful to understand the penetrated state's coping with the powerful state on the former's soil.

A Brief Overview of Theories Relevant to this Study

'Simple Realism': States as Rational Actors Facing External Threats

A state's formation and its power position in the international arena are decisive factors in shaping its external relations. In regards to its state formation, Lebanon has not been a unitary state and non-governmental actors in the country have been generally powerful enough to threaten the government and have, in most cases, kept trans-state ties with Syria. When it comes to its international power position, Lebanon has been a small state in terms of its military strength, which, according to the theory of classical realism represented by Morgenthau (1948), should limit the scope of its external behaviour. Yet the systemic insecurity in the Middle East, which still seems among the most intense in the world, could still be expected to determine Lebanon's external behaviour, as the theory of neo-realism in the writings of those like Waltz (1979) assumes.

Although classical realism focuses on the unit level and neo-realism stresses the systemic one, both theories, which might be termed here a theory of 'simple realism', presume states as unitary actors, and the actual and potential threats that states face as external. In other words, simple realism assumes that since a government represents the whole society, its chief foreign policy concern is security threats, and that since the threats are external, the political leadership of the state behaves as a rational actor trying to manage the international scene. This assumption seems applicable to Syria as a regional middle power.[4]

Once President Hafiz al-Asad consolidated his authoritarian rule,[5] the Ba'th regime – by subordinating and restricting activities of non-governmental actors in Syria – started to enjoy internal stability. This has made it possible for the Syrian regime to conduct its foreign policy relatively free from domestic constraints. Thus, Syria has behaved as a rational actor, effectively coping with external threats posed by Israel by accommodating its foreign policy to the changing regional circumstances in the Middle East. Although Syria aligned itself with the Soviet Union to increase its military capabilities during the Cold War period, Asad, who recognized that strong US support for Israel was paralleled by US concern for maintaining stability in the Middle East, sought to put pressure on Israel to withdraw its army from the occupied Arab territories by exploiting US anxiety.[6] While the United States under President Ronald Reagan 'treated Syria as a Soviet surrogate to be punished',[7] Asad tried to retain a degree of Syria's independence by refusing to sign a friendship treaty with the Soviet Union, although he reluctantly ended up doing so.

After the end of the Cold War, the collapse of the Soviet Union and the emergence of US military hegemony have had great impacts on the Middle East. For Middle Eastern states, such as Iran and Syria, the bipolarity, which made it possible for the Soviet Union to put a check on US power in the region and which also made it possible for them to use the superpower rivalry to their advantage, provided ideal circumstances for the maintenance of regional autonomy.[8] However, the current US-dominated global military hegemony has reduced the autonomy of many regional states in the Middle East and forced them into a greater dependency on the United States, although some have tried to counter US military hegemony by reinforcing their ties with potentially countervailing powers. Under the increased constraints on its foreign policy options, Syria, aiming to dilute the US hegemony, attempted to cultivate ties with Russia, China and North Korea in the military field, and with European countries and Japan in the economic field. At the same time, acknowledging the need for US power to pressure Israel, Syria had carefully taken into consideration US interests in the Middle East until the 2003 invasion of Iraq, when they became incompatible with Syria's national interests.

Based on these domestic and external conditions, Syria's foreign behaviour in the Middle East has been shaped. Following the Israeli state's constitution at the expense of 'Greater Syria',[9] its seizure of the Golan Heights – Syria's natural defence against Israel – in 1967 and its permanent military and economic superiority as well as its potential ability to outflank Syria through Jordan and Lebanon, Syrian regime figures have perceived the Israeli threat as the greatest and most urgent facing their nation. Therefore, Israel has been Syria's main enemy and security preoccupation. As Jordan has become a stable country following its repression of Palestinian guerrillas during 1970's 'Black September', the Syrian–Israeli conflict has been displaced from Jordan to Lebanon, with its permeability and turmoil during the civil war especially raising the likelihood of direct Syrian–Israeli military confrontation on Lebanese soil.

Calculating both Syria's military and economic capabilities rationally, the Asad regime has pursued ambitious but realistic goals vis-à-vis Israel, such as its attempts to recover the occupied lands (above all the Golan Heights) and to achieve Palestinian rights, notably in the West Bank and Gaza, as part of a comprehensive peace under UN Security Council Resolution 242. In this context, Israel has also been Syria's main competitor for influence in Greater Syria (including Lebanon), which Syria still considers its natural sphere of influence and over which it has defined itself as a 'parent state' with special rights and responsibilities. Syrian efforts to seek a power balance against any Israeli threats have inevitably affected its policy towards Lebanon, where it has not only developed a 'deterrence relationship'[10] with Israel, but also alliances with Lebanon's governmental leaders and various non-governmental groups and figures to increase its security.

Unlike the Syrian case, simple realism seems less generally relevant to Lebanon's external behaviour because of the characteristic of its state formation, i.e. the existence of strong non-governmental actors threatening the government, although the theory manages partially to identify external threats, opportunities and options for the state.

How can simple realism deduce Lebanon's external behaviour? Since the weak Lebanese state has been surrounded by the powerful neighbours that have threatened its autonomy – namely, Israel and Syria – simple realism theoretically would expect Lebanon to pursue the following foreign policies: to seek support against these Israeli and Syrian threats among great powers, particularly the United States or France (Lebanon's traditional Western ally); to appease Israel as a counterbalance to Syria; or to appease Syria as a counterbalance to Israel.

However, except in a few cases where Lebanon allied with Israel and the United States against Syria, in general Lebanon has never failed to appease Syria and jump on Syria's bandwagon. As one of the rare cases of Lebanon's balancing against Syria, President Amin al-Jumayyil aligned Lebanon with Israel and the United States against Syria during the first half of the 1980s. In pursuit of winning Western support against the threats posed by Soviet-surrogate Arab neighbours, notably Syria, Jumayyil exaggerated the 'communist threat' and portrayed Lebanon as a barrier to defend the 'capitalist world' in the Middle East under the heightened Cold War context at that time. The other case is that Prime Minister Rafiq al-Hariri on several occasions caused Lebanon to balance against Syria by relying on US and French support. This took place initially from 1992 to 1996 and later in a blatant manner after 2003.

Although the Jumayyil case is explicable by the application of simple realism because of the rare situation where Lebanon's non-governmental actors, especially the Syrian-backed ones, were rather weakened by Israel and thus did not have enough power to threaten the government, Hariri's case was different. This is because under the situation of the non-unitary Lebanese state, the power and influence of Lebanon's pro-Syrian groups and figures and the resulting internal political calculations were non-negligible for Hariri. A neo-realist might say that the change in the international and regional balance of power, which has given the United States an unchallenged hegemony over the world after the 2003 invasion of Iraq, was what was really behind Lebanon's balancing against Syria after that year. However, this explanation using simple realism as theory is undermined by the fact that the strong opposition from half of Lebanon, led by Hizbullah, to the country's balancing against Syria posed domestic constraints on Hariri and thus prevented him from pursing a diplomacy that was free from them. As internal division in a state is what simple realism would never anticipate, it is possible to say that the explanatory power of simple realism is very limited in the case of Lebanon's external behaviour, even though it can be admitted that the international and regional dynamics has influenced it (as neo-realism predicts).

'Complex Realism': Interrelated External and Internal Threats

The theory of simple realism presumes that a state's alignment decision ('balancing' or 'bandwagoning') is predominantly affected by its external constraints and opportunities. In contrast, society-centred approaches such as pluralism view a state's alignment decisions as primarily driven by its internal political incentives and risks. David's (1991) work represents an effort to bridge the gap between the external and internal factors, and the backbone of his theory of 'omnibalancing' is 'that [simple] realism must be broadened to examine internal threats in addition to focusing on external threats and capabilities (that is, structural arguments), and that the leader of the state rather than the state itself should be used as the level of analysis'.[11] His work is based on the assumption that since the political process in many developing countries lacks legitimacy for a majority of the population, internal threats to state leaders may be more urgent than external threats. The omnibalancing theory predicts that most political leaders in these countries who face more immediate and dangerous internal than external threats often appease other states in order to protect the regime from these internal threats.

David's omnibalancing theory, which sees more pressing internal threats as an explanatory factor, influenced the theory of 'omnialignment' advocated by Harknett and Vandenberg (1997), a modified or 'complex' version of realism, and thus their omnialignment theory is termed 'complex realism' in this book. However, in their analysis, states are presumed to face interrelated external and internal threats, which are theoretically 'distinct from responses to primary external or primary internal threats'.[12] A state's leaders thus need to react to interrelated threats by taking the behavioural pattern of 'omnialignments – international alignments that use a combined strategy to deal with internal and external security challenges that feed off one another'.[13]

According to Harknett and Vandenberg (1997), interrelated threats generally occur when externally powerful states exploit a targeted state's domestic instability and support domestic opposition actors in the state.[14] In this situation, the theory of omnialignment, i.e. complex realism, presumes that a state's leaders 'must deal with multiple threats from different quarters'.[15] Regarding Lebanon's relations with Syria since 1970, it is impossible to neglect the fact that Syria has not only managed to maintain various trans-state relations with Lebanon's non-governmental groups and figures in the context of the non-unitary Lebanese state, but also managed to pursue 'divide and rule' in Lebanon's governing body as the government itself has not been generally unitary. As these Syrian-supported Lebanese actors have been, in most cases, in opposition to their presidents and/or prime ministers, the top leaders have had simultaneously to counter both the external threats in terms of Lebanon's disadvantageous power balance vis-à-vis Syria under an anarchic international system and the internal threats posed by these pro-Syrian actors.

Under these circumstances, deducing from Harknett and Vandenberg's (1997) interrelated external and internal threats and strategies used by a state's leadership to cope with these multiple threats, Lebanon's presidents and prime ministers could have the following strategies for Lebanon in relation to Syria. First, they could resist, by relying on the Israeli, US, and/or French authorities, the Syrian regime in order to contain Syrian-backed Lebanese groups and figures ('double balance'). Second, they could resist, with the help of the Israeli, US and/or French authorities, the Syrian regime as a perceived greater threat, while appeasing Syrian-backed Lebanese groups and figures as a perceived less immediate threat ('balance–bandwagon'), though this scenario would be less predictable in reality considering Syria's status quo policies towards Lebanon. Third, they could appease the Syrian regime, as a perceived less immediate threat, while resisting Syrian-backed Lebanese groups and figures as a perceived greater threat ('bandwagon–balance'), although this scenario would be more likely when these groups became less important for Syria or started to violate its national interest. Fourth, they could appease the Syrian regime in order to get support from Syrian-backed Lebanese groups and figures ('double bandwagon').[16]

However, occurrences of the former two, i.e. Lebanon's alignment with Israel, the United States and/or France, have been rare in reality. In general, Lebanon's presidents and prime ministers have appeased the Syrian regime as a perceived less immediate threat, while resisting Syrian-backed Lebanese groups and figures as a perceived greater threat ('bandwagon–balance'); or they have appeased the Syrian regime in order to win support from these powerful groups and figures ('double bandwagon'). Although Prime Minister Hariri on several occasions balanced against the Syrian regime with international support, in particular the US and French after 2003 (when the shift in the regional dynamics of the Middle East, i.e. their negative perception of Syria, enabled Lebanon to find international allies against Syria), in order to contain Syrian-backed Lebanese groups and figures ('double balance'), in general he bandwagoned with the Syrian regime.

The main reason why Lebanese presidents and prime ministers have generally aligned themselves with the Syrian regime seems to be partially due to Syria's status quo policies towards Lebanon. Since the Lebanese state has traditionally (and also in common with many developing countries) had little power to regulate social relations, strong non-governmental actors have emerged in Lebanon, threatening the government and maintaining trans-state ties with other states, especially Syria. Therefore it is unlikely that the Lebanese leaders have ignored the effects of penetration and manipulation of the domestic political system by Syria. In general, penetration is 'more effective against open societies',[17] and the success of penetration is dependent on the intention of the penetrating state.[18] If a state seeks to establish or strengthen an alliance with a targeted state by manipulating the attitudes of the leaders and general public, it is unlikely that this behaviour is perceived as a grave threat to the state's independence.[19] However, if a state seeks alignment in order to subvert the regime of the other state, it is likely that the regime takes a hostile attitude towards the penetrating state.[20] Since the Syrian case has generally been of the former category, the Lebanese leaders, not only the pro-Syrian, but also the anti-Syrian ones, have usually found it worthwhile to align themselves with the Syrian regime so as to be able to resist or appease powerful Syrian-backed Lebanese groups and figures.

These interrelated threats have been especially sensitive for Lebanon's Maronite leaders, particularly the presidents,[21] who have emphasized Lebanese sovereignty. However, since they have mostly recognized Syria's status quo policies towards their state, they have, reluctantly or not, tended to bandwagon with Damascus, except for the staunchest anti-Syrian figures like President Jumayyil.

The viewpoint of the realist school (including both simple and complex versions) considers threats from the powerful Syrian state as an explanatory factor shaping Lebanon's relations with Syria, and it is also true that the Syrian status quo behaviour has affected Lebanese perception. However, considering the tendency of Lebanon's bandwagoning with Syria, there seem to exist more 'positive' factors. In this regard, whether or not constructivism (identity) and liberalism's concept of complex interdependence (involving multiple transnational and interstate ties and shared interests) could also explain the Lebanese–Syrian case is discussed in the following two subsections.

Constructivism: Sovereignty vs. Trans-state Identity

According to Hinnebusch (2002a), 'Constructivists insist that interstate relations are contingent on the way *identity* is constructed; in the Middle East, sub- and supra[-]state identities compete with state identity, inspire trans[-]state movements, and constrain purely state-centric behavio[u]r.'[22] This is because, as Gause (1997) says, 'borders [in the Middle East] were not established through a historical process of domestic consolidation and external war' and that '[t]he power of the [centre] over society, in many cases divided along ethnic, sectarian, tribal, and/or linguistic lines, was limited and open to challenge'.[23]

Under the situation of 'the uneasy relation of identity and state sovereignty',[24] some Middle Eastern States are still challenged from both inside and outside.

In the process of Western colonial states drawing boundaries without paying attention to the hopes and history of local people in the Middle East, the boundaries of Lebanon and Syria were indeed drawn on the basis of imperial calculations. The resulting division of the two countries with the arbitrary Lebanese–Syrian border and the tensions between their states and national identities have led to a situation in which loyalty to each state has been contested by both sub-state (sectarian) and supra-state (pan-Arabism, pan-Islamism) identities in each society and thus irredentist feelings have been historically preserved.

However, Egypt's disastrous defeat in the 1967 war against Israel, the death of Egyptian President 'Abd al-Nasir in 1970 and the dramatic changes in Egyptian foreign and domestic policies (*infitah*) have damaged the prestige and appeal of pan-Arabism and accompanied the consolidation of state sovereignty in the Arab region. President Asad of Syria soon started this process by subordinating non-governmental actors in the country after assuming the control of the Ba'th regime in 1970. However, the consolidation of state sovereignty in the Middle East has not completely freed Arab states from the pressure of pan-Arabism. Since state identity has not fully replaced pan-Arab identity in most Arab states, the legitimacy of a regime remains dependent on the extent to which it voices its support for Arab causes; even though this is often confined to lip-service.[25]

While Syria has largely conducted its foreign policy based on its national interests, and while its concern for an Israeli intervention in Lebanon indeed prompted it to align itself with the Maronites against the Muslim–PLO coalition (as the theory of simple realism predicts), pan-Arab sentiments and Syria's ties with both Lebanese governmental and non-governmental actors – not all necessarily based on pan-Arabism – have not only given the Syrian regime a motivation to intervene, but also helped legitimize its behaviour with respect to the neighbouring states in the Arab world. On the other hand, as Gause (1992) points out, 'Syria has been most careful to maintain the forms of Lebanese sovereignty while consolidating its protectorate there.'[26] To summarize, although most Arab states, including Syria, still take into consideration the symbols of pan-Arabism – as the norm of sovereignty has increasingly undermined that of pan-Arabism – their policies have become consistent with the states' sovereignty. Nevertheless, respect for sovereignty when combined with a residue of pan-Arabism is not inconsistent with stronger regional powers seeking the building of spheres of influence, which has been generally seen as a legitimate pursuit. The Syrian case indeed falls into this category.

In contrast, it is Lebanon which has been the noteworthy exception to the process of consolidating state sovereignty in the Arab region. While state control over society has been consolidated in other Arab states, Lebanon is still subjected to penetration by outside powers where its non-governmental actors, mostly sectarian-based, have maintained trans-state relations and sought support. Indeed, Lebanon's major sectarian communities, i.e. the Maronites, Sunnis, Shi'as and Druzes, have had various co-religious ties with their counterparts in Syria. More importantly, Lebanon's political organizations, mostly formed on the basis of these sectarian affiliations, have generally aligned themselves with external powers, and some of these organizations, especially the Shi'a-based Amal Movement and Hizbullah, have kept close relationships with the Asad regime. In consequence, Lebanese trans-state identity continues to influence external behaviour by the state and as a significant portion of the Lebanese has held identification with Syrians, it is possible to say that Lebanon has not been in a position readily to balance against Syria.

However, the long history of unequal relations between Lebanon and Syria seems to have been strengthening an anti-Syrian feeling among the Lebanese people, including Muslims. One example is that, after the withdrawal of the Israeli army from the 'security zone' in southern Lebanon in May 2000, influential Muslims joined in the discussions calling into question the legitimacy of Syria's dominant position in Lebanon, and some have indeed demanded that Syria show greater respect for Lebanese sovereignty, while admitting the 'special' bonds between the two countries. After the US defeat of Iraq in 2003, Prime Minister Hariri balanced against the Asad regime, especially over the extension of President Emile Lahoud's term, by relying on the increased anti-Syrian trend in Lebanon and exploiting the favourable international climate, although Hariri eventually turned back to align himself with the Syrian regime. Later, the assassination of Hariri in February 2005 further strengthened the anti-Syrian tendency in Lebanon, albeit not among the significant pro-Syrian groups such as Hizbullah, bringing about the end of the Syrian hegemony in Lebanon.

As Wendt (1999), a representative of the theory of constructivism, notes: 'Structural change occurs when actors redefine who they are and what they want.'[27] Thus, it is possible to say that the identity change in Lebanon has arguably affected the transformation in Lebanese–Syrian relations. However, the continuing split in Lebanese identities still prevents Lebanon's anti-Syrian factions from consolidating their hold over the state and fully asserting its sovereignty against Syria.

As Wendt (1999) also points out the importance of the redefinition of actors' interests, it is worth addressing them in detail. At this point, the theory of complex interdependence seems to be relevant to the Lebanese–Syrian case and, in particular, to have an explanatory power for Lebanon's historic, long-term bandwagoning with Syria and some Lebanese leaders' recent detachment from the Asad regime.

Complex Interdependence: Shared Economic and Political Interests[28]

According to Keohane and Nye (2001), the theory of complex interdependence has three main characteristics: the participation of actors other than state governments; '[an] agenda of inter-state relationships consist[ing] of multiple issues that are not arranged in a clear or consistent hierarchy'; and ineffectiveness of the use of armed forces in regard to certain issues, notably economic relations.[29] In addition, the two academics distinguish between the two concepts of 'sensitivity' and 'vulnerability' as keys to an understanding of power in complex interdependence: complex interdependence makes countries sensitive to what happens in other countries and vulnerable to high risks and costs if they attempt to sever their connection with the countries in question.[30] In other words, complex interdependence assumes a cooperative relationship between states which is based on multiple ties created by various actors and accompanies their shared interests and resulting interdependency.

Regarding Lebanese–Syrian relations since 1970, reflecting the characteristic of the non-unitary Lebanese state, not only governmental, but also non-governmental actors in Lebanon have maintained multiple ties with Syria, which has generated some cooperative relations between the two states. In addition, there have been Lebanese and Syrian leaders' shared economic as well as political interests and their resulting interdependency, leading to Lebanon's general tendency to bandwagon with Syria.

Basically, Lebanon and Syria have maintained strong economic relations. First, Syria is still one of the main markets for Lebanon's exports and imports. Second, since the Ba'th regime openly encouraged the private sector to play a greater role in Syria by introducing Investment Law 10 in 1991, Lebanese banks, with other Lebanese entrepreneurs, have been able to operate in Syria, greatly benefiting from their geographical proximity. On the other hand, Syrian officials, politicians and businessmen have traditionally had an amount of foreign reserves in Lebanese banks. For example, under a 'Pax-Syriana' in 1976 Lebanon's banking sector was able to resume its activities and Syrian enterprises were again given an opportunity to utilize Lebanese investment capital.[31] Third, the presence of Syrian workers in

Lebanon has generally yielded some benefits for the latter country, although it is admitted that their presence has definitely raised the unemployment rate in Lebanon and provided Syrian regime figures with a pretext for intervention on behalf of the workers. Lebanese business elites have indeed enjoyed a supply of unskilled labourers willing to work at menial jobs for extremely low wages. On the other hand, their presence in Lebanon has significantly benefited the Ba'th regime, including a decrease in the unemployment rate in Syria and annual remittances of billions of dollars from Lebanon.

Their shared political interests include the fact that Lebanese leaders, on the one hand, have exploited Syrians to their advantage, while the Syrian regime, on the other hand, has used these figures to consolidate the country's power in Lebanon. As this phenomenon was especially observed from 1975 to 2005 (when Syria exerted a dominant influence in Lebanon), if one applies the concepts of 'sensitivity' and 'vulnerability' advocated by Keohane and Nye (2001) to Lebanon's political field during those 30 years, to the extent that Lebanon's political leaders relied heavily on Syria as their power base, one could conclude that their sensitivity to Syria was high. In contrast, if they had relied on other states and thereby diversified their power base, their vulnerability to Syria would have decreased. However, as these political interests actually became vested ones, most of Lebanon's leaders had no interest in giving them up and generally bandwagoned with the Asad regime until the assassination of Hariri in February 2005.

As a result, presumed by complex interdependence, the existence of shared economic and political interests and the resulting interdependency could explain Lebanon's bandwagoning with Syria. Nevertheless, it is necessary to note that Bashar al-Asad's succession in 2000 and his marginalization of the regime's Sunni 'old' elites (such as 'Abd al-Halim Khaddam and Hikmat al-Shihabi) detrimentally affected their Lebanese Sunni partners (such as Prime Minister Hariri) and, thus, their interest in cooperating with the Syrian regime. As Hariri's explicit, but temporary balancing against the Asad regime after the US conquest of Iraq in 2003 (he ultimately cooperated with the Syrian regime in extending Lahoud's presidential term) was largely affected by a shift in the Lebanese and Syrian leaders' shared interests, the changed actions and attitudes taken by Hariri could also be explained by complex interdependence. The factor of 'interests' indeed influenced Hariri and thus reshaped Lebanese–Syrian relations, along with the previously mentioned factors, i.e. the shift in the regional dynamics of the Middle East and in the identity among the Lebanese.

In summary, Lebanese presidents and prime ministers, although they have viewed the Syrian regime differently, either positively or negatively, have had their own reasons to align themselves with Damascus and thus Lebanon's bandwagoning with Syria has on the whole been maintained.

Outline of this Book

To answer the question brought up in the opening sentence, Chapter 2 (from 1970 to 1988), Chapter 3 (from 1988 to 2005) and Chapter 4 (since 2005) look closely at the actions and attitudes taken by Lebanon's presidents or prime ministers towards the Syrian regime, after reviewing the external and internal circumstances affecting their relations. Because Syria has penetrated into Lebanon, its domestic developments where its leaders' 'diplomacy' vis-à-vis Damascus has been observed will be largely examined in detail.

The hypothesis of this study is based on the following theories of international relations: simple realism, complex realism, constructivism and complex interdependence. Specifically, it is based on the assumption that Lebanon's relations with Syria since 1970 must be understood in terms of (a) Lebanon's reactions to external threats (which could explain very few episodes); (b) strategies adopted by Lebanon's top political leaders to cope with interrelated external and internal threats from Syria; (c) Lebanon's still powerful trans-state ties with Syria under the contradiction between Lebanese sovereignty and identity; and (d) Lebanese and Syrian leaders' shared economic as well as political interests and their resulting interdependency. Chapter 5, then, discusses both the validity of these theories and more wide-ranging methodological issues.

CHAPTER 2

DISRUPTION OF THE LEBANESE STATE AND SYRIAN INTERVENTION (1970–1988)

The early 1970s, first, witnessed the paralysis of the Lebanese state, in contrast to its relative stability prior to 1970, and thus Lebanon's consociational democracy[1] became gradually dysfunctional. On the other hand, Syria under President Hafiz al-Asad was in the process of promoting its internal stability (although there had been a succession of military coups in the 1950s and 1960s) and gradually transformed the state into a regional middle power. Given these contrasting situations, Syria started its involvement in Lebanon, which made Lebanese–Syrian relations asymmetrical.

As most government structures came close to collapse following the outbreak of the Lebanese Civil War in 1975, 'semi-anarchy', a situation having the following characteristics, emerged in Lebanon. First, a government lacks a monopoly over the use of force or legitimacy, and non-governmental actors are armed and struggling for power, in most cases backed by external actors (these features are generally common to 'anarchy'). Second, a 'unitary' government nevertheless continues to exist formally and sustains efforts to restore order, unlike in anarchy.

In fact, it was surprising that the 'unitary' Lebanese government continued to exist formally until 1988 and its leaders to some extent continued to attempt to restore internal order and defend Lebanon's sovereignty by political, military and/or economic means. These included reconciliation attempts, the formation of cabinets and endeavours to reunify the Lebanese army and carry out economic reconstruction. Regarding the formation of cabinets, there are theoretically three types of cabinets which could contribute to the re-establishment of order: a 'salvation cabinet' in which almost all important non-governmental groups' leaders should participate, in the case of Lebanon, especially the *zuama* (plural of *za'im*);[2] a 'technocrat cabinet' focusing on economic reconstruction; and a 'military cabinet' formed mainly by army officers.

When the Lebanese government attempted to restore 'normal' state functions by these political, military and/or economic means, its leaders had to be mindful of Syrian policy towards their state and were forced to cope with Syrians mostly in Lebanon's domestic contexts, as Syria exerted a dominant influence on Lebanese soil. For its part, Syria took an interest in restoring order in Lebanon, so as not to give Israel any cause for intervention and, more importantly, so as to be able to maintain that its presence was 'widely perceived as "beneficial" by the international community'.[3] As a result, the Asad regime not only interfered in the attempts undertaken by the Lebanese government, but also mediated between warring Lebanese factions, convened reconciliatory meetings and arranged its own peace plans for Lebanon, although at the same time the regime sometimes encouraged sectarian conflicts in order to enact 'divide and rule'.

As Syrian policy towards Lebanon, having largely been a reflection of the regional dynamics in the Middle East (as the theory of 'simple realism' presumes), was characterized by using its trans-state ties with Lebanon's non-governmental actors (mostly sectarian-based) more than its official ties with the Lebanese government, its top leaders had to keep an eye on both the regional and trans-state factors. Therefore, it is helpful, first, to describe these factors, before discussing in detail the political, military and economic aspects of the Lebanese–Syrian relationship.

Among top Lebanese leaders, this chapter primarily examines the actions and attitudes taken by President Sulayman Franjiya, President Ilyas Sarkis and President Amin al-Jumayyil towards the Asad regime of Syria. This is because until the amendment of the Lebanese constitution in 1990, the presidency possessed a degree of power superior to that of its counterparts, the premiership and the parliament speakership. In addition, it is necessary to mention that while the civil war in Lebanon continued until 1990, this chapter deals with the period until 1988. This is mainly because the year witnessed the end of the existence of a 'unitary' government, one of the characteristics of semi-anarchy, and the emergence of two rival governments with no president in Lebanon. The other reason is that many events happening in the last two years of the civil war, the most important of which being the formation of the Ta'if Agreement, have definitely affected the post-war Lebanon.

Middle East International Relations and the Impact on Syria and Lebanon

Introduction

The international relations of the Middle East had a considerable impact on Syrian policy towards Lebanon, which Lebanon's presidents had to consider when they took action and formed attitudes towards the Asad regime. A series of inter-Arab cooperations and conflicts affected Syrian–Lebanese relations, notably the formation of the Riyadh–Damascus–Cairo axis, the disputes between Egypt and Syria over Egyptian President Anwar Sadat's separate diplomacy with Israel and the Iraqi–Syrian rivalry that existed after the outbreak of the Iran–Iraq War. However, at the same time, the Arab League (typically led by Saudi Arabia) made efforts to mediate the inter-Arab struggles over Lebanon.

In addition, regional conflicts in the Middle East, such as the Israeli–Syrian struggle and the Iran–Iraq War, had an impact on Syrian–Lebanese relations. Finally, at the international level, the USA–USSR Cold War was played out in the region, specifically in Lebanon. The United States intervened in the Middle East and in the Lebanese conflict, often on the Israeli side but occasionally to support Maronite actors, while the Soviet Union provided some support to Syria.

Formation of the Riyadh–Damascus–Cairo Axis

While stabilizing Syria's domestic front in order to maximize its power and resources for the struggle with Israel, President Asad set up new alliances between Syria and the Gulf oil states by halting the ideologically-based verbal attacks against them. The Asad regime thus received financial assistance, which was desperately needed to rebuild and expand the military capabilities of the Syrian army and also to co-opt, appease or subdue elements of Syria's Sunni bourgeoisie who had contested the legitimacy of the 'Alawi-dominated regime.[4] Asad also maintained Syria's close relations with the Soviet Union in order to secure a supply of arms.

Asad's success in creating a 'presidential monarchy'[5] by subordinating non-governmental actors in Syria as well as playing them off against each other allowed him to pursue a foreign policy that was relatively unconstrained by domestic concerns, as the theory of simple realism can explain. Under the rein of Asad, Syria changed from being a victim to a regional player and this new status made it possible for the state 'to effectively adapt foreign policy to the changing geopolitical power balance'.[6] Syria improved its relations with Egypt and the pragmatic trend in Arab politics that had begun after the 1967 Arab–Israeli War was reflected in the foreign policies adopted by both Asad and Egyptian President Anwar Sadat.[7] They aligned with King Faysal of Saudi Arabia, consequently forming the

Riyadh–Damascus–Cairo axis.[8] However, these relations were soon worsened by Egypt's unilateral conclusion of the first disengagement agreement with Israel in January 1974 (Sinai I) and by the hasty lifting of the oil embargo by the Gulf oil states.[9]

Egypt's Separate Diplomacy towards Israel

When the civil war erupted in Lebanon on 13 April 1975, relations between Syria and Egypt were poor. Concerned about their relationship, Saudi Arabia took the initiative with the aim of reconciling disputes between Syria and Egypt. In mid-April 1975, a Saudi-initiated trilateral conference in Riyadh led to reconciliation, albeit partial and temporary, between Syria and Egypt.[10]

Indeed, Syrian–Egyptian relations soon deteriorated after the conclusion of the second disengagement agreement in September 1975 (Sinai II) between Egypt and Israel.[11] The agreement did not refer to the situation in the Golan Heights and made Syria more vulnerable to Israel while at the same time securing the Egyptian–Israeli border. Then, Syrian President Asad regarded the Egyptian behaviour as a further betrayal following the events of the military operation during the 1973 October War.

It is this that led Syria to focus serious attention on Lebanon. The Syrian–Egyptian disputes spilled over into Lebanon, with each having local proxies. Moreover, with Lebanon's border stretching across the western part of southern Syria, this made it possible for Israel to attack Syria via Lebanon and thus made Syria vulnerable to that kind of attack. As Weinberger (1986) notes, '[a]lthough Lebanon was a "confrontational state" only in the 1948 Arab–Israeli war, Syria had long recognized its neighbo[u]r's potential military significance in both a defensive and offensive capacity.'[12] Given Syria's increased vulnerability to Israel as Egypt withdrew from the Arab–Israeli power balance, Asad paid increased attention to the civil war situation in Lebanon and attempted to dampen the conflict, as it could potentially give Israel a cause for intervention in Lebanon. Over time, Syria's initial mediatory activities and indirect intervention through its proxy forces were stepped up to the level of direct military intervention.

US and Israeli Roles in the Entrance of the Syrian Army into Lebanon

At the same time, the increased Syrian involvement in Lebanon caused considerable Israeli concern. In 1976, the escalation of the Lebanese conflict threatened to bring about a direct military confrontation between Syria and Israel over Lebanon. Under these circumstances, the 'Red Line Agreement', the aim of which was to prevent this happening by guaranteeing respect for mutual security needs between Syria and Israel, was arranged with the support of the United States. US Secretary of State Henry Kissinger recognized Syrian President Asad's fear of possible Israeli intervention in Lebanon to protect Christians. In fact, Asad attempted to keep the Lebanese National Movement (LNM)[13] and the PLO under his control in order to avoid the Maronites being forced into a corner by these factions. Since such a Syrian attempt to pacify Lebanon would be beneficial to Israel, the latter made a secret agreement, allowing the entry of a small number of Syrian troops into northern Lebanon.[14]

As Sela (1998) pointed out, the Red Line Agreement also 'entailed Asad's renewed commitment to take part in the peace process under American supervision with the aim of reaching an agreement with Israel on ending the state of war in return for its withdrawal to the pre-June 1967 borders'.[15] Since Asad expected 'Golan II' to be the eventual outcome, Syria needed to show the United States that its behaviour in Lebanon was moderate and that it did not pose a threat to Israel. The agreement stimulated a Syrian–Maronite alliance, and Syria's policy of taking the side of the Maronites presented a favourable opportunity to Lebanese President Franjiya (a Maronite). Having been heavily handicapped by the powerful LNM–PLO coalition, Franjiya managed to deal with the coalition by aligning himself with Asad during the spring and summer of 1976.

Saudi Intervention and Creation of the Arab Deterrent Force

While Syria aligned with the Maronites, Egypt had been supporting the LNM–PLO coalition. As a result, tensions between Syria and Egypt were at their worst. This situation heightened Saudi Arabia's concern and led to Riyadh's efforts to resolve both the Lebanese conflict and the Egyptian–Syrian discord. On the one hand, Egypt had traditionally opposed attempts to unify the Eastern Arab region, and it interpreted Syrian policy under President Asad towards Lebanon as a move in this direction. On the other hand, Syria had, by the end of September 1976, gained a sufficiently dominant position in Lebanon to push its own settlement backed by the military presence.[16]

However, Asad calculated that supporting the inter-Arab solution sponsored by Saudi Arabia would be politically and financially advantageous in regard to the Syrian position on Lebanese soil. In addition, as Asad worried about the backlash against his decision to suppress the Palestinians and the Muslims in Lebanon, which was de-legitimized not only in Syria, but also in the Arab world, he needed to get out of the anti-Palestinian and Muslim conflict. Since Saudi–Egyptian relations were still good, Saudi Arabia managed to convene a preliminary meeting in Riyadh in mid-October, and an Arab League conference was held in Cairo a week later.[17]

Syrian and Egyptian cooperative behaviour in both meetings led to some positive measures to end the Lebanese conflict. In fact, the symbolic Arab Security Force (ASF) which consisted of 2,500 troops, whose creation had resulted from an Arab League conference in Cairo on 10 June 1976 and whose aim had been largely to replace the Syrian army having already entered Lebanon on 1 June, was expanded to become the 30,000-strong Arab Deterrent Force (ADF).[18] The ADF's mandate was to secure a ceasefire by facilitating the withdrawal of all Lebanese militia groups and Palestinian forces to the locations they had held before the start of the civil war, and to support the Lebanese government in regaining its authority and implementing its policies.[19] Although this decision by the Arab League might have intended, as in the creation of the ASF, to contain Syria's role in Lebanon, it led to the legitimization of the Syrian presence under the ADF banner.

Since the Arab states could not reach an agreement on the sizes of each national contingent in the ADF, the Arab League left this issue to the newly elected Lebanese President Sarkis.[20] His own election to the presidency having been due to Syrian help,[21] Sarkis determined that up to 25,000 Syrian troops should be included in the ADF, despite the PLO's demand for the maximum number to be 10,000.[22]

Sadat's Trip to Jerusalem and Israeli Aggression under the Likud Government

After the creation of the ADF, the Lebanese situation was relatively calm for the first half of 1977. However, Egyptian President Sadat's trip to Jerusalem in 1977, the Camp David Accords in 1978 and the Egyptian–Israeli Peace Treaty in 1979 had a profound impact on inter-Arab politics as well as, by extension, on the Syrian and Lebanese situations. Syria's vulnerability increased considerably, since the Egyptian policies made it possible for the Israeli army to concentrate on its northern and eastern borders.

In addition, the establishment in 1977 of the Likud government in Israel, led by Prime Minister Menachem Begin, increased Syrian President Asad's concern. This aggressive government actually aimed to expel Syria and the PLO from Lebanon by upgrading its alliance with the Maronites, which dated back to early 1976, when the Maronites received military support from Israel.[23] Begin ordered the Litani Operation in southern Lebanon in 1978, the beginning of Israeli aggression which would culminate in the massive operation in Lebanon in June 1982. Due to Egypt's expulsion from the Arab world and the resulting major Arab–Israeli power imbalance, Israel was able to afford overt support to the Maronites, both militarily and politically. These circumstances led Syria to shift its alliance from the Maronites to the Muslims and the Palestinians, i.e. its traditional allies in Lebanon, in order to contain the Israeli threat. Since Asad had no hope of recovering the Golan Heights through US mediation after the conclusion of the Camp David Accords, he had no need to show that Syrian policy towards Lebanon was moderate by facilitating the calm of the Lebanese–Israeli border.

Despite the Syrian policy shift, which opened the possibility of increased turmoil in Lebanon, President Sarkis generally avoided explicitly antagonizing the Asad regime and instead attempted to seek Arab intervention.[24] Sarkis requested some Arab and international backing for Lebanese sovereignty and aimed to secure Lebanon's autonomy from Syria without provoking it.[25] After the failure of international efforts in the autumn of 1979 by France and the United States (the latter sent the former Under-Secretary of State for Political Affairs, Philip Habib) to resolve the Lebanese turmoil, Sarkis put more emphasis on an inter-Arab settlement for southern Lebanon.[26] Since the PLO's military presence in the south was also a great concern for Sarkis's Sunni counterpart, Prime Minister Salim al-Huss,[27] who had been designated by Sarkis in December 1976 and was grappling with economic reconstruction,[28] Sarkis gained support from Huss. In consequence, the Lebanese government adopted a unitary stance at the 1979 Arab League summit in Tunis. However, the differences of positions between the PLO and the Lebanese side remained large.[29] Since Syria needed an armed Palestinian presence in southern Lebanon to counter the increased pressure from both Israel and the Maronites, it inevitably supported the PLO rather than the Lebanese government.[30] Eventually, the summit rejected Lebanon's foremost demand, i.e. the withdrawal of the PLO from the area south of the Litani River,[31] and was finally closed without a final communiqué.[32]

Since the situation in southern Lebanon continued to be highly volatile, in July 1981 the Lebanese government required the Arab League to hold a summit focusing on the south.[33] The Lebanese demand was finally realized at the Fez summit in November. Lebanon managed, in spite of disagreements by the Arab states over the Saudi-proposed 'Fahd Plan' for the Arab–Israeli conflict, to obtain a unanimous resolution, the most important recommendation of which was the deployment of the Lebanese army in southern Lebanon.[34] However, the effect of this resolution was impeded by the antagonism between the hard-line and moderate Arab states and by the confrontation between Saudi Arabia and Syria, mainly deriving from the Islamic Revolution in Iran and the Iran–Iraq War, in which Syria backed Iran.

Fragmentation in the Arab World and the Emergence of the Syrian–Iranian Alliance

The Iran–Iraq War brought about new and immediate fragmentation in the Arab world, which manifested itself in the formation of the two axes. On the one hand, there was an Iraqi–Saudi–Jordanian axis, which became a powerful alignment within the Arab system in the early 1980s.[35] On the other hand, resulting from the regional isolation of these two countries, there emerged a Syrian–Libyan axis.[36] Syria was excluded from the Iraqi–Saudi–Jordanian axis because of the collapse of its brief unity talks with Iraq in 1979, its support for Iran in the Iran–Iraq War and the worsened relations that resulted. At the same time, Syria and Iran were forced into a close alliance by their common hostility or vulnerability to Iraq and Israel. Libya was isolated by its leader Mu'ammar al-Qadhafi's many adventures and destructive activities with regard to its neighbouring countries.

As a result, relations between Syria and Saudi Arabia, which were rather important for the former position in Lebanon, became strained. At the same time, Syria's alliance with Iran had repercussions in Lebanon and made Israel's military operation in Lebanon increasingly costly for Israeli itself. With Syria's agreement, Iran sent members of the Revolutionary Guard to Lebanon during the Israeli invasion in the summer of 1982. The Pasdaran troops that were sent into Lebanon by Iran were training future Hizbullah militants in the Biqa' region, along the Syrian border, and thus the Syrian–Iranian alliance played an important role in creating Hizbullah in 1982. While Iran supported Islamic movements such as the Islamic Unification Movement in Tripoli and Islamic Amal in the Biqa' region, its main pillar in Lebanon became Hizbullah.

Under the establishment of the Israeli hegemony in Lebanon as a result of its summer invasion in 1982, the alliance between Syria and Iran made it possible for Hizbullah to attack the Israeli army and Lebanese President Jumayyil. He was elected in September 1982 under Israeli supervision after the assassination of his elder brother, Bashir al-Jumayyil, and was viewed by Hizbullah as a Western surrogate. In October 1983, Hizbullah orchestrated twin suicide bombings against the American and French army bases that were part of the Multi-National Force (MNF), with the aim of expelling the Western powers from Lebanon and shaking the authority of Jumayyil.[37] These attacks actually contributed not only to the MNF's withdrawal in February 1984 and the abrogation of the May 17 Agreement (which was concluded in 1983 between Israel and Lebanon under US guidance and was a virtual 'separate' peace treaty) in March 1984,[38] but also the resulting recovery of Syria's hegemony in Lebanon.

However, Iran's support for 'radical' Hizbullah was later at odds with Syria's well-calculated and cautious policy towards Lebanon, and President Asad was specifically concerned about Hizbullah's activities such as hijacking airplanes and kidnapping Westerners. The Damascus–Tehran axis became consequently strained, and the most important example of such tensions was the confrontation between the Amal Movement (supported by Syria) and Hizbullah (backed by Iran) that took place in the latter part of the 1980s.[39] Following the confrontation between their respective allies, Syria and Iran eventually managed to rein in their rivalry and to keep their alliance intact by forming the Damascus Agreement in 1989.[40]

USA–USSR Rivalry and Israeli Hegemony in Lebanon

Since the détente between the superpowers was ended by the Soviet invasion in Afghanistan in 1979 and by the subsequent coming to power of US President Ronald Reagan in 1980, the Middle East, as is usual for the Third World, became an arena for superpower rivalries and surrogate conflicts. Israel and its Lebanese allies, especially the Maronites, exploited the new situation to contain the Syrian–Muslim–Palestinian advance in Lebanon and to create an Israeli-dominated order. They realized that the Reagan administration tended to see issues in the Third World as an extension of the Cold War and thus articulated their own causes in terms of the USA–USSR confrontation.

These circumstances led President Jumayyil to conclude the May 17 Agreement between Lebanon and Israel in 1983, under the pretext of defending the Middle East from the 'communist threats' posed by the Soviet Union and its regional allies. He may have also calculated that encouraging the United States to consider Lebanon in the context of the Cold War might result in Lebanon being able to negotiate more equally with both Syria and Israel.

During the Lebanese–Israeli negotiations, Jumayyil considered a peace treaty with Israel as to be out of the question,[41] since it would run the risk of encouraging further domestic conflicts and outside interventions, especially from Syria. However, Israel hoped, in reward for its withdrawal from Lebanon, both to conclude a peace treaty and to normalize relations with Lebanon, and it became clear that the United States had no intention of pressuring Israel to change its position.[42] The Lebanese–Israeli negotiations thus reached a stalemate. Later, it was the shuttle diplomacy between Israel and Lebanon by US Secretary of State George Shultz that helped them to complete a draft agreement, which was finally signed by both Lebanon and Israel on 17 May 1983 (the May 17 Agreement).[43] However, Shultz, despite his earlier pro-Arab stance, did not assume the role of an impartial mediator and surrendered to the powerful pro-Israeli lobby in the United States, ignoring Syria's interests. The agreement was, in spite of Lebanese objections, a virtual 'separate' peace treaty. The Lebanese government expressed disappointment at both the contents of the agreement and the role of the US mediator.[44]

The May 17 Agreement would have imposed Israel's hegemony over Lebanon by opening the latter country to Israeli armed forces and products and by banning Arab forces from being stationed in Lebanon, with the simultaneous withdrawal of the Syrian army being stipulated as a condition for the Israeli army's withdrawal.[45] Although the United States and Israel calculated that 'a militarily weakened Syria had no choice but to accept withdrawal or face continued Israeli occupation of Lebanon',[46] Syria refused to withdraw its forces from Lebanon on the basis of the agreement and demanded its complete abrogation.[47]

This demand was based, primarily, on Syria's assertion that the May 17 Agreement violated Lebanese sovereignty and that it would strengthen Israeli–Maronite ties.[48] In this regard, Syria objected particularly to the formation of Lebanese–Israeli Joint Supervisory Teams, which were to be under the control of Israeli military officers and whose role was to patrol the Lebanese–Israeli border.[49] Furthermore, the agreement had the enormous potential to threaten Syria's national security. This was because the agreement accorded considerable control to Israel over the whole of southern Lebanon, prohibited any opposition to Israel on Lebanese soil and banned the passage through Lebanon or its air space of troops, weapons and equipment to or from any state not having diplomatic relations with Israel.[50] Third, as a self-proclaimed champion of the Arab cause, Syria calculated that any separate accord with Israel would weaken Palestinian power,[51] not to mention its own bargaining position over the Golan Heights. In total, Syria dismissed the May 17 Agreement as it did the second 'Camp David' accord.[52]

Syria in the end refused to withdraw from Lebanon on the basis of the May 17 Agreement, and its initiatives to promote Lebanese opposition to the agreement resulted in the formation of the National Salvation Front (NSF).[53] The Syrian army and the NSF confronted the Israeli army and its allies in Lebanon, notably President Jumayyil and the Maronites in the Shuf area during the summer and autumn of 1983, the 'Shuf War'.[54]

Although Jumayyil relied on Israeli and US power to contain the Syrian-backed NSF, the Israeli army suffered a large number of casualties. Mindful of the risks that would follow a confrontation with a Syrian army that was reinforced by USSR aid,[55] the Israeli army withdrew in September 1983 from the Shuf area to the Awali River in southern Lebanon.[56] Based on the Treaty of Friendship and Cooperation with the Soviet Union that Syria had concluded in October 1980, their negotiations led the USSR in late 1982 and early 1983 to dispatch some 5,000 military advisors and SAM-5 missiles to Syria.[57] The Syrian army thus gained enough power to confront the Israeli army in the battle with the aim of destroying the May 17 Agreement, which would have dragged Lebanon into Israel's orbit.

In addition, a succession of fierce Shi'a attacks against the US presence on Lebanese soil in 1983 – the April bombing of its embassy and the October bombings of MNF facilities including the US Marine Corps barracks – had a tremendous impact on the Reagan administration. The United States finally decided in February 1984 to withdraw its troops from the MNF.[58] In the end, Jumayyil's reliance on the Israeli and US military presence evoked disapproval in Lebanon's Muslim communities, most of which were supported by Syria and Iran, and also led to huge and violent uprisings, which ultimately resulted, in March 1984, in Lebanon's abrogation of the May 17 Agreement.[59] As US and Israeli power dwindled in Lebanon, Jumayyil now attempted to mend Lebanon's relations with Syria, which resulted in failure.[60]

With Israel's hegemony in Lebanon decreasing, Syria began to rebuild its hegemony there.[61] However, Lebanon continued to be in a dangerous condition during the latter part of the 1980s. In fact, Syria and its important ally, the Amal Movement, were in confrontation with the PLO, especially the Fatah faction and its leader Yasir 'Arafat, and with Iranian-backed Hizbullah in the battle of Palestinian refugee camps, the so-called 'Camps War'.[62]

Brief Summary

In summation, it could be said that Lebanon's collapsed and penetrated situation was not only affected by the international/regional rivalries in the Middle East, but also provided an arena for these rivalries. This was true particularly in terms of the inter-Arab antagonism between Syria and Egypt and that between Syria and Iraq; the regional struggles, manifestations of which were the conflict between Syria and Israel and the Iran–Iraq War; and a dimension of the USA–USSR Cold War confrontation in the Third World. While the Arab League, notably Saudi Arabia, tried to contain the inter-Arab antagonism and to stabilize Lebanon, for example through the introduction of the ADF, these efforts tended to end up legitimizing Syria's role in Lebanon.

Lebanese Non-Governmental Actors and Syria: Their Basic Interests and Relations

Introduction

With the Lebanese state increasingly dysfunctional, non-governmental actors in Lebanon stepped up their activities and became more or less organized and armed militias. The main groups – such as the Maronites, Sunnis, Shi'as, Druzes and Palestinians – all had trans-state relations in one form or another with Syria, which Lebanon's presidents had to examine when they took action and formed attitudes towards the Asad regime. The trans-state relations between the Lebanese non-governmental actors and Syria were largely determined for the former by power calculations and identities, for the latter by its position as a regional middle power in the Middle East and by its domestic circumstances. On the one hand, Syria used these non-governmental actors to serve its own national interests, acting as a balancer, aggressor and/or patron during the civil war in Lebanon. Syria also attempted to minimize its reliance on any single group or identification with a particular side in the conflict for the purpose of legitimizing its presence in Lebanon, even though the characterization by Abukhalil (1994) of its policy as one of drawing a distinction between friends and enemies at particular junctures seems valid.[63] For their part, the Lebanese non-governmental actors saw Syria's involvement as an opportunity for them to pursue or protect their own interests, and their behaviour was mainly determined by a combination of power calculations and the identity of each group.

The Maronites and Syria

As Rabinovich (1984) pointed out, the three main parties with a Christian-Maronite orientation and their militias constituted the political and military pillars in Lebanon's Maronite community. They were Pierre al-Jumayyil's Kata'ib Party, Kamil Sham'un's National Liberal Party (NLP) and Franjiya's group.[64] Maronite identity would, all things being equal, have made them opponents of Syria's influence in Lebanon; however, their power calculations could either reinforce or dilute this orientation, depending on the context.

The Kata'ib Party initially took a position between Franjiya's cooperative attitude towards President Asad and Sham'un's long-term antagonism against him.[65] As Asad managed to improve his relations with the Kata'ib Party in the early 1970s, Jumayyil actually visited Syria in December 1975.[66] Despite their original conflicting views, Jumayyil and Sham'un later formed the Lebanese Front in January 1976, with Sham'un as the president and with Jumayyil leading the Lebanese Forces (LF) as its joint militia against the powerful LNM–PLO coalition.[67]

In addition to these figures, there were 'moderate' Christian leaders who had flexible views on power sharing with Muslims in Lebanon's political system, and in order to preserve Lebanese sovereignty they attempted to find a modus vivendi with the Palestinians. After the spring of 1975, Sarkis became the most prominent representative of this trend.[68]

Lebanon's Maronites' relations with Syria changed dramatically as their needs and circumstances altered. Fearing that the LF would not be able to withstand the heavy offensive by the LNM–PLO coalition, Franjiya and Jumayyil requested Asad in May 1976 to send the Syrian army into Lebanon.[69] The conditions of the deal were as follows. Syria would protect the Maronites from the coalition and force a political solution based on the Constitutional Document, which had been formed under Syrian supervision in February, and which stipulated the preservation of Lebanon's sectarian system. On the other hand, the Maronites in turn would recognize Syria's 'special status' in Lebanon.[70] However, once the Maronites were free from the threat of their military and political defeat, they gradually came to oppose the Syrian military presence, partly because Syria was renewing its alliances with Muslims and Palestinians in Lebanon.

Under these circumstances, as Zamir (1999) pointed out, there emerged three types of attitudes towards Syria among Lebanon's Maronite leaders after 1976. First, Franjiya, who had maintained close ties with the Syrian regime and particularly with Asad, and who also owed the prevention of his earlier ousting from the presidency to Syrian help, advocated that Lebanon's close relations with Syria be maintained. Second, Sarkis accepted Syria as the dominant force in Lebanon, but sought to contain it by relying on the power of the United States and other Arab countries. A third, but prevailing, Maronite attitude towards Syria, advocated by the Lebanese Front, sought the recovery of Maronite political and military power against Syria by seeking a strategic alliance with Israel. At the same time, it took the form of the LF leading a series of armed struggles against the ADF in Lebanon.[71] Aware that the Maronites could not restore their hegemony over Lebanon, the Lebanese Front also sought a Christian 'mini-state' as part of Lebanon's 'cantonization', which provoked strong Syrian opposition, since it would strengthen Israel's role in Lebanon.

In addition, the Lebanese Front also sought leverage over Syria by allegedly supporting the Muslim Brotherhood in Syria,[72] which inflicted severe blows on the Asad regime during the late 1970s and early 1980s. Although Syria accused the Kata'ib Party of facilitating the Muslim Brotherhood's activities in Lebanon and also being involved with them inside Syria, it hoped to put an end to this alleged involvement by improving relations with the Lebanese Front.[73] On the other hand, Syria put emphasis on terminating the new relations between its hostile neighbour Iraq and the Lebanese Front, after the leader, Sham'un, stated that Iraq should play a more active role inside Lebanon.[74]

After the assassination of Bashir al-Jumayyil by an alleged Syrian agent, Lebanon's Maronites realized that their alliance with Israel had become too costly and was also a threat to their solidarity, as the alliance split the community between pro-Israeli and pro-Syrian figures. In May 1983, Franjiya formed the NSF with Rashid Karami and Walid Junblat, which was established at the behest of Syria and through mediation between the three leaders, and which aimed to abrogate the May 17 Agreement between Lebanon and Israel.[75]

The solidarity of the Maronites was also shattered by their internal conflict. Faced with such younger militia leaders as Ilyas Hubayqa and Samir Ja'ja', who had gradually consolidated their power after the outbreak of the civil war by challenging traditional leaders in Lebanon's Maronite community, the ageing Sham'un and Pierre al-Jumayyil began to lose the power they had once possessed within the community.[76] According to Petran (1987), the death of Jumayyil in August 1984 had a particularly strong impact on Maronite solidarity.[77] In February 1985 the LF, led by pro-Israeli Ja'ja', revolted against the Kata'ib Party and its leaders.[78] Ja'ja' objected especially to President Amin al-Jumayyil's attempts to improve his relationship with Asad and declared the LF's independence of the Kata'ib Party regarding the issues of security, politics, finance and information.[79]

However, perceptions within the LF changed, and the idea of reaching an accommodation with Damascus, which had been advocated by the intelligence chief, Hubayqa, began to gain support within the organization.[80] This was primarily due to the Israeli army's withdrawal in stages between January and June 1985 from most of southern Lebanon and southern Biqa' to the 'security zone' along Israel's northern border. Also, it was due to the heavy defeat of the LF by the NSF in Sidon, for which Ja'ja' had been responsible.[81] However, since Hubayqa's alignment with the Asad regime was largely based on his desires to contain Ja'ja' and to consolidate his position within the LF by using recovering Syrian power in Lebanon, he did not receive solid support from Lebanon's Maronite community at large. After Hubayqa signed the 'Tripartite Agreement' with Nabih Berri and Junblat in December 1985 to stabilize Lebanon under Syrian hegemony, the LF actually splintered.[82] Backed by strong Maronite opposition to the agreement stemming partly from the Syrian regime's disregard for and bypassing of President Jumayyil and supported by a majority in the Lebanese army command and the anti-Syrian Maronites, Ja'ja' managed to have Hubayqa and his followers ousted to Syrian-controlled Biqa'.[83] After this, Maronite–Syrian relations remained poor, and the Asad regime was unsuccessful in finding reliable leaders in the community other than Franjiya.

The Sunnis and Syria

Among Lebanon's Sunnis the major actors were 'traditional' leaders (*zuama*), 'moderate' political leaders, Nasserist organizations and Sunni fundamentalists. From a Syrian point of view, the Sunnis constituted one of its natural allies because of their Arab-oriented identity. Syria also needed to maintain good relations with Lebanon's Sunni community, since the 'Alawi-dominated and secular-oriented Asad regime was viewed with suspicion by Sunnis in Syria, especially in the 1970s and early 1980s, when the regime was engaged in violent military confrontation with a Sunni fundamentalist group, the Muslim Brotherhood. Also, with the Sunnis holding Lebanon's premiership, cooperation with them was necessary if Syria was to put its Lebanese policy into effect smoothly. On the other hand, because the Sunnis in Lebanon lacked military forces, apart from the relatively weak Nasserist organizations, the community needed the protection offered by Syria's military and political power. Although the Lebanese Sunnis could conceivably have relied on other Arab states to compensate for their relatively decreasing power during the civil war, it appears that Lebanon's geographical proximity with Syria and the weakened Egyptian influence in the Arab world after the death of President 'Abd al-Nasir played an important role in making Syria their natural protector.

The power of Sunni *zuama* had diminished during the conflict because of the rising power of the so-called 'radical' groups in the Muslim community such as the LNM and Hizbullah. However, the Asad regime relied on Lebanon's Sunni *zuama* to counter the powerful LNM–PLO coalition and, in particular, to confront the Israeli-backed Maronite forces. Among the Sunni *zuama*, the Syrian regime's relations with Karami were generally stable, and he indeed participated in the NSF, which was formed under the Syrian initiative to counter the May 17 Agreement between Israel and Lebanon. Sa'ib Salam initially hesitated to align himself with the Syrian-backed NSF,[84] even though he condemned Amin al-Jumayyil's election to the presidency.[85] However, once it was clear to him that President Jumayyil had failed to restore security in West Beirut, the seat of his own power base, Salam associated himself more closely with the NSF.[86]

President Asad relied mainly on 'moderate' Sunni political leaders in Lebanon for his stabilization efforts. Both Huss and Shafiq al-Wazzan held the premiership during the term of President Sarkis, and they tried to pacify the country in cooperation with the Syrian regime.[87]

On the contrary, Syria's relations with Nasserist organizations such as the Independent Nasserist Movement and its militia, Murabitun, remained strained, except during the first phase of the civil war when Syria supported the LNM–PLO coalition. These organizations demanded the abolition of Lebanon's sectarian system and attempted to drive the Maronites into a corner and to further fortify Lebanon as a power base for Palestinian armed struggles against Israel. The Asad regime was concerned about Nasserist behaviour, since it would provide a base for Syrian dissidents and a pretext for Israel's penetration into Lebanon. Syria's relations with Muslim fundamentalists in Tripoli were also poor, since many of the members of the Muslim Brotherhood were flowing into the city and finding protection there, especially after the Hama massacre by the Syrian regime in 1982.[88]

The Shi'a and Syria

The Shi'a community in Lebanon had two main political groups. One was the Amal Movement, led by Berri and calling for moderate reforms of Lebanon's political system. The other was Hizbullah (the Party of God), guided by its 'spiritual leader', Sheikh Muhammad Husayn Fadlallah, and taking more radical stances that sometimes brought about clashes with Syria.[89] Although both groups had connections with Syria, the Amal Movement was the closer ally. This was because after the anti-Ba'th Sunni disturbances in Syria in 1973, Musa al-Sadr, the then head of the Higher Shi'a Council in Lebanon, responded to Syrian President Asad's need by issuing a religious sanction (*fatwa*) which stated that the 'Alawis constituted a community of the Shi'as.[90] Asad indeed welcomed the Sadr statement, as it would help him control a majority of Sunnis at home who had deep misgivings about his 'Alawi-dominated regime.[91] Asad, on the other hand, acknowledged the increasing power of the Lebanese Shi'as under Sadr and was able to meet his need for a strong external patron to further consolidate his power in Lebanon.

After the outbreak of the civil war, the Amal Movement benefited in a number of ways from its relations with Syria. After the disappearance of Sadr, the Amal Movement's founder, its leader Husayn al-Husayni (from 1978 to 1980) and his successor Berri ensured that there were good relations with Asad.[92] Having become a dominant force in Lebanon's Shi'a community, the Amal Movement decided to break ranks with the LNM–PLO coalition. This was because the LNM–PLO coalition controlled Shi'a areas in southern Lebanon using harsh measures, including torture, which led to Shi'a antagonism against the coalition.[93] Thus, the 'Amal [Movement] became one of a small number of pro-Syrian organizations', when Damascus aligned in June 1976 with the Maronites, to contain the LNM–PLO coalition.[94] Since most Muslims regarded the alignment as a case of betrayal by the Asad regime, Syria thereafter treated the Amal Movement as one of its most reliable allies in Lebanon. Syria was motivated in so doing not only by the rising Shi'a political, military and demographic power in Lebanon,[95] but also by its need to have a Muslim force in Lebanon to counterbalance the Sunnis, especially when the Asad regime confronted the Muslim Brotherhood inside the country.[96] In fact, the Amal Movement had a reliable militia, and its strong sympathy towards the Asad regime was well-preserved during the period.

In addition, as Abukhalil (1990) pointed out, 'Syria also needed the Amal Movement as a tool for Syria's regional policies'.[97] Since the penetrated and fragmented Lebanese state was an arena for regional power rivalries, the Asad regime used the Amal Movement as a proxy for its anti-Iraqi campaigns.[98] Indeed, many pro-Iraqi Ba'th leaders were assassinated by the Amal Movement,[99] which was against Saddam Husayn's war on Shi'a Iran.

After the Israeli invasion in 1982, Iranian-backed Hizbullah increased its power in Lebanon, and the Amal Movement emerged as an important tool by which Syria could prevent Iran from dominating the Shi'as in Lebanon. Syria's relations with the Amal Movement temporarily worsened as a result of the movement's initial tacit collaboration with the Israeli army, its initial hesitation to join the Syrian-initiated NSF and its attempt to improve the relations between the NSF and President Jumayyil.[100] However, their relations were soon improved, since Jumayyil's refusal to discuss even the moderate reform plans advocated by the Shi'as drove the Amal Movement into the opposition and made the NSF more powerful.[101] The Amal Movement was subsequently a pillar of the 1985 Tripartite Agreement, which had been brokered by Syria among the leaders of the three main Maronite, Druze and Shi'a militias. In addition, Syria and the Amal Movement had a shared interest in preventing the resettlement of PLO forces in southern Lebanon (one of the main strongholds of the Amal Movement). This was because it risked bringing about an Israeli retaliation that could result in massive destruction of Lebanese infrastructure, as had taken place in 1982. The Amal Movement needed both a patron and arms in order to achieve this goal, and Syria supplied the organization with large amounts of weapons.

As a result, Syria used the Amal Movement to attack the PLO during the Camps War in the late 1980s, through which the movement sought to prevent a resurgence of 'Arafat's presence in Lebanon. However, Berri's alignment against Palestinian forces harmed the credibility of the Amal Movement among Lebanese Muslims. In addition, the Amal Movement's influence was badly affected by its growing corruption and inefficient leadership.[102] However, the Amal Movement still retained a broad power base, especially in the villages of southern Lebanon, while Hizbullah displaced the Amal Movement in southern Beirut.[103] Since Syria recognized and supported the Amal Movement's intentions and actions to prevent the resurrection of Palestinian power in Lebanon, their relations continued to be close until the end of the Syria–PLO conflict.

According to Abukhalil (1990), 'Syria's relations with Hizbullah (the Party of God) [were] more problematic. The Syrian regime [had] to walk a tight-rope in its dealings with the . . . movement.'[104] The reasons were, first, that Hizbullah was ideologically opposed to the Asad regime's advocacy of secular pan-Arabism. Second, Hizbullah's 'extreme' activities, such as taking Westerners hostage and suicide bombings, had the potential to worsen Syria's image in the international community,[105] and Asad was indeed strongly criticized for his connections with Hizbullah.

Since Iran had a powerful influence over Hizbullah, relations between Syria and Hizbullah reflected Asad's efforts to balance Syria's stakes in the alliance with Iran and its interests in Lebanon. What happened, as a result, was that when Syrian and Iranian interests converged, Syria and Hizbullah were able to coordinate their activities. In the early 1980s, Hizbullah supported Syrian struggles against Israeli and MNF forces in Lebanon, and their coordination contributed to a political climate which forced Jumayyil to abrogate the May 17 Agreement. Hizbullah played an important role in Syria re-establishing its dominant position in Lebanon, after the brief decrease in its power as a result of the Israeli invasion in 1982.

However, in the late 1980s, the alliance between Iran and Syria became strained by the Camps War. Iran, which was trying to create a Palestinian–Shi'a alliance against Israel, demanded that Syria stop the Amal Movement's attacks on the PLO.[106] In addition, Hizbullah was opposed to the Amal Movement's attempts to calm the southern border with Israel and continued to side with the PLO.[107] Consequently, clashes between the Amal Movement and Hizbullah occurred frequently, with Hizbullah insisting that it should have positions and freedom of activities against the Israeli army in the south, while the Amal Movement rejected these demands. Later, the Syrian army was forced to enter into West Beirut to save the Amal Movement from Hizbullah's advances,[108] which culminated in February 1987 when confrontations between Syrian troops and Hizbullah fighters resulted in the massacre of 23 members of Hizbullah.[109]

Afterwards, Syria's relations with Hizbullah, and by extension with Iran, seriously deteriorated over the issue of Western hostages. When Ayatollah Husayn Ali Montazeri turned down Asad's appeal to release an American military officer, William Higgins, who was abducted by Hizbullah in February 1988, Asad ordered the Amal Movement to attack Hizbullah, a decision which angered 'radical' figures in the Iranian government.[110]

Under the continuing fighting between the Amal Movement and Hizbullah, Iran's attempts to mediate between them were unsuccessful, because the Iranian leadership itself was split.[111] Since the 'radical' Ali Akbar Mohtashemi strongly supported Hizbullah, and since the 'moderate' Hashemi Rafsanjani condemned both the Amal Movement and Hizbullah equally for the catastrophic situation in Lebanon, a reflection of the Iranian power struggle could be seen in the situation.[112] However, as soon as the dual leadership by President Rafsanjani and Ayatollah Khamenei became consolidated in Iran,[113] it began to contain the clashes between the Amal Movement and Hizbullah.

In addition, Iran cooperated with Syria to form the Damascus Agreement in January 1989, by which Syria permitted a Hizbullah presence in southern Lebanon on condition that Hizbullah would restrain its military operations against Israel so as not to invite massive retaliation by the latter.[114] Now that Syria had finally secured good relations with both the Amal Movement and Hizbullah, it was in a position to balance and mediate the two main groups of Lebanon's Shi'a community and this has become an important asset for Syria in implementing its post-war Lebanese policies.

The Druze and Syria

Syrian–Druze relations were further strengthened after Kamal Junblat supported Franjiya's election to the Lebanese presidency in 1970, as Franjiya had been a close friend of the Asad family. While Interior Minister Junblat, who had retained his position until 1972,[115] was responsible for regulating Palestinian military activities, his closeness to the Palestinians and the increasing power of the LNM under his guidance led President Asad to maintain close relations with him. Junblat, on the other hand, understood that the Palestinian activities in Lebanon relied largely on the supply of arms from Syria and that this supply and their Lebanon-based operations against Israel could be jeopardized or impeded by deterioration in Lebanese–Syrian relations.[116] Furthermore, such a development could weaken Junblat's power and threaten his position, since the LNM was aligned with the Palestinians in a common struggle against the sectarian-based Lebanese state.

After the outbreak of the civil war in Lebanon, relations between the LNM and Syria were initially good, because of their mutual interest in containing Maronite power. However, relations soon deteriorated dramatically, since Junblat's demands for thorough reforms of Lebanon's political system were not acceptable to Asad, who hoped for moderate reforms in Lebanon.[117] When the Syrian intention was manifested in the Constitutional Document in February 1976, Junblat strongly rejected it on the basis that it would not change the sectarian character of Lebanon's political system, which prevented Druzes from occupying the top posts such as the presidency, premiership and parliament speakership.[118] Indeed, Jumblat was not satisfied with the Syrian plan and sought to force Asad to take a more radical stance for political reforms in Lebanon,[119] since the LNM was at that time militarily superior to the LF. The LNM renewed hostilities and engaged in attacks against Syrian-supported President Franjiya, who, in keeping with Pierre al-Jumayyil, asked for the entry of the Syrian army into Lebanon.

Junblat's rejection of the Constitutional Document, as well as his refusal to cooperate with Asad over his pragmatic strategy towards Lebanon, led to their fierce battle during the summer of 1976, and Junblat was finally defeated by the Syrian regime both militarily and politically.[120] As a result, Syria succeeded in assuming a dominant role in Lebanon and persuading other Arab states to accept its role. After Junblat was assassinated in March 1977, possibly by a Syrian agent, his son Walid Junblat and his followers improved relations with Asad.[121] It seemed that the weakened LNM, especially after the assassination of its experienced leader, had no choice, but to accept Syrian hegemony in Lebanon.

The restoration of this alliance benefited the Asad regime, especially when it fought against the Israeli army in Lebanon and against President Amin al-Jumayyil in the 1980s. The Druzes became a reliable pillar for Syria, and Junblat actually joined the NSF in 1983 and later supported the Tripartite Agreement in 1985, both of which were initiated by Syria. The improved relations with Asad made it possible for Lebanese Druzes to receive financial assistance, weapons and munitions from Syria.[122]

However, during the late 1980s Junblat confronted Asad over Syria's strategy with regard to the Camps War. Although he fought with Berri against Jumayyil and the Israeli army during the Shuf War in order to abrogate the May 17 Agreement, his force did not align with Berri against the Palestinians during the Camps War. As Petran (1987) pointed out, this was because Junblat's armed forces substantially included Palestinians and the Druze community's sympathy for them, which was inherited from his father, remained strong.[123] Neglecting Syrian pressure, Junblat's militias blocked the coastal highway to prevent the reinforcements of the Amal Movement from reaching Palestinian camps and attempted to secure supplies to the camps.[124]

Relations between the Druzes and Syria were decisively worsened in February 1987, when the Syrian army was deployed in West Beirut to save the Amal Movement, and when Junblat tried to establish a strong foothold there.[125] Junblat's goal seems to have been not only making it easier to provide support to Palestinian forces, but also to increase his power among the Muslims in Beirut. However, Asad now made it a top priority to weaken the Druzes, calculating that stripping pro-Palestinian groups outside the camps of their power would badly affect Palestinian military operations.[126] A series of attacks on Junblat, which took the form of forcing him to hand his aide over to the Syrian authorities and to reshuffle his command in a manner acceptable to them, incurred bitter Druze resentment against Asad.[127]

The Palestinians and Syria

Syria used its ties with a number of Palestinian groups in Lebanon as a means to secure its own national security against Israel and its political and economic interests in Lebanon. Syria's relations with Fatah and its leader 'Arafat had initially been poor. This was because at the time of 'Black September' in 1970, Asad, the then commander of the Syrian air force, had declined to provide air cover for the Syrian ground forces entering Jordan to support the Palestinians, which resulted in their slaughter by the Jordanian army.[128] In contrast, Syria's relations with radical Palestinian groups were fairly good, and it thereby gained a position to exert influence over them by 1973.[129] The balance was further tipped towards Syria in mid-1974, when it was able to get its proxy organization, Sa'iqa, to soften its radicalism.[130] Being thus dissociated from radicalism, President Asad demonstrated to US Secretary of State Kissinger Syria's acceptance of his diplomatic approach towards the Arab–Israeli conflict.

As the possibility of Israel's attack against Syria through Lebanon was growing after the outbreak of the civil war, Asad sought both to control the PLO's military activities against Israel on Lebanese soil and to avoid Israeli penetration into Lebanon. In pursuit of this end, Syria dramatically changed its relations with the PLO during the conflict. Syria had initially supported the LNM–PLO coalition. Later, when Maronite militias launched a heavy offensive in January 1976 with the aim of partitioning Lebanon and establishing a Maronite 'mini-state', thereby risking an Israeli invasion, Asad ordered the dispatch of units of the Palestine Liberation Army (PLA) into Lebanon to prevent the Maronites from realizing their goal.[131]

However, Palestinian–Syrian relations soon deteriorated over the Syrian-initiated Constitutional Document in February 1976, because the PLO finally decided to align with the LNM.[132] Ultimately, the Syrian army invaded Lebanon, siding with the Maronites in June 1976 and aiming to prevent the radicalization of Lebanon by the LNM–PLO coalition, since this situation threatened to give Israel a pretext to invade Lebanon and thus would endanger the Syrian state itself.

After the Likud government upgraded Israel's alliance with the Maronites as a consequence of Egypt's withdrawal from the Arab–Israeli power balance, Asad attempted to contain Israel's aggression towards Lebanon by resuming ties with the PLO. However, his renewed relations with the PLO were not firm. During Israel's Litani Operation in 1978 and the Israeli invasion in 1982, the Syrian army stationed in Lebanon did not positively engage in the battles, which allowed the Palestinians to be attacked by the Israeli army. The PLO realized that Syrian devotion to the Palestinian cause was suspect and that Syria would not risk its own security for the sake of the Palestinians. After 1982, Syria, even though it supported guerrilla operations against the Israeli army in Lebanon, had no intention of directly confronting Israel by allowing the PLO to engage in 'free' military activities.[133] Syria also controlled Palestinian activities in the Biqa' area.[134] While Syria claimed to be a patron of the PLO, it did not fulfil the responsibilities attached to this self-assumed role, apparent in the cases of 1978 and 1982.

Despite the Syrian claim, the PLO had no intention of ceding its autonomy to Syria, and 'Arafat and his Fatah organization struggled to maximize the freedom of their military actions. On the other hand, Asad attempted to reshape the PLO's leadership to make it more subject to him, and particularly encouraged dissidents within the PLO to challenge 'Arafat.[135] After the PLO withdrew from Beirut in September 1982,[136] splits within the PLO occurred mainly over differing attitudes towards the 'Reagan Plan', a version of 'Camp David'-style autonomy for the West Bank, and over relations with Jordan.[137] Believing that Syria had no right to be a 'protector' over the PLO because of its failure to defend Palestinians in 1978 and 1982, and with considerably reduced options after the PLO's expulsion from Lebanon, 'Arafat gave the Reagan Plan serious consideration and began to consult with the Jordanian monarchy over it.[138] In addition, 'Arafat kept pace with King Husayn of Jordan 'in proposing negotiations with Israel over the West Bank'.[139]

'Arafat's renewed alliance with Husayn was not acceptable to Asad, and when revolts against 'Arafat actually occurred within the PLO, the Syrian regime exploited them, trying to oust him and reshape the organization in a manner more favourable to it. In 1983, Syrian-backed Palestinian forces launched a heavy offensive against 'Arafat, which led to his eventual evacuation from Tripoli.[140] Later, during the Camps War, Syria sponsored the Palestine National Salvation Front (PNSF), which, though it was composed of anti-'Arafat factions, did not give Syria a reliable alternative to 'Arafat's PLO.[141]

In sum, despite its desire to control the PLO and a series of attacks against it, Syria was caught in a dilemma. Since the Asad regime assumed a self-imaged role as the champion of Arab nationalism and at the same time continued open conflict with the PLO, a symbol of the Arab cause, there was danger of damaging the regime's credibility. Therefore, Syria generally negotiated and dialogued with the PLO while putting pressure on the Palestinians, and never actually severed relations with the PLO during the civil war period in Lebanon.

Brief Summary

Overall, the identity of each non-governmental actor in Lebanon shaped an underlying predisposition in its relations with Syria: relations between the Muslim and Palestinian groups and Syria were generally better than those between the Maronites and Syria, and the Asad regime, in terms of advocating Arab nationalism, did not want to confront the Muslims and the Palestinians. However, the Lebanese and Syrian power calculations occasionally affected their relations. In fact, Syria aligned itself with the Maronites and antagonized the LNM–PLO coalition in 1976. Later, during the Camps War in the late 1980s, there were clashes between the Hizbullah-backed Palestinian forces and the Syrian-supported Amal Movement.

In addition, there was interdependency between the Asad regime and Lebanese non-governmental actors. The former used these groups to justify Syria's presence and consolidate its hegemony in Lebanon, and the latter exploited Syrian power to promote their own interests.

President Sulayman Franjiya and the Asad Regime

Introduction

President Franjiya was primarily concerned about Palestinian military activities on Lebanese soil in the early 1970s, to which President Asad also had to pay attention in terms of Syria's national security. Later, after the outbreak of the civil war in Lebanon, he was confronted by the powerful LNM–PLO coalition. The emergence of semi-anarchy in Lebanon prompted Syria to make efforts to stabilize Lebanon, and the Asad regime interfered in the formation of the Karami cabinet, initiated the formation of the National Dialogue Committee (NDC) and the Constitutional Document, and arranged the presidential election for a successor to Franjiya. Franjiya's actions and attitudes towards the Syrian regime over these issues are examined in this section.

Palestinian Military Activities on Lebanese Soil

The heavy losses inflicted on the PLO by the events of 1970's Black September in Jordan were a major factor in determining Fatah's cautious approach in Lebanon. However, while the PLO spokesman officially announced in January 1972 the continuation of a temporary freeze in its guerrilla activities in southern Lebanon, the PLO leadership sometimes found it difficult to ensure that this order was actually executed.[142] This was because the Popular Front for the Liberation of Palestine–General Command (PFLP–GC) and some Fatah field commanders opposed the order.[143] In fact, a number of small incidents occurred between the Palestinian guerrillas and the Lebanese army, since it attempted to restrict the guerrilla activities in terms of Lebanon's national security.

In May 1973, the Palestinian seizure of parts of suburban Beirut and subsequent clashes between the Lebanese army and the radical Palestinian groups, such as the Popular Front for the Liberation of Palestine (PFLP), the Democratic Front for the Liberation of Palestine (DFLP) and Sa'iqa, all associated with the LNM, forced President Franjiya to take some harsh measures.[144] When the DFLP kidnapped several Lebanese soldiers at the beginning of May, the army, in its largest operation against the Palestinians since 1969, surrounded the Palestinian refugee camps in Beirut, and Fatah was quickly drawn into the confrontation.[145] 'Despite a succession of [ceasefire] agreements, the clashes between the [Lebanese army] and the [Palestinian] commandos continued for over two weeks, spreading from Beirut to other parts of [Lebanon].'[146] The climax in these clashes was Franjiya's decision to use the Lebanese air force against the Palestinian camps where the commandos stationed.[147]

However, Franjiya was soon forced to halt the air raids because of the enormous pressure exerted on Lebanon by Syria and other Arab countries.[148] In particular, Egypt and Syria, which were planning what became the October War in 1973, had a strong will not to escalate the situation.[149] President Asad ordered not only the closure of the Lebanese–Syrian border on 8 May, but also that the Fatah and Sa'iqa forces move from Syria and cross into Lebanon.[150] Although relations between Franjiya and Asad were seriously aggravated by the crisis, the fact that they had maintained a close relationship helped to make it possible for them to reach an accommodation.[151] Egypt's interest in containing the Lebanese turmoil may also have contributed to the halting of Lebanese air raids on the Palestinians. Under these measures of pressure, especially those exerted by his 'friend' in Damascus, Franjiya finally suspended military operations by the Lebanese army.[152] He also concluded the Milkart Agreement with the leadership of the PLO on 17 May, which was based on the principles of the 1969 Cairo Agreement.[153]

While Franjiya was forced to halt the Lebanese army operations against the Palestinians, by realigning himself with the Asad regime he might have expected their restrictions on military activities in Lebanon. Although the fighting between the Lebanese army and the Palestinians continued on Lebanese soil, Lebanon allowed Syria to make use of its radar bases when Israeli and Syrian fighters clashed over Lebanese airspace during the 1973 October War.[154] Finally, in December 1974, Lebanon revealed its intention to buy Soviet-made SAM missiles for use against Israel's air raids and soon discussed this issue with Syria.[155] While Syria, from the viewpoint of pan-Arabism, opposed Lebanon's restrictions on Palestinian military activities, it showed a supportive attitude towards the Lebanese effort to strengthen its own military capability.

Formation of the Karami Cabinet

After the Ayn al-Rummaneh clashes between the Kata'ib Party and the Palestinians on 13 April 1975, the spread of fighting between rival militias further polarized Lebanon's internal situation. On the one hand, the Maronites pledged support for the Kata'ib Party and the NLP, and demanded that the Lebanese army intervene to stop the fighting.[156] On the other hand, the LNM protested against the slaughter of Palestinians and 'called for a political and economic boycott of the Kata'ib Party'.[157] In protest against the call from LNM leader Junblat, the Kata'ib Party and the NLP withdrew its members from the cabinet under Prime Minister Rashid al-Sulh, who was strongly supported by Junblat, which brought about the collapse of the Sulh cabinet on 15 May.[158]

Under these circumstances, President Franjiya ordered an ex-commander of Lebanon's Internal Security Forces, Nur al-Din al-Rifai, to form a cabinet mainly composed of military officers.[159] While the Kata'ib Party and the NLP appreciated the president's move to initiate the formation of a military cabinet, the LNM and its ally, the PLO, strongly condemned it.[160] Since Muslims and Palestinians considered the Lebanese army to be a Maronite symbol, and since the high-ranking officers were actually dominated by Maronites, Franjiya's designation of Rifai was considered to be an example of his sectarian bias. In addition, Franjiya ignored Lebanon's constitutional practice by not taking heed of the parliamentary recommendation for the premiership, as a majority in the parliament endorsed Karami.[161] In consequence, strong opposition from the LNM–PLO coalition forced Franjiya to dismantle the Rifai cabinet and to appoint as the premier his traditional opponent, Karami, on 28 May 1975, with whom President Asad had good relations.[162]

According to Weinberger (1986), until the formation of the Rifai cabinet, Syria had been rather passively involved in Lebanese affairs and had only issued press statements expressing support for the rights of the Palestinians.[163] However, since Franjiya's decision to establish the military cabinet had resulted in armed clashes and political stalemate in Lebanon, Syrian leaders were forced to involve themselves more actively in Lebanese affairs. In particular, as Salibi (1976) pointed out: 'Syria could have been seriously embarrassed by a new confrontation between the Lebanese [a]rmy and the [PLO] commandos, which would have forced the Syrian government to intervene on the Palestinian side.'[164] This scenario was not at all favoured by the Syrian government. As Asad relied on US Secretary of State Kissinger to recover the Golan Heights, he did not want to take any action that would be viewed unfavourably by the US administration. Asad thus immediately launched a diplomatic initiative with Foreign Minister 'Abd al-Halim Khaddam, Air Force Commander Naji Jamil and Chief of Staff Hikmat al-Shihabi.[165]

The Syrians, especially Khaddam, Jamil and Shihabi, played an important role in forming the Karami cabinet,[166] taking into consideration the preferences of Lebanon's Sunni establishment, the LNM and the PLO, all of which perceived him as the sole candidate for the premiership.[167] This was desirable for Syria, since Karami was traditionally a strong supporter of its influence in Lebanon. With domestic support for Karami, Asad managed to force Franjiya to designate Karami, Franjiya's long-term political rival in northern Lebanon, to the premiership.[168]

Prime Minister Karami had to remove two major obstacles in forming his cabinet. On the one hand, Junblat was still calling for the boycott of the Kata'ib Party and stated his refusal to take part in any cabinet in which members from the party would be included.[169] Pierre al-Jumayyil, on the other hand, was not willing to cede to Junblat's demands.[170] As Karami soon faced a political deadlock, which was accompanied by heavy fighting,[171] he had to rely on Asad for the breakthrough. The Syrian regime then suggested the formation of a temporary 'mini-cabinet', which led to the establishment of a six-member cabinet on 1 July 1975.[172] In addition to the appointment of Karami, the cabinet formation was a further blow to Franjiya, since he hoped the forthcoming cabinet would include members from both the Kata'ib Party and the LNM.[173] Karami made a bitter choice in designating Sham'un as Interior Minister, as they had been antagonists since the 1958 Civil War.[174] Since the appointment of Sham'un was welcomed by Jumayyil and not rejected by Junblat,[175] Karami and Asad may have calculated that Sham'un's presence in the cabinet would appease or at least decrease the opposition from Jumayyil and Junblat to the Karami cabinet, and thus would stabilize the country.

However, according to Petran (1987), Sham'un 'refused even to consult with Karami and used his position at every opportunity to sabotage the government's policy and to advance the rightist [Maronite] cause'.[176] Karami's effort to stabilize the country by forming a 'neutral' cabinet, which was strongly backed by Asad, consequently faced a severe blow from Sham'un.

Asad, in fact, forced both Franjiya and Karami to relinquish some of their political preferences in helping to form the cabinet. However, Franjiya had to make more of a concession by nominating Karami and excluding Jumayyil and Junblat from the cabinet than Karami was obliged to make by including Sham'un in his cabinet. On the one hand, Franjiya may have believed that the inclusion of Kata'ib Party and LNM members in the cabinet would contain their 'radical' activities on the battlefield. Asad, on the other hand, might have been calculating that their inclusion would further paralyse the country because of a political deadlock among cabinet members that would have resulted. Under a heavy offensive against the Maronites by the LNM–PLO coalition bolstered by Syria, Franjiya was forced to obey the Asad initiative.

Formation of the National Dialogue Committee

After the conclusion of Sinai II in September 1975, the intensity of sectarian fighting in Lebanon forced the Karami cabinet to ask President Asad to intervene to stop it.[177] However, since President Franjiya's relations with Asad had worsened after the formation of the cabinet, Franjiya blamed the Syrian-supported LNM–PLO coalition for initiating the fighting and even indicated the possibility of asking the Arab League or key Arab countries to enter into a conflict-resolution process.[178] Since Syria did not want those actors to be involved in the process, Foreign Minister Khaddam immediately initiated negotiations for a ceasefire and the formation of the NDC to discuss political reforms and achieve reconciliation in Lebanon.[179]

The NDC was finally formed on 20 September 1975 and had in total 20 members, equally divided between Muslims and Christians.[180] The committee actually included most leading politicians: Junblat; the notable Sunni politicians, Salam, 'Abdallah al-Yafi and Prime Minister Karami; Parliament Speaker Kamil al-As'ad; Secretary-General of the pro-Syrian faction of the Ba'th Party, 'Asim Qansu; leader of the Kata'ib Party, Jumayyil; ex-President and leader of the NLP, Sham'un; and leader of the National Bloc Party, Raymond Iddi.[181] As Khazen (2000a) pointed out, the fact that the pro-Iraqi faction of the Ba'th Party had no representative on the NDC was an indication of increasing Syrian influence in Lebanese politics.[182]

However, the result of this Syrian mediation was disappointing, and the NDC meeting finally became, as Khazen (2000a) described it, a 'national deaf talk'.[183] This was because, while the Kata'ib Party and its allies focused on the issue of Lebanon's territorial sovereignty, the LNM and its allies stuck to the issue of political reforms in Lebanon, including the abolition of sectarianism.[184] When the members of the Kata'ib Party and the NLP decided to boycott the NDC, the subcommittee responsible for political issues managed to propose the reforms to cancel Article 95 of the Lebanese constitution (stipulating the sectarian allocation of its parliamentary seats), to lower the suffrage age to 18 and to establish an economic and social council, all of which were demanded by the LNM.[185] Then, the Maronite side 'promptly took to speaking of the NDC as "the supreme revolutionary command"',[186] and Franjiya and Karami reached a compromise deal the contents of which were not the abolition of Article 95, but its reinterpretation.[187] While they were keen on preserving Lebanon's sectarianism as their key power base, they were also fearful of further polarization in Lebanon. Asad might have tolerated the compromise deal, since the worsened situation in Lebanon would have seriously threatened Syria's national security.

Formation of the Constitutional Document

The escalation of violence between Lebanon's Maronite militias and the LNM–PLO coalition, especially in the areas around the Palestinian refugee camps of Tall al-Za'tar and Jisr al-Basha during December 1975 and January 1976,[188] forced President Asad to appease each side. First, in order to prevent the Maronites from attempting to partition Lebanon and establish their own 'mini-state', which might have drawn Israel into Lebanon, in mid-January Asad decided to dispatch units of the Syrian-based PLA,[189] which was officially part of the PLO, but in reality was part of the Syrian army.[190] Next, after stopping the Maronite progress, Syria imposed a ceasefire on 21 January.[191] As Khazen (2000a) noted: 'While Asad sought to tame the Maronite establishment, his objective, in early 1976, was not to defeat Christian forces militarily.'[192] On the contrary, Syria needed the cooperation of Lebanon's Maronite and Sunni *zuama* in order to curb the LNM–PLO coalition, whose military offensive against the Maronites had the potential of giving Israel a cause for intervention.

A delegation from the Kata'ib Party had already visited Syria in December 1975, which failed to improve their relations.[193] However, a heavy military offensive conducted by the LNM–PLO coalition in January 1976, which led to the fall of Sham'un's stronghold, Damur,[194] might have changed the Maronite perception of Syria and led to a situation in which cooperation with Syria was an option to prevent the community's further damage. Until then, Franjiya had not managed to convince Lebanon's Maronite leaders of the merits of working with Syria, although he had been secretly negotiating with Asad over political settlement for Lebanon since November 1975.[195] Franjiya seems to have calculated that by aligning the Maronites with Syria he could redress Lebanon's power balance in favour of the Maronite community. In the end, the weakened Maronite situation made it possible for Franjiya to go to Syria along with Prime Minister Karami in February 1976 in order to finalize a Syrian-initiated peace plan, which later became the Constitutional Document.[196] While the plan reassigned the allocation of Lebanon's major political posts to specific religious sects, it stipulated the equal division of the parliamentary seats between Christians and Muslims, the strengthening of premiership power and the conditions concerning Palestinian respect for Lebanese sovereignty.[197]

Karami, who also went to Syria along with Franjiya, resisted the idea of abolishing Lebanon's present sectarian allocation of the premiership and parliament speakership, which had been stipulated in the original Syrian plan to satisfy Junblat, and instead maintained the continuation of the existing political formula.[198] As a result, the plan for the nullification of the sectarian distribution of the above two posts was not adopted in the final official text of the Constitutional Document. Karami might have recognized Asad's need to cooperate with him in the attempt to pacify Lebanon and succeeded in maintaining the allocation of the premiership to the Sunni community. After Franjiya announced the Constitutional Document on 14 February 1976, Junblat criticized it vehemently. According to Khazen (2000a), one of the reasons for this was that while the Constitutional Document formulated a more balanced sectarian composition of Lebanon's government posts and provided a moderate resolution for the Lebanese conflict, the document did not adopt the LNM's most crucial programme: the abolition of political sectarianism in Lebanon. The other reason seems to be that Junblat's desire to hold the premiership or parliament speakership was blocked.[199] However, since the military balance was still in favour of the LNM–PLO coalition, compromise was not a real choice for Junblat, which brought about the resumption of heavy fighting.

Franjiya's Refusal to Resign Earlier

Along with a series of massive attacks led by the LNM–PLO coalition primarily against President Franjiya, there was heavy pressure in March 1976 for his resignation.[200] As a result, Syria's future position in Lebanon, especially as a mediator, became dependent on the outcome of an early presidential election for a successor to Franjiya, whose wide unpopularity surely deprived him of sufficient power to stabilize the Lebanese state. Asad suggested that, prior to the end of Franjiya's term, his successor would be elected on the condition that the incumbent should resign immediately after the election.[201] Asad's three main envoys, Khaddam, Jamil and Shihabi, negotiated with Franjiya, who initially opposed this idea explored by Asad.[202] However, under the enormous Maronite and Syrian pressure put on Franjiya to resign and a mounting threat by the LNM to establish a 'revolutionary government', the unanimous adoption of a constitutional amendment (Article 73) by the Lebanese parliament on 9 April, which would make possible the early election of Franjiya's successor, finally led him to sign the amendment.[203]

Two main candidates for the Lebanese presidential election emerged in late April 1976. One was Iddi, who had criticized not only the behaviour of the Kata'ib Party in the initial phase of the civil war, but also Syria's role in Lebanon.[204] Since Iddi had alienated the Maronite leadership, he was supported by the LNM–PLO coalition.[205] The other was Sarkis, who was supported by the Kata'ib Party, the NLP and Prime Minister Karami.[206] While Syria's official position towards the candidates was that the election was Lebanon's internal affair and thus Syria would not intervene,[207] its favour for Sarkis was obvious, considering Iddi's anti-Syrian stance. In addition, Sarkis's 'neutral' political stand was acceptable to both Lebanese Christians and Muslims and was seen favourably by Asad in the light of Syrian attempts to stabilize the Lebanese state. However, as Sarkis lacked a wide popular power base and the Lebanese army's support, he depended on the Asad regime.[208]

When the Lebanese parliamentary deputies met on 8 May 1976 to elect a new president, Syrian pressure on them (based on its military presence in Lebanon through Sa'iqa and the PLA), especially on some deputies reluctant to vote for Sarkis, influenced the final result of the election.[209] Indeed, a group of deputies from the Biqa' area was forced to vote for Sarkis, since the Syrian military presence in the area was overwhelming.[210] It is also said that Sa'iqa members forced anti-Syrian deputies suspected of boycotting the election to attend the parliament session.[211] Sarkis, then, gained 66 votes out of 69 deputies present and only three deputies actually boycotted the election: Iddi, Salam and Sulh,[212] who were all on bad terms with Asad and/or his close ally, Franjiya. Even though the Syrian influence in the election was obvious, almost all the Lebanese deputies, forced or not, chose to elect Sarkis to the presidency, and their actions seemed to be based on his 'neutral' stance.

While Sarkis's election raised the Lebanese hope of terminating the civil war, this hope did not last, since Franjiya stated that he would hold the presidency until September 1976, when his term was formally to be concluded.[213] Franjiya might have calculated that if he resigned under a series of massive attacks launched by the LNM–PLO coalition, his position within the Maronite community would be further weakened. This was because his political rivals in the community, Jumayyil and Sham'un, had increased their power by forming the Lebanese Front. In addition, it seems that the Asad regime tolerated Franjiya's unwillingness to resign, because of its indirect benefit of having the well-known figure in the Lebanese presidency. As the LNM–PLO coalition further escalated its military activities with the aim of forcing Franjiya to resign, he asked for the direct intervention of a sizeable part of the Syrian army on the side of the Maronites, and the intervention indeed started in June 1976.

Summary

During the early 1970s, Palestinian military activities on Lebanese soil had been a great concern for President Franjiya, who attempted to regulate their operations especially in 1973. Although Franjiya was forced to suspend his use of the Lebanese air force against the Palestinian camps by the pressure exerted by President Asad, his calculation seemed to be that realigning with the Syrian regime could encourage Palestinian cooperation on military activities. In the aftermath, despite the continued clashes between the Lebanese army and the Palestinians, Lebanon and Syria cooperated during the 1973 October War and over the issue of the Lebanese plan to purchase Soviet-made missiles.

Immediately after the outbreak of the civil war in Lebanon, Franjiya faced a series of fierce attacks from the strong LNM–PLO coalition. Asad likely forced Franjiya to designate Karami, who was supported by the coalition and Sunni establishment in Lebanon, to the premiership. However, it is equally likely that Franjiya did so and thus appeased Asad in order to obtain the support of the Syrian-backed LNM–PLO coalition, which was necessary to maintain his status.

Although Asad's imposition of Karami temporarily worsened his relationsip with Franjiya, they remained in contact on the basis of their shared political interests. Asad, for his part, did not want to antagonize Franjiya, as Syria needed to obtain the broad support and acceptance of the Lebanese government to increase its involvement in Lebanese affairs. Consequently, when Franjiya modified a recommendation proposed by the Syrian-led NDC, i.e. the abolition of the sectarian allocation in the

Lebanese parliament, Asad did not overtly oppose it, although the recommendation had been originally aimed at taming the Syrian-supported LNM–PLO coalition. Later in the spring of 1976, when Franjiya retracted the promise of his earlier resignation, Asad permitted him to hold office until his official term expired. This was because Asad might have calculated that his regime would be able to exert more influence through such a well-known figure than through a lesser-known figure. In turn, gaining the Syrian support allowed Franjiya to defend his power against that of Sham'un and Jumayyil, his rivals in Lebanon's Maronite community, who were increasing their power by forming the Lebanese Front. It appears that Franjiya's long-term reliance on Asad increased his 'sensitivity' towards Damascus and encouraged his consistent alignment with it.

After the LNM–PLO coalition militarily defeated Lebanon's Maronite militias during the severe fighting of late 1975 and early 1976, the community showed willingness to align with Syria in order to prevent further losses. The changed Maronite perception enabled Franjiya to associate himself with the Syrian-initiated Constitutional Document in February 1976, which aimed to preserve the status quo in Lebanon, i.e. the sectarian-based political system, with some modifications. After Junblat criticized the document and escalated military attacks against Franjiya in particular and the Maronite community in general, both of which were now being backed by Asad, Franjiya asked the Syrian army to protect them from the LNM–PLO coalition. Franjiya's request suited Asad's interests, since he feared the increasing power and popularity of the LNM–PLO coalition among Lebanese Muslims, which had the potential to draw Israel into Lebanon. Owing to this fear, in June 1976 Asad decided to deploy Syria's regular army to Lebanon, mainly to contain the powerful LNM–PLO coalition and partly to avoid giving Israel a pretext for intervention in Lebanon. Syria inevitably became a more pivotal player in Lebanese affairs, once its troops had settled down in Lebanon.

President Ilyas Sarkis and the Asad Regime

Introduction

President Sarkis designated initially Huss and later Wazzan to Lebanon's premiership, both of whom had good terms with the Asad regime. However, under the changed regional circumstances in the Middle East, Syria improved its relations with the PLO, and the strengthening of the Lebanese army's role, to which Sarkis gave priority as a key stabilizing force, was not fully implemented. While Sarkis began to distance himself from the Syrian regime, he acknowledged the necessity of Lebanon's cooperation with Syria in order to reconstruct the Lebanese state. Sarkis had periodically extended the Syrian-dominated ADF mandate (although he finally abolished it) and attempted to maintain good economic relations between Lebanon and Syria under the flourishing militia economy in Lebanon. Sarkis's actions and attitudes towards the Asad regime over these issues are explored in this section.

Designation of Huss and Wazzan to Lebanon's Premierhip

Although he was elected with the help of the Asad regime and although his inauguration ceremony in September 1976 took place at Shtura in the Biqa' region under a Syrian armed presence,[214] President Sarkis initially tried to implement a 'neutral' policy to pacify Lebanon.[215] In the process of forming a new cabinet in Lebanon, Sarkis's decision might have been influenced by his debt to the Syrian regime for his election to the Lebanese presidency. Despite this, Sarkis persisted in his 'neutral' political views, and while he took into consideration Syrian opposition to the LNM's participation in the cabinet,[216] he managed to put in place a cabinet without representatives from any of the warlord factions in Lebanon. Sarkis designated Huss, a respected economist, to the premiership, who formed a technocrat cabinet composed of four Christians and four Muslims in December 1976.[217] Sarkis and Huss began to take measures to restore public order in Lebanon, on the basis of which they hoped to launch a process of its economic rehabilitation. As Huss himself noted, the Lebanese government was strongly opposed to any attempts by radical Maronites and the PLO in Lebanon to injure political integrity.[218] Also, the government's engagement in constructing such a centrally controlled state in Lebanon matched with Syrian interests, since the stabilization of its western flank under a Syrian-influenced regime would decrease the potential for Israeli penetration into it through Lebanon.

However, the common desire of Sarkis and Huss to establish a strong state faced tough opposition from the *zuama* in Lebanon, especially the Maronite warlords, who were oscillating between reality, i.e. the goal of establishing their own 'mini-state', and hope, i.e. to control entire parts of Lebanon. As the Maronite attitudes were incompatible with Syria, their relations, which had already come under increasing strain, were further worsened. In fact, the Maronites, having managed to restore their power by aligning with Syria in 1976, no longer felt they needed Damascus.

Although the Maronite–Syrian relations changed, Sarkis continued to take into consideration both Asad's and Lebanese Muslims' preference for Huss, and relations between Sarkis and Huss were generally good.[219] When Huss tendered his resignation in May 1979 in protest against the fighting between the LF and the Syrian army on Lebanese soil,[220] Sarkis asked Huss to form a new cabinet, which was realized in July.[221] After Huss finally resigned in July 1980, Sarkis initially designated Taqi al-Din al-Sulh to the premiership. However, as Sulh failed to form a new cabinet, Sarkis later designated a technocrat, Wazzan, as the successor in October.[222] Sarkis and Wazzan cooperated and made joint peace efforts until Sarkis left the presidency in 1982.

Deployment of the Lebanese Army and the Mandate of the Arab Deterrent Force

After assuming the post, President Sarkis started his attempts to pacify Lebanon by using the army. In doing so he had to consider the Syrian military presence in Lebanon, which had been legitimized by the Arab League as part of the ADF, and the Syrian army later constituted the majority in it. The relationship between the Lebanese army and the Syrian-dominated ADF is the main focus of this subsection.

After the Arab League conferences of Riyadh and Cairo in October 1976, the PLO began to refortify its military bases in southern Lebanon. As a result, the PLO brought about violent confrontation with a newly-created Christian militia group, later known as the South Lebanese Army (SLA), which was led by Major Sa'd Haddad and armed and financed by Israel. Both the LNM–PLO coalition and Haddad's forces intensified their fighting, and the cycle of violence continued from the latter part of 1976 to the first part of 1977.

Under these circumstances, Syria found itself caught in a dilemma. While Syria sought the containment of the Israeli influence in southern Lebanon and favoured the LNM–PLO coalition in the region, it also feared that the resumption of fighting in the south would invite further military intervention by Israel. In addition, Syria could not send the ADF to southern Lebanon, because of Israel's opposition on the basis of the Red Line Agreement.

To resolve the perilous situation in southern Lebanon, Syria sponsored a meeting with the PLO and the Lebanese government in Shtura, Lebanon, and the Syrian effort brought into existence the Shtura Agreement in July 1977.[223] According to Hinnebusch (1986), the agreement stipulated that 'the Palestinians would respect Lebanese sovereignty, stay out of Lebanese politics, move their military forces to restricted areas in the south, and refrain from attacks across the [Israeli–Lebanese] border, while the Lebanese army would move south and take control of the border area from Haddad'.[224]

Although the peace process based on the Shtura Agreement was to take place in two stages,[225] it was not carried out completely. Indeed, the agreement was fully applied to northern Lebanon, but was not implemented in southern Lebanon.[226]

Although Syria was the power broker of the agreement, it began to lose interest in the implementation because of the regional political shifts. The installation of the Likud government in Israel and its initiatives to strengthen its ties with the Lebanese Maronites, particularly the LF and SLA, led Syria, deterred by Israel from maintaining a direct presence in southern Lebanon (the Red Line Agreement), to require controllable Palestinian armed forces as a proxy in the region.[227]

Although Sarkis continuously attempted to bring about the Palestinian withdrawal from southern Lebanon and the deployment of the Lebanese army there on the basis of the Shtura agreement,[228] because of the Asad regime's passive attitudes these measures were not put into effect. Sarkis's disappointment at the Syrian regime gradually caused him to distance himself from it. While Sarkis moved closer to the Lebanese Front during the fighting between the LF and Syrian forces in 1978, he carefully tried not to alienate and antagonize the Muslims and the Palestinians in Lebanon and avoided an all-out confrontation with the Asad regime.

At the same time Sarkis probably understood the difficulty of rebuilding the Lebanese army. Instead of the Lebanese army, Sarkis attempted to have UN forces stationed in southern Lebanon, but this did not materialize. This was because the introduction of such a force would reduce the power of the Syrian-dominated ADF and thus threaten its status in Lebanon, and hence Asad strongly objected to Sarkis's attempt.[229]

However, after Israel's Litani Operation in March 1978, Lebanon and Syria agreed to send the Lebanese army to southern Lebanon, with Syria securing Palestinian cooperation.[230] This situation appears to have been achieved as a result of the following calculations. On the one hand, President Asad may have thought that the containment of Haddad's force in the south would in turn weaken Lebanon's Maronite forces, especially the LF in northern Lebanon, which the Syrian-led ADF had militarily confronted since February 1978. In addition, Asad appears to have calculated that further objection to the deployment of the Lebanese army in the south would decrease the legitimacy of the Syrian presence in Lebanon. On the other hand, by exploiting the neighbouring country's delicate position in his country, Sarkis may have hoped to increase the legitimacy of the Lebanese government by having the army in the south and to turn Syria's focus from northern Lebanon to southern Lebanon. In May, the Litani Brigade of the Lebanese army, which was numbered at 650 and put together under Huss, was newly created and it aimed, by passing through the area controlled by Haddad, to reach the southern border region under the jurisdiction of the United Nations Interim Force in Lebanon (UNIFIL).[231] However, Haddad's militias attacked the brigade and halted the process.[232]

After the Syrian army, in defiance of Sarkis, did not stop fighting against the LF in northern Lebanon, he announced his resignation in July 1978,[233] probably calculating that he was irreplaceable and indispensable to Asad. Immediately, he asked Sarkis to remain in office, since Syria's military presence in Lebanon under the umbrella of the ADF owed its legitimacy to Sarkis, who had the right to end the mandate of the ADF. Thus, the Syrian army ceased a series of attacks against the LF, and Sarkis withdrew his resignation.[234] However, as Sarkis's resignation attempt resulted in halting the fighting against the LF and saving its losses, it is possible to say that he leaned towards sectarianism based on his Christian identity.

Nevertheless, the LF called for the replacement of the ADF by an international peacekeeping force. Pressured by Lebanese Maronites,[235] and by securing support from the Arab countries financing the ADF, Sarkis managed to negotiate successfully with Asad – who feared Lebanon's refusal to renew the ADF's mandate – at Bayt al-Din, Lebanon, in mid-October 1978. The conference called for the rebuilding of the Lebanese army, with a balanced sectarian composition, to replace the ADF.[236] This was followed by the Lebanese parliament's approval of the new army law in March 1979.[237] Although non-Syrian ADF troops withdrew from Lebanon completely by May, Syrian troops still held some strategic positions, especially in the centre of Beirut.[238] This Syrian attitude was explicable by the rejection of the new law by Sarkis, who, fearing that any military reform would strip the Maronites of their prerogatives, sided with the LF.[239] The continuing strained relations between Syria and the LF clearly affected Sarkis's behaviour.

In January 1980, Syria further redeployed most of its troops which had been stationed in northern Lebanon and East Beirut to Biqa', although it still kept several thousand troops in West Beirut.[240] The Syrian redeployment appears to have been influenced by the following factors. First, by concentrating its forces in Biqa', Syria attempted to ensure additional protection for its most vulnerable flank in the event of future Israeli attacks, the probability of which increased after the establishment of the Likud government. Second, since the Asad regime was facing a series of military attacks at home from the Muslim Brotherhood, the concentration of Syrian troops in an area relatively close to its capital made it easy for security forces in Syria to be reinforced by units of the ADF. Third, but most importantly, since the mandate of the ADF had to be renewed every six months, Asad might have calculated that it was necessary to appease Sarkis in view of the continuation of hostilities between the ADF and the LF. However, in March Syria rejected the demand by Butrus Khuri, commander of the Lebanese army, for the complete withdrawal of the Syrian army from all districts of Beirut and maintained its sizeable presence.[241]

Considering the desire of Syria to preserve its prestige and power in Lebanon, Sarkis continued to extend the ADF's mandate on its periodic expirations. This appears to have been influenced not only by Syria's still dominant power in Lebanon and Asad's occasional gesture of appeasement towards Sarkis, but also by the following regional factors and his own perception. In fact, since Sarkis relied on other Arab states as counterbalances to Syria, their views may have influenced him. Regarding the ADF's mandate, the Arab states actually held the view that the termination would lead to an alternative bilateral agreement between Lebanon and Syria, one that would only decrease whatever influence the Arab states could exert on Syria to soften its Lebanese policies.[242] Also Sarkis, as a 'neutral' figure, probably did not want to provoke Asad, which would alienate the Lebanese Muslims.

However, Sarkis's reliance on the Arab community to resolve the hostilities between the ADF and the LF to secure the deployment of the Lebanese army in all of Lebanon's territories resulted in failure. Although the Arab League summit in November 1981 stipulated its support for the Lebanese government's plan for the army's deployment in southern Lebanon,[243] this was not realized. It was largely due to the polarization among the Arab states, especially antagonism between Saudi Arabia and Syria, which resulted from the former supporting Iraq and the latter aligning with Iran in the Iran–Iraq War.

Later, Sarkis adopted increasingly unfriendly attitudes towards the Asad regime. One example is that Sarkis did not ask for the extension of the ADF's mandate in July 1982, although he had previously agreed to the continuation of the mandate whenever it periodically expired.[244] Furthermore, Sarkis demanded the complete withdrawal of the ADF and Israeli army from Lebanon, and finally the Arab states, including Syria, agreed to terminate the ADF's mandate at the Arab summit in September.[245]

However, it is impossible to neglect the fact that Sarkis still took Syrian concerns into account even after he clearly sided with the Lebanese Front in the 1980s. During the 'Missile Crisis' in 1981, which threatened to bring about a direct Syrian–Israeli military confrontation in Zahla, Lebanon, Sarkis dispatched his envoy to Syria to resolve the dangerous situation.[246] After the end of the crisis, Sarkis and Wazzan presented a joint peace programme, including the termination of all contacts with Israel by the Lebanese Front; the strict observance of the 1969 Cairo

Agreement by the Palestinians; and the gradual withdrawal of the Syrian army, which should be complete by August 1982.[247] Later, at the Arab summit in September, Sarkis agreed that the implementation of the withdrawal of Syrian forces from Lebanon at the end of the ADF's mission would be determined by Lebanese–Syrian negotiations.[248] Thus, as Thompson (2002) explained: 'Asad was able to maintain the legitimacy of Arab League sanctioning of the presence of Syrian forces in Lebanon even after the termination of the ADF mandate. As long as the Israelis maintained forces in Lebanon, Syria would have a written endorsement of its continued presence.'[249]

Sarkis could have put more pressure on the Asad regime with the aim of the Syrian army's complete and immediate withdrawal, but he did not. There were two reasons for this. First, Syria was isolated in the Arab world by virtue of its siding with Iran in the Iran–Iraq War. Second, Syria's dominant position in Lebanon was largely shattered by the Israeli invasion in June 1982, although Syrian forces remained entrenched in the Biqa' region.

Thus, it is possible to say that Lebanon was theoretically in a better power position to balance against Syria in the initial period of the 1980s. However, Sarkis perhaps took other internal threats against his position into consideration – such as the growing power of the Shi'as in Lebanon, their relations with Syria and Israel's alignment with the Maronites – and so avoided antagonizing the Asad regime. Consequently, it appears possible to say that Sarkis avoided all-out confrontation with the Syrian-led ADF and even attempted to appease the Syrian regime with the help of the Arab League.

Lebanon's Militia Economy and Reconstruction Efforts

As the civil war progressed, so did the fragmentation in Lebanon. This situation affected the economy: as the militia economy emerged, the 'normal' economic system nearly ceased to function.

Under the flourishing militia economy, attempts by Lebanon's political leadership to reconstruct a national economy were one of its main activities to restore the state's functions. In doing so, the Lebanese leaders had to take into consideration Syrian economic interests, since the country was involved not only in Lebanon's militia economy, through smuggling, but also in their reconstruction efforts.

As Picard (2000) explained, the militia economy came into being with 'the transition from the local mobilization of armed defence groups in villages or neighbourhoods that operated within the framework of a unified state to the monopolization of resources and means of coercion by large, organized, and hierarchical militias that gradually carved up Lebanese territory after 1976'.[250] In fact, the LF, the Amal Movement and the Progressive Socialist Party (PSP) attempted to consolidate their power in their own communities by looting Lebanon's national property and by depriving opponents of strategic resources, such as oil and electricity. They gave priority to securing access to those resources without having to rely on the mediation of their enemies, for example, by constructing separate ports, since Lebanon imported more than 50 per cent of its consumer goods.[251]

More importantly, Lebanese militias began to be involved in criminal economic activities, and the Syrian army stationed in Lebanon became deeply engaged in smuggling in the 1980s. Indeed, after the Syrian army started to station in Lebanon, a series of illegal economic networks between Lebanon and Syria was formed, especially in the Biqa' region, so as to smuggle drugs, consumer goods and other materials.

Despite the spread of the illegal militia economy in Lebanon and the Syrians' deep involvement, Syria sometimes brought benefits to Lebanon, which resulted in President Sarkis's initial good relationship with President Asad. As Lawson (1996) pointed out, in the autumn of 1976 the Syrian-led ADF created conditions in Beirut for Lebanon's banking system to work normally. This was favourable not only for Beirut's financial community, since the precarious security situation after the outbreak of the civil war made it impossible for Lebanon's banking sector to find domestic outlets for its holdings, but also for Syrian enterprises, which had used the highly respected banking system in Lebanon.[252]

During the late 1970s and early 1980s, reflecting the strained relations between Sarkis and Asad, the Lebanese–Syrian economic relationship was not always close. However, Syria finally agreed with Lebanon in 1981 to amend the 1953 trade pact to allow the export of a greater variety of Lebanese goods to Syria.[253] Since Syria was moving into self-sufficiency in cement production and Lebanon had traditionally exported both black and white cement to Syria,[254] Lebanon clearly needed to diversify its exports to Syria. Asad may well have been attending to Lebanon's economic needs so as not to further antagonize Sarkis.

However, the closure of the trans-Syrian pipeline and the halt of the export of Iraqi crude oil to Tripoli in April 1982, which were the result of the hostilities between Syria and Iraq,[255] further worsened the Lebanese–Syrian relationship. After a delegation composed of Lebanese businessmen visited Iraq,[256] the Lebanese cabinet approved a plan to establish a centre in Baghdad with the aim of marketing Lebanese industrial goods.[257] However, Sarkis avoided the severance of Lebanon's economic relations with Syria, since the former economic life, including the smuggling, largely depended on the latter country. For example, the Electricité du Liban network, which covered 85 per cent of Lebanon's electricity requirements and suffered from great losses as a result of the illegal tapping of its electricity lines by Lebanese individuals and militias, was forced to import electricity from Syria through the Biqa' region.[258] In addition, Syria was an important transit route for Lebanese goods to the Gulf states.

Summary

President Sarkis largely attempted to keep his policies as 'neutral' as possible, although he owed his election to Syrian power and although his inauguration was performed under its guidance. Sarkis was successful in putting in place a cabinet that did not contain representatives from warlord factions in Lebanon while designating Syrian-supported Huss to the premiership and deferring to Syrian opposition to the LNM's participation in the cabinet.

However, Sarkis soon began gradually distancing himself from President Asad. By 1978 Sarkis had become closer to the Lebanese Front, mainly as a result of the deteriorating relationship between Syria and the Maronite community in Lebanon, particularly between Syria and the LF, as well as the Asad regime's passive attitude towards the implementation of the Shtura Agreement, which had been concluded in July 1977. While Sarkis had anticipated Syrian support in containing the Palestinian military activities in southern Lebanon and in deploying the Lebanese army to the south, the changes in the international relations of the Middle East gave Syria an interest in maintaining a Palestinian military presence on the Lebanon–Israel border.

To counter this Syrian policy shift, Sarkis attempted to build inter-Arab support to confront the PLO presence in southern Lebanon and enable the Lebanese army to be dispatched to the area. His efforts were ultimately disrupted by the polarization among the Arab states owing to the Islamic Revolution in Iran and the Iran–Iraq War, as well as by Syria, which needed armed Palestinians in southern Lebanon to counter Israeli provocation under the Likud government.

At the same time, Sarkis avoided alienating Lebanon's Muslim community and the Asad regime by continuing to support his Sunni counterpart, i.e. Prime Minister Huss. Indeed, when Huss threatened to resign in May 1979, Sarkis asked him to form a new cabinet. As Huss prioritized economic reconstruction, he consistently backed Sarkis's regional policy of seeking inter-Arab support to stabilize southern Lebanon. In the 1981 Missile Crisis, Sarkis sent his envoy to Syria and cooperated with Prime Minister Wazzan to propose a joint peace programme.

Ultimately, Sarkis deferred to Syrian interests in Lebanon by continuing to extend the ADF's mandate at its periodic expiration. Even after he finally decided to let its mandate expire in July 1982, he later agreed at the September Arab League summit that the withdrawal of the Syrian army would be contingent on future Lebanese–Syrian negotiations and on the Israeli army's withdrawal from Lebanon.

It appears likely that Asad's occasional manifestations of appeasement, notably the Syrian army's partial redeployment from Christian-dominated areas of northern Lebanon and East Beirut to the Biqa' region in January 1980, as well as Sarkis's recognition of the growing power of Lebanon's Shi'a community and its close relationship with Syria, encouraged his deference to the Syrian regime. In addition, the Lebanese–Syrian economic interdependency, which Sarkis's Sunni counterparts Huss and Wazzan emphasized to a greater extent, was likely another important factor for Sarkis's alignment with the Asad regime, particularly considering the priority Sarkis gave to cooperation with Huss and Wassan.

In the autumn of 1976, the Syrian-led ADF established an economic environment in Beirut that made it possible for Lebanon's banking sector to resume its operations and thus enabled Syrian investors to access its services once again. At the same time, Lebanon exported various goods to Syria itself and the Gulf states through it. Under Lebanon's flourishing militia economy and the illegal economic activities that resulted from it, even one of the most important lifelines in Lebanon – electricity – had to be imported from Syria. These factors clearly affected Sarkis's relationship with the Asad regime.

President Amin al-Jumayyil and the Asad Regime

Introduction

Under the weakening power of Syria and its allies in Lebanon, i.e. Muslim forces and the PLO, President Jumayyil aligned

Lebanon with the United States and Israel against Syria, and Lebanon indeed concluded the May 17 Agreement with Israel in 1983. However, as Syria soon recovered much of its power on Lebanese soil by using its allies in Lebanon, it caused Jumayyil to decide to abrogate the agreement in 1984. Although Jumayyil began to take Syrian interests into consideration, the Tripartite Agreement, which was arranged and concluded in 1985 under the auspices of Syria, antagonized him and his relationship with the Asad regime was not much improved until the end of his presidential term. Their relations were further defined by the role and deployment of the Lebanese army, and Lebanon's efforts for economic recovery and social stability.

Treatment of the May 17 Agreement

After the assassination of his younger brother, Bashir al-Jumayyil, on 14 September, 1982, Amin al-Jumayyil was elected to the Lebanese presidency by an overwhelming majority of the Lebanese parliament, i.e. the votes of 77 of the 80 representatives, and he took office on 23 September.[259] Unlike Bashir, who was said to have links with the Central Intelligence Agency (CIA) and Mossad,[260] Amin had been considered to be a 'balanced' man because of his friendly relations with not only Christian, but also Muslim political leaders in Lebanon,[261] although he was also a member of the Kata'ib Party. President Jumayyil retained Prime Minister Wazzan, and Wazzan selected as the cabinet ministers nine competent technocrats who had no political or governmental background.[262] Jumayyil himself might have been eager for Wazzan to form a broad coalition cabinet consisting of all the important political groups in Lebanon, but since he was elected under Israel's occupation, his policies needed to take its dominant position in Lebanon into consideration. Thus, Jumayyil did not strongly assert that Syria's main allies in Lebanon, Berri and Walid Junblat, would be included in a new cabinet.[263] It appears that as a secondary choice a 'neutral' technocrat cabinet, which would not so harm the personal reputation of Jumayyil, was formed while he was appeasing Israelis.

Jumayyil initially attempted to take an even-handed stance towards each of the 'occupation forces' in Lebanon, and many Lebanese indeed wanted the US-led MNF, which was created after the Israeli invasion in June 1982, to supervise the evacuation of Palestinian guerrillas, as well as Israeli and Syrian forces, from Lebanon.[264] However, these attempts by Jumayyil faced difficulties, since the United States did not seriously pressure Israel into withdrawing its troops.[265]

Indeed, Jumayyil came to ally himself closely with Israel's Likud government and the US Reagan administration and, in turn, to antagonize the Asad regime and Syria's Lebanese proxies. These outcomes were the results of the further strengthened Maronite–Israeli connections and the weakening of Syrian influence in Lebanon, both of which were caused by the Israeli invasion in 1982, the resulting emergence of the Israeli hegemony in Lebanon and the strengthened Cold War context in the Middle East after the end of the détente between the superpowers.

Consequently, Lebanese Muslims' hope for Jumayyil to develop a policy of national reconciliation evaporated, and their increasingly negative attitudes towards him constituted a basis for them to strengthen alliances with Syria in the hope of destroying the US-backed Israeli-dominated order in Lebanon. The Asad regime thus managed to form the NSF in 1983, which caused the Israeli army huge damage.

With the beginning of the Israeli army's partial withdrawal from the Shuf region in July 1983, Syrian President Asad's main allies in Lebanon, Junblat and Berri, voiced their opposition to the deployment of the Lebanese army in the region, based on their understanding of the sectarian nature of the army.[266] In fact, Jumayyil nominated Ibrahim Tannus, who had supervised the Kata'ib Party's military training for the past nine years, as the Lebanese army's new commander.[267] Jumayyil then exploited Tannus's power to purge officers considered politically undesirable by the LF.[268] In addition, by issuing Decree Law 10, Jumayyil also managed to regain the Lebanese army commander's absolute authority, where the new army law in March 1979 had imposed restrictions.[269] As a result, since the Lebanese army was staffed with officers favoured by the LF and since those officers won rapid promotion, the army's 'Christian character' was rather strengthened and this prevented the army from functioning as a symbol of 'national reconciliation'. In addition, reflecting Jumayyil's initial reliance on the Reagan administration, massive amounts of arms and military equipment were supplied by the United States,[270] which also sent its army's advisors to help train the staff of the Lebanese army.[271]

However, Jumayyil managed, with the help of the US and French authorities, to hold meetings with Junblat in order to achieve the dispatch of the Lebanese army to the Shuf region.[272] Junblat may have been concerned about the probable resumption of hostilities in his home ground and the further damage and casualties that might result there, if a political arrangement were not reached. In late August 1983, a series of meetings between the Lebanese authorities and Junblat was held in Paris, and an agreement (the Paris Accord) was concluded; this was to be implemented by Lebanon's legal authorities, including the army, and would provide security for the Shuf region.[273] However, although '[i]t was also agreed that Junblat would seek the consent of Syria and his allies',[274] Asad rejected the accord.[275] Since Syria desperately needed strong coalitions between its Lebanese allies in order to abrogate the May 17 Agreement, Asad may have considered a series of Junblat's actions to be destructive of the solidarity of those opposed to Jumayyil. As a result, the Syrian rejection undermined stabilization efforts in the Shuf region assigned to the Lebanese army.

After the Israeli army started to withdraw its troops on a large scale from the Shuf region in the autumn of 1983 because of its heavy casualties caused by the NSF's attacks during the Shuf War, Syria once again began to play an important role in

Lebanon, although the initial phase did not see much success. As a first step, Foreign Minister Khaddam arranged a national reconciliation meeting in Geneva, called the 'Geneva Conference', in late October. After the struggles over the sequence of issues between the Lebanese Front and the NSF, it was determined that the conference would address the following issues: Lebanese identity, the May 17 Agreement and Lebanon's internal reforms,[276] but it was clear that the May 17 Agreement was arguably the principal topic.[277] Despite Syria's demand for the abrogation of the May 17 Agreement, Jumayyil managed to secure a mandate for Lebanon to work with the United States on renegotiations of the agreement. This was because the two staunch Syrian allies in Lebanon, Karami and Berri, followed Franjiya and softened their hostile attitude towards the agreement in exchange for the Maronites' recognition of the Arab character of the Lebanese state.[278] These three figures indeed advocated the temporary freezing of the agreement to give Jumayyil more time to negotiate with the US administration.[279] Franjiya, Karami and Berri 'agreed that while, of course, the agreement should not be ratified it also could not be abrogated'.[280] This was because both paths would lead to the continuation of Israel's occupation in Lebanon: if ratified, Syria would not withdraw and consequently Israel would stay; if abrogated, Israel would not withdraw and consequently Syria would stay. As a result, although Junblat (who was bolstered by his military victory over the Maronites in the Shuf War, which actually contributed to the Israeli withdrawal in the autumn) consistently supported the Syrian position to abrogate the agreement,[281] Khaddam's attempts to persuade Syria's Lebanese allies to support its stance for the abrogation of the agreement resulted in failure.

Jumayyil's trip to the United States in December 1983, with the aim of getting its support to resolve the Lebanese deadlock over the May 17 Agreement, was unsuccessful. Although Lebanon's internal support for the renegotiations with the United States (even among the pro-Syrian figures) and Jumayyil's continued confidence in the country to check the power of Syria and its Lebanese allies made it possible for him to defy the Asad regime and gain manoeuvrability, the Reagan administration now viewed the Syrian regime very negatively. Since the US facilities in Lebanon had been attacked twice that year by Shi'as allegedly having connections with and supported by Syrian intelligence forces in Lebanon, and since Washington perceived Damascus as obstructing its stabilization efforts in Lebanon, the United States had no intention of pressuring Israel, whose relations with it were particularly excellent, to renegotiate with Lebanon.[282] In the strengthened Cold War context, as Gerges (1997) pointed out, Jumayyil 'discovered belatedly that the US was unwilling to over-invest in Lebanon, and it could not afford the high costs involved: Lebanon was not worth it'.[283]

Once the MNF, his strong patron, evacuated Lebanon in February 1984,[284] Jumayyil acknowledged the danger of neglecting pan-Arab and anti-Israeli feelings among the Lebanese, especially the Muslims. As a result, he found himself left with no choice but to establish a new relationship with the Asad regime to protect his presidency from strong NSF (especially Druze and Shi'a) pressure. In exchange for Jumayyil's statement on 29 February that he was prepared to abrogate the May 17 Agreement,[285] Junblat and Berri were persuaded by Asad not to drive Jumayyil into a corner and not to force him to resign.[286] This episode showed that Jumayyil aligned himself with the Syrian regime to appease the pro-Syrian actors in Lebanon. As a result, the battle was now off, and the Lebanese government took the necessary constitutional step formally to cancel the May 17 Agreement, which was realized on 5 March.[287]

Formation of the 'Tripartite Agreement'

Under these favourable circumstances, Syria initiated the second national meeting, called the 'Lausanne Conference', in the middle of March 1984.[288] The meeting was supposed to be more or less under Syrian guidance. However, the Syrian regime was racked by the fraternal antagonism between President Asad and his younger brother, Ri'fat al-Asad, because of the leader's illness, and so did not have enough power to 'orchestrate' the conference.[289] Damascus's important allies in Lebanon, Berri and Junblat, stuck to their demands to force President Jumayyil to resign, to put him on trial and to gain more political power for themselves, although Foreign Minister Khaddam put pressure on them to drop these demands.[290] Moreover, Franjiya demanded the preservation of all Maronite privileges just when a reconciliation plan submitted by Jumayyil was about to be agreed upon.[291] Since there appears to be no evidence that the Syrian regime attempted to persuade its traditional ally, Franjiya, to withdraw his demand,[292] Jumayyil was probably disappointed at the regime, even though he would have recognized its extraordinary situation.

Late April 1984 saw the formation of a 'national unity cabinet' led by Karami, which was delicately balanced both between and within Lebanon's various sects, although important posts relating to foreign and defence issues were allocated either to Muslims or pro-Syrian figures.[293] Although the cabinet attempted to reunite the country and to restore state sovereignty in all parts of Lebanon, by the time it gained a vote of confidence from the Lebanese parliament on 12 June, the cabinet itself had become as fragmented as the country.[294] The division between Christian and Muslim ministers on major issues was indeed sharp, and it became more difficult for them to control their own militias.[295]

In these circumstances of increasing disintegration, Jumayyil initially relied on the Asad regime in order to gain support from Syria's Lebanese allies, i.e. Franjiya, Karami, Berri and Junblat, but to no avail. This was because since these politicians possessed their own militias, it was difficult for Damascus to force them to support Jumayyil. Moreover, as Salem (1995) recalls: 'Syria was not especially interested in strengthening the president at the expense of its trusted allies.'[296] Later, even when Jumayyil's leadership of the Kata'ib Party was challenged by Ja'ja' in the spring of 1985, he did not ask for Syrian help, even though President Asad had offered to provide assistance to help contain Ja'ja'.[297]

Bitter relations between Jumayyil and the Asad regime, as well as the failure of the Karami cabinet to end the conflict and achieve both national reconciliation among the Lebanese and the Israeli army's full withdrawal from Lebanon,[298] led Asad to sideline the Lebanese authorities and to promote an accord between the three main pro-Syrian militia leaders. They were Hubayqa of the pro-Syrian faction of the LF, Berri of the Amal Movement and Junblat of the PSP. As Rabinovich (1987) pointed out, this was Syria's 'explicit recognition given to the militias as the effective wielders of power in Lebanon'.[299] In late December 1985, the Tripartite Agreement between the three leaders was formed under the guidance of Syria. The agreement called for an end to the civil war in Lebanon, the gradual abolishment of Lebanon's sectarian political system, the deprivation of the power of the Lebanese presidency and the recognition of the 'special' relationship between Syria and Lebanon.[300]

The Tripartite Agreement aimed to be a 'Pax-Syriana' that would pacify Lebanon, but this agreement soon collapsed in January 1986. Resentful of the provisions relating to the transfers of the prerogatives of Lebanon's presidency partly to the premiership and partly to the cabinet, and of the more clearly defined relationship between Lebanon and Syria, almost all Maronite leaders in Lebanon, including Franjiya, opposed the terms that Hubayqa had accepted in their name.[301] Backed by these strong anti-Hubayqa feelings among the Maronites and also resenting Asad's sidelining of him in the formation of the Tripartite Agreement, Jumayyil – with the help of Ja'ja', who shared his bitter feelings towards Hubayqa and Asad – militarily defeated Hubayqa and his faction in the LF.[302] Thus, any hope of the agreement being implemented was dashed.

After the collapse of the Tripartite Agreement, Syria attempted, mainly by using its proxy, the Amal Movement, to contain Hizbullah and to prevent the PLO from restoring their power in Lebanon.[303] The Syrian efforts towards what they called 'normalization' may have influenced Jumayyil's perception of the country, causing him to improve his relations with Asad. However, Asad set the condition that they should address all issues on the basis of the Tripartite Agreement.[304] Although Jumayyil actually acknowledged the necessity of taking Syrian interests into consideration in controlling conflict situations in Lebanon, he opposed the condition imposed by Asad.[305]

Finally, Jumayyil's disappointment in Asad, as well as the fact that his presidential power was largely owed to Ja'ja' and the LF after the United States and Israel diminished their power in Lebanon, reinforced his tendency to pursue Maronite-oriented policies, which continued until the last phase of his presidential term. In September 1988, the Lebanese parliament was unable to elect his successor because of the fierce antagonism that existed between factional groups in Lebanon. After a Syrian attempt to elect Franjiya resulted in failure, Jumayyil stepped down without nominating his successor and appointed the Christian commander of the Lebanese army, 'Awn, to the premiership.[306] This was unacceptable to the Lebanese Muslims and the Asad regime, as they recognized Prime Minister Huss, who had succeeded Karami after his assassination in June 1987, and his cabinet as legitimate. Since Huss refused to step down, the existence of a 'unitary government' ended and two rival cabinets appeared in Lebanon: the 'Awn cabinet, supported by the LF and most of the Maronites; and the Huss cabinet, backed by Syria and its Muslim allies.

Role and Deployment of the Lebanese Army

With his external patrons, the United States and Israel, decreasing their presence in Lebanon, President Jumayyil increasingly used the Lebanese army against his rivals, especially from the Druze and Shi'a community, and as a result the army further drifted towards full alignment with the LF. While Syria succeeded in inserting a clause in the 1985 Tripartite Agreement that the Lebanese army command should be rehabilitated under its guidance,[307] this action strongly antagonized not only the army's Maronite leadership, but also Jumayyil. After the streets of West Beirut had no militias because of Syria's military campaign in March 1987, it was presumed that Jumayyil and 'Awn, the then commander of the Lebanese army, would take the same measure in East Beirut against LF leader Ja'ja'.[308] However, due to Jumayyil's reliance on Ja'ja' and the close relations between 'Awn and Ja'ja', this Syrian calculation did not materialize.

Indeed, the strong relationship between the Lebanese army and the LF had considerably deepened Syrian suspicion of the army's 'neutrality'. When furious clashes and great tension persisted between the Amal Movement and the Palestinians during the Camps War, the deployment of the Lebanese army's 'special forces', which were composed of a number of different army brigades, as a buffer force around the camps was planned.[309] Although the Lebanese army's role in easing the tension was sometimes helped by the Syrian army, Jumayyil could not rely completely on President Asad for full support. Even when the Lebanese army tried to implement the Syrian-arranged security plan for West Beirut in July 1986, Asad decided to dispatch only symbolic numbers – about 200 men – from Syrian troops.[310]

Lebanon's Efforts for Economic Reconstruction and Social Stability

Although the spread of an illegal militia economy in Lebanon created a situation where the government lost control over public revenues and income but 'continue[d] to spend in order to maintain essential services, pay wages and salaries and subsidize some basic imported goods',[311] the Lebanese authorities attempted to reconstruct its economy. In fact, the Lebanese cabinet decided to close the illegal ports in September 1986 so as to secure customs revenue.[312] However, the LF, the Amal Movement and the PSP were not cooperative.[313] Since there seems to be no evidence that Damascus pressured its Lebanese allies, i.e. the Amal Movement and the PSP, to side with the Lebanese authorities, it appears that President Jumayyil was disappointed at President Asad.

However, when Lebanon's poor Muslims, especially the Shi'as, protested against a probable rise in the cost of living in late August 1987 after the Lebanese government made a decision to cut subsidies to basic goods in order to contain its spiralling deficit, the Syrian army intervened to disperse the demonstrations.[314] Although the decision had been briefly suspended because of widespread opposition in Lebanon, the government finally cut its petrol subsidy in September (though only partially),[315] and it could be said that regarding this case Syria, though indirectly, helped Lebanon to stabilize its own society as was necessary for economic reconstruction.

Summary

Being elected at a time when both Israel and the Western states were intervening in Lebanon to contain Syria, President Jumayyil had initially aligned Lebanon with the United States and Israel against Syria. Lebanon indeed concluded the May 17 Agreement with Israel in 1983 and had been able to align with the United States and Israel because of the weakened power of Syria and its Lebanese allies – Muslim forces and the PLO – the establishment of Israeli hegemony in Lebanon and the revival of the Cold War within the context of the Middle East, which led the United States to seek support from Lebanon. However, Jumayyil's policies provoked heavy opposition from the Syrian-led NSF and led to the fierce Shuf War and a succession of heavy Shi'a attacks on the MNF. In response, Jumayyil called on the United States and Israel to contain the NSF, but both reacted by decreasing rather than increasing their presence in Lebanon because of their numerous casualties.

Under these circumstances, Jumayyil saw the danger of failing to recognize the strong Arab identity assumed by most of the Lebanese population, and began to align Lebanon with Syria to protect himself from the fierce Druze and Shi'a attacks. In exchange for Jumayyil's abrogation of the May 17 Agreement, President Asad pressured Syria's prominent Lebanese allies, Junblat and Berri, to back down on Jumayyil's resignation. However, despite facing Syrian pressure, Junblat and Berri still made what Jumayyil considered to be unreasonable demands on him during the Lausanne Conference in March 1984, and the Syrian regime, in the midst of an internal crisis caused by President Asad's illness, could not persuade them to moderate their demands. Later, in April, as fragmentation within Lebanon further mounted, and when Jumayyil requested the Asad regime to persuade Syria's Lebanese allies to cooperate with him, Damascus refused to strengthen his position at their own expense.

Although Jumayyil soon discovered that the 1985 Tripartite Agreement resulted in a military conflict between the pro-Syrian faction of the LF and the Lebanese army, which led to his additional disappointment with the Syrian regime, he restarted a dialogue with Asad in the autumn of 1986. Syrian efforts to contain Hizbullah and the PLO by using the Amal Movement in order to prevent the 'radicalization' of the Lebanese population could well have appeased him. However, Asad insisted the dialogue should be based on the spirit of the Tripartite Agreement, which Jumayyil found unacceptable. This led Jumayyil to become increasingly reliant on the LF and the Lebanese army. In March 1987, Jumayyil failed to fulfil Syrian expectations by refusing to instruct the Lebanese army to take actions necessary to clear LF militias from East Beirut. Although Asad refused to pressure Berri and Junblat to cooperate with the Lebanese government over the closure of Lebanon's illegal ports in September 1986, the Syrian army later sided with Jumayyil in late August

1987 after observing Lebanon's poor Shi'a community's demonstrations against the government's decision to cut subsidies for basic goods. Although the Syrian regime occasionally cooperated with Jumayyil, he demonstrated favouritism towards the Maronite community until the end of his presidential term in September 1988.

CHAPTER 3

LEBANON FROM 'ANARCHY' TO 'INDIRECT RULE' UNDER SYRIA (1988–2005)

After the Lebanese Civil War had ended in 1990, the Lebanese government was forced to confront the reality of 'indirect rule' under Syria, which frequently intervened in Lebanon's political, economic, social, military and diplomatic affairs to further its own interests even as Lebanese leaders attempted to exploit Syrians for their own benefit.

As Syrian policy towards Lebanon was still largely defined by regional dynamics in the Middle East (as the theory of 'simple realism' presumes) and was pursued by use of its trans-state ties with Lebanon's mostly sectarian-based non-governmental actors more than its official ties with the Lebanese government, Lebanon's top leaders had to maintain a careful watch on both the regional and trans-state factors. Thus, after briefly examining the processes of the termination of the civil war and the consolidation of Syrian hegemony in Lebanon under 'anarchy' (1988–1990), this chapter first describes the regional and trans-state factors and then examines in detail the political, economic, social, military and diplomatic aspects of Lebanese–Syrian relations during the indirect rule (1990–2005).

Among top Lebanese leaders, Prime Minister Rafiq al-Hariri is a central figure in this chapter, because of the increased power of Lebanon's premiership as a result of the amendment of its constitution in 1990, his occupation of the position for a total of 10 years and his considerable domestic and international influence even when he did not hold the post. More importantly, Hariri occasionally attempted to act 'independently' of the Syrian regime with strong Lebanese and international backing, although his power was curtailed by Syrian allies in Lebanon's governing body and Syrian-backed non-governmental actors such as Hizbullah. In contrast, Hariri's counterparts, i.e. President Ilyas al-Hirawi, his successor Emile Lahoud and Parliament Speaker Nabih Berri, remained fairly dependent on the Syrian regime throughout their terms.

Termination of the Lebanese Civil War and Consolidation of Syrian Hegemony in Lebanon

Introduction

In order to understand post-war Lebanese–Syrian relations, it seems essential to consider the Lebanese situation which led to the termination of the civil war and the consolidation of Syrian hegemony in Lebanon, as these largely affected their relationship from 1990 to 2005.

Formation of the Ta'if Agreement

Since Michel 'Awn claimed to be Lebanon's premier in place of Salim al-Huss after the aborted Lebanese presidential election in September 1988, this resulted in a period when Lebanon had no president but two rival governments. All guise of a 'unitary' government having ended and the situation of anarchy emerged in Lebanon, its real division became highly probable. Had this division been realized, it would have been dangerous for Syria and the other Arab states, because the collapse of the Lebanese state would not only have created a cause for Israel's intervention in Lebanon, but also had a knock-on effect on the entire Arab state system.

Under these circumstances, a new phase in the rivalry between Syria and Iraq over Lebanon started, since Iraq, as a result of the end of the Iran–Iraq War in August 1988, found itself free from having to attend to its eastern border with Iran and began focusing on its western border. In a manifestation of Iraq's desire for vengeance against Syria for the latter state's support to Iran during the war, Iraq increased its involvement in Lebanon by extending aid to the anti-Syrian government led by 'Awn, while Syria supported the rival government led by Huss. Iraq's backing allowed 'Awn, in March 1989, to declare the 'Liberation War' against Syria. Despite their initial antagonism, which originated in 'Awn's open battle with Samir Ja'ja', leader of the LF, over control of the Port of Beirut while 'Awn was attempting to consolidate his authority over Lebanon, he received aid from Ja'ja' and they cooperated to confront their common enemy: Syria.[1] An escalation in violence and heavy warfare between the Syrian army and 'Awn's forces throughout the spring and summer put enormous pressure on Arab, especially Saudi, mediation efforts, ultimately leading to the formation of the Ta'if Agreement in October 1989, under the auspices of the Arab League, as the basis of Lebanon's national reconciliation.

The prime objective of the Ta'if Agreement was to lay the foundation for the establishment of a new political order in Lebanon, which was later realized by the amendment of the Lebanese constitution in September 1990. First, the agreement stipulated a reduction in the power of the presidency (held by the Maronites) that, in effect, placed the post on an equal footing with the premiership (held by the Sunnis) and parliament speakership (held by the Shi'as); an expansion of the power of the Lebanese parliament; and the establishment of parity in the numerical distribution of parliamentary seats between Christian and Muslim deputies (even though Lebanese Christians were now a demographic minority). Second, the agreement called for disarming of Lebanese militias and restoration and extension of the authority of the central government in Beirut throughout Lebanon, including the south. Third, the agreement formalized Lebanon's 'special' relations with Syria that granted it the legal right to maintain its army presence on Lebanese soil of the size and period to be specified by the two governments and that enabled it to respond to perceived threats against its security on that soil. The agreement also defined the role of the Syrian army in assisting the Lebanese government to establish its authority throughout Lebanon. Fourth, the agreement demanded the Israeli withdrawal from the 'security zone' in southern Lebanon in compliance with UN Security Council Resolution 425 and other resolutions.[2] As the Ta'if Agreement was sanctioned not only by the Lebanese government, but also by the Arab League and the United Nations, Syria was able to secure an internationally recognized legal basis for its presence in Lebanon.

Defeat of 'Awn

After the conclusion of the Ta'if Agreement, Syrian President Hafiz al-Asad and his Lebanese allies – President Hirawi, who had been elected after the assassination of Rene Mu'awwad in November 1989, and Prime Minister Huss – began endeavouring to implement the agreement with international and regional backing. However, Syrian hegemony in Lebanon continued to be challenged by 'Awn. Indeed, 'Awn not only defended his government, but also rejected the agreement, leading to his dismissal as a commander of the Lebanese army, suspension of payments to civil servants under him and imposition of an economic blockade on the districts controlled by him.[3]

As Norton (1991) argued, ''Awn's rejection of the Ta'if Agreement was due to the fact that it did not call for the withdrawal of the Syrian army from all Lebanese territories, but instead only called for redeployment to the Biqa' region'.[4] While

'Awn enjoyed popularity among Lebanon's Christian community, with his followers launching a series of attacks against pro-Ta'if figures, that of Ja'ja' decreased to such an extent that he came to fear being marginalized within the community.[5] As a result, Ja'ja' began to distance himself from 'Awn, which was later manifested in his acceptance of the Ta'if Agreement and tacit willingness to participate in the Huss cabinet.[6] The split resulted in an open battle between Lebanese army units under 'Awn and LF forces in January 1990, in which 'Awn's massive support among the Maronites made it possible for him to launch military attacks against the LF.[7]

Syria initially did not react out of concern that a direct attack against 'Awn might lead to mounting violence in Lebanon, arousing opposition not only within the country, but also in the regional and international arena and, more importantly, provoke outside, especially Israeli, intervention in Lebanon against it. However, taking military action against 'Awn became a favourable option for Asad in the latter half of 1990. First, Syria gained broad Lebanese support for the Ta'if Agreement, including Hizbullah, the LF and the Maronite religious establishment,[8] all of which had experienced bitter dealings with the Asad regime. As for the LF, Hirawi, backed by Damascus, had engaged in negotiations with Ja'ja', ultimately resulting in the LF's acceptance of the post-Ta'if process.[9] At the same time, increased Maronite support for the process enabled Hirawi officially to request Syrian assistance necessary to oust 'Awn in October.[10]

Moreover, Syria's participation in the US-led anti-Iraqi coalition in 1990, resulting from the decreased power of the Soviet Union – its long-time principal patron – greatly contributed to the improvement of its relations with the United States and several European countries. Through the United States, Syria secured Israel's tacit permission to use Syrian ground and air forces against 'Awn, a clear violation of the 'Red Line Agreement', to defeat him.[11] This domestic and international support led Asad to order the Syrian army to attack 'Awn's enclave around the Lebanese presidential palace in Ba'abda in October, an act that eventually led to the capture of all of East Beirut and the end of the civil war.[12] 'Awn initially took refuge in the French Embassy of Beirut before going into exile in France. The subsequent assassination of the NLP's leader Dani Sham'un, a leading supporter of 'Awn and, hence, one of Syria's main remaining opponents in Lebanon – allegedly by Syrian intelligence forces – demonstrated its strong will to dominate the post-war Lebanon.

Brief Summary

While the Ta'if Agreement stipulated Syria's 'special' status in Lebanon, its power on Lebanese soil was still fiercely challenged by 'Awn. However, his surrender in October 1990 not only marked the end of the civil war, but also firmly established Syrian hegemony in Lebanon, which was to be further consolidated in May 1991 with the conclusion of the Lebanese–Syrian Treaty of Brotherhood, Cooperation and Coordination. The Syrian hegemony thereafter enabled it to 'play the Lebanon card', especially in the context of Arab–Israeli diplomacy.

Middle East International Relations and the Impact on Syria and Lebanon

Introduction

From 1990 to 2005, the international relations of the Middle East continued to have a crucial impact on Syrian policy towards Lebanon, which Lebanese Prime Minister Hariri had to consider when he took action and formed attitudes towards the Syrian regime. Specifically, the Arab–Israeli peace process, particularly the progress of the Syria–Israel track, affected the Syrian–Lebanese relationship. More recently, the US-led Iraq War in 2003 not only changed US perception of Syria, but also made it possible for some Lebanese leaders to resist the Syrian hegemony, which ultimately contributed to the termination of Syrian indirect rule in Lebanon.

Syrian–Israeli Negotiations

As mentioned, the breakdown of the global bipolarity system was a crucial factor behind the Syrian decision to join the US-led anti-Iraqi coalition during the Gulf Crisis/War from 1990 to 1991. The decline of the Soviet Union stripped Syria of the option of going to war as a means of settling the Arab–Israeli conflict. Syria's lack of any real alternative to entering into the peace process forced President Asad to abandon its traditional conditions for the participation: UN sponsorship and a united Arab delegation.[13] Because of the disadvantageous international situation within which Syria was embroiled, Asad had no choice but to accept US procedural terms, 'which were designed to shape the course of the negotiations to Israel's advantage'.[14] Indeed, Syria attended the Madrid Peace Conference in October 1991, and a succession of Middle East peace negotiations continuously largely defined Syria's regional policy, especially towards Lebanon, as well as Lebanon's foreign relations.

The Madrid Peace Conference stipulated two means by which peace negotiations for the Middle East could proceed: via multilateral talks concerning development, refugees, security, water and environment in the region or via bilateral talks between Israel and the frontline Arab states. After Syria decided to enter direct negotiations with Israel, such a conflict soon emerged that it was not until June 1992, when the Labour government under Yitzhaq Rabin was established in Israel, that any true progress was observed.[15] The stalemate in the negotiation process during this period intensified Hizbullah's military activities against the Israeli-occupied security zone in southern Lebanon. Faced with Syrian determination to use its proxy, Hizbullah, to acquire negotiating leverage with Israel, the weak Lebanese government had no choice but to accept Syrian terms.

At the Syrian–Israeli negotiations in August 1992, Israel stated that although UN Security Council Resolution 242 applied to the Golan Heights, it did not call for Israeli withdrawal from all the occupied territories.[16] In opposition, Syria maintained that since Resolution 242 clearly required full Israeli withdrawal, a partial withdrawal was not acceptable.[17] Despite this disagreement, Asad continued to demonstrate Syria's eagerness to engage in negotiations with Israel. Indeed, he initiated encouraging the Palestinians, Jordanians and Lebanese to resume peace talks, and even supported continuation of the talks when they were interrupted by Israel's expulsion of Hamas members to southern Lebanon in December.[18]

Despite such vigorous efforts made by Asad, disagreements between Syria and Israel regarding the Golan Heights ultimately stalled their negotiations in 1993. Frustrated and claiming to respond to Hizbullah's attacks on its presence in southern Lebanon, Israel launched a massive military campaign against Hizbullah in July as part of what it referred to as Operation Accountability. The heavy Israeli attacks against both Hizbullah in southern Lebanon and the Syrian army in the Biqa' region were aimed at forcing Syria to make concessions to Israel. Although Asad's cooperation with the Israeli government in the resolution of the crisis led the Israeli side to consider him to be a serious negotiating partner who desired peace, the continued Syrian–Israeli differences regarding the 'Golan-for-peace equation' pushed Israel to give priority to the Israeli–Palestinian peace negotiations.[19] Israel's signing of the Oslo Accords in September and conclusion of subsequent separate agreements with the PLO and Jordan not only made it possible for Syria to focus on the issue of the recovery of the Golan Heights, but also diminished its bargaining power vis-à-vis Israel.

In this context, Lebanon, especially Hizbullah's military operations against the security zone in southern Lebanon, became an important asset for Syria, a condition which, arguably, led Asad to focus strongly on considering the means by which the

Lebanese situation might give Syria an edge on negotiations with Israel. First, as Asad realized that Israel could benefit from a Syrian move against Hizbullah's military activities in southern Lebanon, he linked a resolution regarding Hizbullah not only to an overall resolution of the Arab–Israeli conflict, but also a resolution to the Golan Heights question that would be in his favour. Second, when Prime Minister Hariri announced in February 1993 Lebanon's readiness to seek a settlement with Israel under Resolution 425 (calling for an immediate end to Israel's occupation in southern Lebanon), Asad quickly countered him,[20] fearing Hariri's announcement could reduce Syria's negotiating power vis-à-vis Israel.

As stated by Ehteshami and Hinnebusch (1997), the year 1995 was crucial in Syrian–Israeli negotiations, which accelerated after the assassination of Rabin.[21] His successor, Prime Minister Shimon Peres, publicly declared that the Golan Heights was Syrian territory, and his eagerness to reach an agreement with Syria, combined with the shift in Israeli public opinion in favour of doing so after Rabin's assassination, created the conditions necessary to begin negotiations with Asad in late 1995.[22]

Nevertheless, no breakthrough ensued, and in April 1996, as it had in July 1993, Israel launched a massive military campaign against Hizbullah and Lebanon's infrastructure in what it termed as Operation Grapes of Wrath. Observing the exacerbated tension between Syria and Israel and needing to campaign for the upcoming Israeli parliamentary elections, Peres suspended the peace negotiations.[23]

After the Likud Party won the majority in the May 1996 Israeli parliamentary elections, Prime Minister Benjamin Netanyahu began to separate the Lebanese–Israeli peace track from the Syrian–Israeli peace track. In addition, Netanyahu insisted that '[future] Israeli–Syrian negotiations [should] be resumed with no preconditions and irrespective of progress [in precedent negotiations] between the Syrians and the [former] Labo[u]r government'.[24] In opposition, Asad maintained that 'peace {was} a strategic choice' for Syria, all negotiations between Syria and Israel should 'be resumed from the point at which they {had been} interrupted', all agreements reached with respect to the withdrawal of the Israeli army from the Golan Heights and security affairs should remain valid and 'the Syrian and Lebanese {peace} tracks {were} inseparable'.[25]

To promote the separation of the Lebanese–Israeli peace track from the Syrian–Israeli peace track, Netanyahu advocated the so-called 'Lebanon first' option in July 1996.[26] The offer of this option had been influenced by the perception of the Israeli army, which, especially after the conclusion of Operation Grapes of Wrath, had begun to doubt effectiveness of its presence in the security zone of southern Lebanon.[27] As the 'Lebanon first' option aimed to divide Lebanon and Syria, and as its advocating of the Israeli army's unilateral withdrawal from southern Lebanon could rid Syria of the trump card, it was not surprising that Syria rejected the option.[28] Consequently, Hariri's attempts to promote the 'Lebanon first' option met with stubborn Syrian objections and ultimately resulted in failure. The resulting stalemate in Syrian–Israeli negotiations intensified Hizbullah's military activities in southern Lebanon.

With casualties among Israeli soldiers increasing in southern Lebanon, the security zone became a liability for Israel. In 1998, Netanyahu announced Israel's readiness to accept Resolution 425 and demanded that Lebanon ease the conflict along its border with Israel by working out security arrangements.[29] In response, Asad rejected the proposal drafted by Netanyahu because it would lead Syria to lose one of its most important bargaining chips with Israel: Hizbullah's military presence in southern Lebanon.[30] Under these circumstances, Lebanon, having no choice, but to follow Syria, also rejected the Israeli offer.[31]

The successor of Netanyahu, Ehud Barak, assumed Israel's premiership in May 1999 and revealed his intentions to withdraw the Israeli army from southern Lebanon within one year and to cooperate with Asad. In order to restart Israeli–Syrian negotiations, Prime Minister Barak and Syrian Foreign Minister Faruq al-Shar' agreed to accept the sponsorship of US President Bill Clinton and met in Washington DC in mid-December.[32] However, this and a subsequent meeting in Shepherdstown led to no true progress. Eventually, Barak announced that peace with Syria was currently impossible;[33] however, the Israeli army started to withdraw from the security zone of southern Lebanon, which was finalized on 24 May 2000.

While the Israeli presence in Lebanon has officially ended, Israel has continued to occupy a sliver of a disputed territory known as the 'Shabaa Farms'. This occupation has not only enabled Hizbullah to justify maintaining its military presence, but also enabled Syria to use Hizbullah's weapons as a trump card. In other words, it is possible for Syria to maintain that Israel will not experience peace along its northern border unless it agrees to a comprehensive settlement with Syria.

Immediately after Ariel Sharon visited the al-Aqsa mosque in Jerusalem in September 2000, the second Palestinian *intifada* erupted, which was manifested in violence against the Israeli army stationed in the West Bank and Gaza. In sympathy, Syria not only tolerated, but also encouraged limited Hizbullah military activities against the Israeli army in the Shabaa Farms, which Syria and Lebanon continue to regard as an Israeli-occupied Lebanese territory. However, the new Syrian leadership under Bashar al-Asad, who had assumed responsibility for the Lebanese policy from Vice President 'Abd al-Halim Khaddam in 1998 and held the presidency after his father's death in June 2000, had no intention to open a conventional military confrontation with the Israeli army.[34] Syria, thus, did not counter the retaliatory Israeli attacks on its military installations in Lebanon in April and July 2001 following Hizbullah's military operations in the Shabaa Farms.[35]

Repeated Palestinian uprisings and strained Palestinian–Israeli relations continued to define Syria's policy towards Lebanon. After Saudi Crown Prince 'Abdullah released a peace proposal in mid-February 2002 as a means of setting the agenda for the forthcoming March Arab League summit in Beirut,[36] President Asad visited Lebanon just before the start of the summit to impress firmly that Syria should be a leading player in the Arab–Israeli peace process.[37]

In the aftermath of the 11 September 2001 terrorist attacks, US officials initially avoided mentioning Hizbullah in the context of its war against terrorism. To secure Arab backing for the US-led war in Afghanistan, Washington calculated that it should not explicitly target Hizbullah and other Syrian-sponsored guerrilla groups in its war on terror as long as Damascus cooperated, primarily by ensuring that Syria's surrogate forces would refrain from launching attacks against Israel. Syria, for its part, hoped that 'its participation in the anti-terrorism campaign could be traded for [US] pressure on Israel over the occupied territories'.[38] However, it soon became clear that this hope would not be realized under US President George W. Bush, who had become reliant on the increased power of US neoconservatives and thus become pro-Israeli. In this context, Hizbullah restarted military operations in October 2001 after a three-month hiatus,[39] an action that led the US administration to add Hizbullah to its 'terrorist list'.[40]

US-led Iraq War in 2003

After the 11 September 2001 terrorist attacks, the Bush administration introduced the doctrine of pre-emption, which targeted not only 'terrorist organizations', but also 'rogue states'. The US administration included the Iraqi regime under President Saddam Husayn in the latter category, and its alleged possession of weapons of mass destruction (WMD) was used as a pretext for the administration to launch military operations in order to topple the Husayn regime in 2003. Syria opposed the US military action, because of its economic stakes in Iraq, its concern about becoming the next target if the United States succeeded in Iraq and its maintaining of Arab nationalist identity.[41]

Syria's opposition to the US policy concerning Iraq led US–Syrian relations to become tense and ultimately caused the US Congress to pass the Syria Accountability and Lebanese Sovereign Restoration Act (SALSRA) in November 2003. The SALSRA would allow the Bush administration 'to apply a combination of diplomatic and economic sanctions against Syria',[42] if it did not end its support to 'terrorists', its development of WMDs and its 'occupation' of Lebanon.[43] Facing the charge that Syria was supporting anti-US militants in Iraq, the Asad regime tightened controls on Syria's border with Iraq, although US neoconservatives continued to perceive Syria negatively as a de facto member of the 'axis of evil' and prepared for regime change in Syria.

In this context, US neoconservatives calculated that, as Hinnebusch (2006) described, '[i]f Syria could be forced out of Lebanon, a pro-Western Lebanese government could be brought to sign a peace treaty with Israel, and the Syrian regime, isolated and having suffered a major loss of prestige, might collapse'.[44] As a result, the neoconservatives began to focus more strongly on Lebanon, which enabled several Lebanese political leaders, including Prime Minister Hariri, to leverage their relations with the US administration against their relations with the Syrian regime.

However, Syria's strong will to maintain its dominance over Lebanon led Damascus to pressure the Lebanese cabinet and parliament to support an amendment of the Lebanese constitution that would allow Syria's main ally in Lebanon, President Lahoud, to serve another term. In opposition, Hariri became increasingly active in the international arena. In cooperation with one of his closest allies, President Jacques Chirac of France, a leader who had his own agenda to improve French relations with the United States, with which France differed regarding how to deal with Iraq's Husayn regime, Hariri contributed to the formation of

UN Security Council Resolution 1559. The resolution, passed on 2 September 2004, called for Syria to halt its interference in Lebanon's internal affairs and fully withdraw from the country and for Hizbullah and Palestinian groups in Lebanon to disarm.[45] However, the Lebanese parliament, under pressure from the Syrians, amended the constitution on 3 September and Lahoud's term was consequently extended for three more years.

Adoption of Resolution 1559 reactivated Lebanese debate regarding whether the Syrian presence was still necessary to maintain the stability of Lebanon and whether Hizbullah should be disarmed, as the Israeli army had withdrawn from all of southern Lebanon except for the Shabaa Farms. With regard to the former dimension, the assassination of Hariri on 14 February 2005 was widely blamed on the Asad regime, and increased Lebanese and Western, especially US and French, pressure to end Syria's indirect rule in Lebanon. Consequently, Syria completely withdrew its army and intelligence by 26 April. With regard to the latter dimension, Hizbullah waged military attacks on the Shabaa Farms in January 2005,[46] an action that may have resulted from Syria's frustration at being internationally isolated as well as the necessity for Hizbullah to show its armed presence, both of which resulted from the adoption of Resolution 1559.

Brief Summary

The regional Syrian–Israeli power struggle assumed a greater number of diplomatic and military forms while continuing to define Syria's policy towards Lebanon. Under these external circumstances, although Prime Minister Hariri occasionally attempted to act 'independently' of the Syrian regime, these efforts were soon contained by it. However, the outbreak of the 2003 Iraq War dramatically changed US perception of Syria in a decidedly negative direction, gave Hariri more room for manoeuvre and initiated a series of events that ultimately ended Syrian indirect rule in Lebanon.

Lebanese Non-Governmental Actors and Syria: Their Basic Interests and Relations

Introduction

Under the indirect Syrian rule, the Maronites, Sunnis, Shi'as and Druzes – the main non-governmental actors in Lebanon – maintained various trans-state relations with Syria,[47] which Lebanese Prime Minister Hariri had to examine when he took action and formed attitudes towards the Syrian regime. Their trans-state relationship, which was characterized by differing degrees of cooperation and conflict, was mainly shaped by Syria's position as a regional middle power in the Middle East, its stakes in Lebanon and the calculations of these sectarian groups. On the one hand, Syria recognized that it needed to secure the support of these groups to justify its presence in Lebanon, and thus struggled to win their endorsement. However, when the behaviour of a sectarian group in Lebanon was clearly against Syria's interests and beyond its tolerance, the regime, in cooperation with its Lebanese allies, clamped down on the group. On the other hand, the Lebanese sectarian groups, even with power inferior to that of Syria, attempted to use the Syrian presence to their advantage. Their behaviour was mainly determined by power struggles both between and within the sectarian communities in the reconstructed Lebanese state. Although a sectarian group's relationship with Syria was affected by its communal identity determining its basic tendencies, it appears that its power calculations had a greater impact on its relations with Syria.

The Maronites and Syria

The Ta'if Agreement provided Syria with an opportunity to neutralize the power of the Maronite community, since it had long opposed the 'Pax-Syriana',[48] because of both its traditional 'Lebanon-oriented' identity and its bitter relations with Syria during most of the Lebanese Civil War. Since the LF, the

Maronite religious establishment, the Kata'ib Party and most of the Maronite *zuama* were left without any reliable external patrons after Israel had decreased its support for them, they accepted the Ta'if Agreement, while 'Awn and his colleagues rejected it.[49] The acceptance of the former groups and figures provided some political legitimacy for the Syrian-initiated post-Ta'if process, although most of them later became disillusioned with it.

Although the LF's head, Ja'ja', had helped the Syrian army to oust 'Awn, he refused to recognize Syria's predominant position in Lebanon. Consequently, President Hafiz al-Asad may well have calculated that Ja'ja' would become an opponent of Syrian rule, and his decreased power and unpopularity within the Maronite community, largely because of the LF's disarmament and his contribution to defeating 'Awn, provided the Syrian regime with a pretext for excluding him. Presumably in line with Syrian wishes, the Lebanese government declared a ban on the LF in March 1994.[50] Ja'ja' was arrested in April for the October 1990 murder of the NLP's leader Sham'un,[51] who had succeeded to the leadership after his father's death in 1987 and had taken a strong anti-Syrian stance, along with 'Awn, during the Liberation War. Ja'ja' was also charged with leading the Zuq bomb incident in February 1994,[52] which had targeted the Marinate community, killing 10 and wounding over 60.[53] In addition, members and supporters of the LF, 'Awn and the NLP had been detained during the 1990s on suspicion of 'plotting against national security'.[54]

Although Maronite Patriarch Nasr Allah Butrus Sufayr supported the Ta'if Agreement and did nothing to stop 'Awn's collapse,[55] he later expressed resentment at Syria's indirect rule in Lebanon, which allowed Damascus to encroach on Lebanese sovereignty. While Sufayr accepted Lebanon's 'privileged relations' with Syria in a joint Christian–Muslim working paper published in March 1994 on the condition that they did not interfere with Lebanese sovereignty,[56] he continued to be the most prominent religious leader in Lebanon who had never visited Syria. Sufayr's stance was mainly based on the traditional Maronite 'Lebanon-oriented' identity, but his stance manifested in the paper provided a basis for Lebanese acceptance of some Syrian presence in Lebanon.

However, facing the realities of Israel's evacuation from the security zone of southern Lebanon in May 2000 and Syria's interference in the parliamentary elections in the summer of that year, Sufayr accelerated discussion on the Syrian presence in September 2000, stressing the need to proceed with the redeployment of the Syrian army in accordance with the Ta'if Agreement. Later, when some 30 anti-Syrian Christian figures, including Amin al-Jumayyil, Matn MP Nasib Lahoud, Batrun MP Butrus Harb, Jubran Tuwayni (publisher of the *al-Nahar* newspaper) and members of the NLP and the Kata'ib Party, formed the Qurnat Shahwan Gathering,[57] Sufyayr became the leading 'spiritual leader' of the group.

The Kata'ib Party reconsidered its allegiance to a 'Lebanon-oriented' identity, which led it to adopt a 'realist' policy and become supportive of the Syrian presence in Lebanon in order to accommodate the post-Ta'if process.[58] When Munir al-Hajj succeeded to the leadership in 1999 following the death of George Sa'ada in 1998, he maintained the party's alignment with the Syrians.[59] During the Lebanese parliamentary elections in 2000, Hajj joined the electoral list led by pro-Syrian Interior Minister Michel al-Murr, but his failure to win a seat seriously undermined his political stature.[60]

In consequence, power struggles within the Kata'ib Party broke out during 2000 and 2001 between one faction wishing to distance itself from Damascus and another wishing to cooperate with it. The leading figure associated with the former faction was Jumayyil, who was, ironically, permitted by the Syrian regime to return to Lebanon in July 2000, while the leading figure associated with the latter faction was Karim Pakraduni. After Pakraduni was eventually elected as the party's new head in

October 2001,[61] he calculated that an excessive amount of anti-Syrian movement under the indirect Syrian rule would strip the party – and, by extension, the Maronite community – of political power, leading him to sustain the party policy of bandwagoning with Damascus. In addition to Pakraduni, the former LF leader Ilyas Hubayqa and a northern *za'im*, Sulayman Tony Franjiya, continued to cooperate with the Syrian regime. As one of the key pro-Syrian pillars in the Lebanese government, Franjiya continuously occupied ministerial posts throughout most of the Syrian rule. Hubayqa, who was never a reliable ally for the Syrians because of his lack of real power and legitimacy within the Maronite community, was later assassinated in January 2002.[62]

Damascus succeeded in installing pro-Syrian Maronite figures such as Hirawi and Lahoud to Lebanon's presidency, whose reduced power has still been important as one of the three pillars in the governing body. However, Syria failed to construct broad and lasting Lebanese Maronite support for its rule. This was largely attributed to Syria's perceived discrimination towards the community as a whole, including Syrian-initiated 'unjust' measures in the Maronite districts during the parliamentary elections, and the treatment of Ja'ja' in particular, who alone stood accused of a series of assassinations during the civil war despite the widespread belief that these acts had been committed by many other militia leaders. These factors arguably contributed to Lebanon's Maronite community's negative perception of the Syrian regime and its allies in the Lebanese government, and ultimately to the community's strong support for the political current questioning the Syrian presence in Lebanon, which was accelerated in September 2000.

The Sunni and Syria

The post-Ta'if regime, which enhanced the power of Lebanon's premiership and disbanded Lebanese militias, a power that the Sunnis largely lacked, 'reversed the deterioration of their position in the civil war and gave them a greater access to government than their cohesion or numbers warranted'.[63] However, Syria's supremacy and the installation of pro-Syrian figures to the presidency and the parliament speakership checked the power of Sunni figures who held the premiership.

Prime Minister Hariri's attempts to reconstruct Lebanon during his assumption of the post from 1992 to 2004, except for the two years under Huss (1998–2000), by counting on his ties with the Saudi monarchy and US and European top leaders were checked by the fact that the Lebanese government 'was no longer the master of Lebanon'.[64] While attempting to act 'independently', especially politically and diplomatically, and to counterbalance the Syrian regime by seeking support from both his international allies and the Lebanese populace, among whom he was popular, his efforts were largely blocked by Damascus and its allies in the Lebanese government. While Hariri largely exercised freedom within the economic sphere, Lebanese economic affairs were connected with Syrians, as Syrian Vice President Khaddam and Hariri had business connections. However, as Hinnebusch (1998) suggested, these ties were not 'readily manipulated to the sole advantage of Syria',[65] as evidenced by the Asad regime's delay in liberalizing its banking sector, leading Syrian entrepreneurs to direct their assets to Lebanese banks.[66]

Hariri was also engaged in power struggles against his communal rivals. Indeed, Hariri attempted, by using his wealth and position, to extend his patronage network in West Beirut so as to compete with Huss and Sa'ib Salam, both of whom maintained their own constituencies in the area, as well as to counter 'Umar Karami, his political opponent in Tripoli, who had a close relationship with the Syrian regime. In fact, these rivals served Syrian interests in checking Hariri's enormous power owing to his domestic and international popularity.

In sum, the Syrian regime's patronage of Sunni leading figures in Lebanon, except for Hariri, appeared to have succeeded. After heated debate regarding the Syrian presence on Lebanese soil arose in 2000, Grand Mufti Muhammad Rashid Qabbani and Karami successfully justified the presence,[67] while Huss stressed the importance of maintaining coordination between Lebanon and Syria as neighbouring countries.

The Shi'as and Syria

The 1989 Damascus Agreement positioned Syria as the sole and ultimate arbiter between the Amal Movement and Hizbullah, two pillars of the Shi'a community in Lebanon. This subsection describes relations between each organization and Syria during the period of its indirect rule.

Syria obtained support from the Amal Movement to implement its policy within Lebanon and stabilize the situation under its rule, as the movement advocated a pluralistic and undivided Lebanon (which was compatible with Syrian aims) and incorporated the secular Shi'a middle class.[68] The Amal Movement had its own reasons for supporting the Syrian-dominated post-Ta'if process. First, as the power of the parliamentary speakership, which has been allocated to the Shi'as, was increased by the Ta'if Agreement, the 'pragmatic' leader of the Amal Movement, Berri, became more interested in aligning himself with Damascus. Indeed, he adapted the Amal Movement to the reality of post-Ta'if politics and maintained his control of the parliamentary speakership. Second, according to Picard (2000), newly established private Shi'a banks replaced the traditional role of the Amal Movement to benefit from the remittances of the Shi'a diaspora,[69] which effectively increased the movement's dependence on Syria. Third, Hizbullah was generally more popular than the Amal Movement among the Shi'a community, because of the Amal Movement's role during the 'Camps War' (when it sided with the Syrian army against the Palestinians) as well as Hizbullah's provision of social services and its vanguard role in the resistance to Israel in southern Lebanon. Overall, the Amal Movement's increasing political stakes in the post-Ta'if process and its vulnerable position within the Shi'a community are likely to have contributed to its consistent alignment with Syria.

In contrast, Syria's relations with Hizbullah passed through periods of agreement and conflict. Although the damage to their relations in the late 1980s was mended by the Damascus Agreement, Hizbullah, initially, was not willing to approve the Syrian-supported Ta'if Agreement for several reasons First, as Zisser (2001) pointed out, Hizbullah's concern was that the Ta'if Agreement would benefit the Maronites and Sunnis and threaten the status that it had gained during the civil war. As the post-war process accompanied the game of politics within Lebanon's government institutions, the generally low educational level of the Shi'as made it difficult to fill the political offices and positions allocated to the community with competent members.[70] Second, the Ta'if Agreement questioned Hizbullah's very raison d'être by calling for disarmament of Lebanese militias.

With Syria consolidating its hegemony in Lebanon, especially after its alignment with the US-led anti-Iraqi coalition in 1990, Hizbullah leaders may have calculated that establishing a close alliance with Syria would preserve or increase their power. While Hizbullah agreed to disarm in Beirut and Biqa', two of its main strongholds, its armed presence in southern Lebanon was accepted because of the continued presence of the Israeli-backed SLA in the region. On the other hand, Hizbullah was required to coordinate its military activities to serve Syria's regional policy, especially towards Israel, '[i]n return for Syria's support for its role at the head of the Islamic resistance in the south'.[71] Syria also needed Hizbullah's support to stabilize Lebanon's political situation, because of Hizbullah's incorporation of the radicalized Shi'a lower class, as opposed to the Amal Movement.[72]

Consequently, Hizbullah's cooperation with the Syrians was clearly manifested in its participation in Lebanon's political process and its concerted military activities in southern Lebanon. With regard to the former aspect, Hizbullah's participation in the

1992 Lebanese parliamentary elections enlarged its stakes within the political process and marked the beginning of its alignment with the Syrian-backed post-Ta'if politics, although its political power was occasionally contained by the Syrians, especially when conflict between Hizbullah and the Amal Movement erupted. With regard to the latter aspect, the progress or lack thereof in the peace talks between Syria and Israel clearly influenced the value and scope of Hizbullah's military activities. When the Israeli government under the Labour Party considered the Asad regime as a serious negotiating partner between 1992 and 1996, the regime generally kept Hizbullah's military activities in check. However, when Israeli Prime Minister Netanyahu neglected President Asad by advocating the 'Lebanon first' option between 1996 and 1999, Damascus encouraged Hizbullah's military activities as a means of putting pressure on Netanyahu.

After the Israeli army pulled out from southern Lebanon in May 2000, Hizbullah faced the problem of justifying its existence. As Hizbullah's legitimacy was largely dependent on its armed struggle against the Israeli army in the security zone, the evacuation might have damaged its power and status. While Syria faced the reality of Israel's unilateral withdrawal, its need to have a surrogate force to pressure the Israeli army to withdraw from the Golan Heights was not changed. In this context, the Syrian and Lebanese authorities soon raised the pretext that the Shabaa Farms remained an Israeli-occupied Lebanese territory, despite the Israeli recognition of the area as part of the Golan Heights. This has made it possible for Hizbullah to act as it had previously, with its leadership stating that it would keep fighting for the liberation of the Shabaa Farms.

Hizbullah's military activities in the Shabaa Farms from the fourth quarter of 2000 to the first half of 2001 were connected with the second Palestinian *intifada*. After the 11 September 2001 terrorist attacks, Hizbullah briefly halted its military activities. However, as Syria's cooperation with the US-led anti-terrorism campaign did not lead the United States to put pressure on Israel regarding the Golan Heights, Hizbullah restarted its military operations in the Shabaa Farms in October.[73] Later, in the context of defying the SALSRA and UN Security Council Resolution 1559, Hizbullah pursued its military activities in the Shabaa Farms.[74] Since then, Syria's military support for Hizbullah has been continuously criticized by the international community, particularly the United States.

The Druze and Syria

When the civil war ended, the most prominent figure in Lebanon's Druze community and the leader of the PSP, Walid Junblat, appeared not to have full confidence in the Asad regime. This was based on his bitter experiences during the civil war, especially after the assassination of his father, allegedly by Syria and/or its Lebanese proxies, and the confrontation between his militias and the Syrian army during the Camps War. However, he had no choice but to align the Druze community with Damascus to ensure its survival and secure his political status. While Syria was consolidating its position in Lebanon after the conclusion of the Ta'if Agreement, he sided with the Syrian regime against 'Awn during the Liberation War and later participated in the post-Ta'if political process. Another factor, the rivalry between Junblat and Talal Arslan (a Druze *za'im*), may have led Junblat to maintain ties with Damascus to prevent it from supporting Arslan. At the same time, Syria needed Junblat's aid in gaining Druze support for its indirect rule in Lebanon because, as Harris (1996) pointed out, of Arslan's close relations with the Maronites,[75] who generally maintained an unfavourable attitude towards the Syrian rule.

The close relationship between Junblat and the Syrian regime was manifested in several ways. One was the Syrian-led gerrymandering of the electoral districts in Mount Lebanon to secure the election of Junblat and his allies in the parliamentary elections of 1992, 1996 and 2000.[76] By joining in the post-Ta'if process, Junblat had held the post of the minister of the displaced between 1992 and 1998 and provided housing for many refugees, a large number of whom were Druzes displaced as a result of the fierce 'Shuf War'. By doing so, Junblat appeared to present himself as the only reliable patron of the Druze community, a reputation that was also favourable for Damascus.

After Bashar al-Asad assumed control of Syria's Lebanese policy from Khaddam in 1998, Junblat was ousted from his cabinet position because of his close relationship with Khaddam. Consequently, Junblat began to criticize President Lahoud, one of the key Lebanese allies of Asad, and the Syrian rule in Lebanon. Although Junblat temporarily toned down his criticism, particularly during the campaign period for the 2000 parliamentary elections in Lebanon, he soon became one of the leading figures to question the Syrian presence. Junblat, in fact, welcomed the September 2000 statement by Maronite Patriarch Sufayr and generally (with occasional concessions) maintained his anti-Syrian stance until 2005.

Brief Summary

Overall, Lebanon's Muslim sects generally maintained better relations with Syria than did the Maronites. Regarding this point, it appears possible to conclude that the communal identity of each sectarian group determined the framework of its relationship with Syria. However, as clearly manifested in the cases of the Kata'ib Party under 'pragmatic' leadership, Prime Minister Hariri and Junblat, the leaders' desire for more power and promotion of their own interests in some situations overrode their communal identity.

Prime Minister Rafiq al-Hariri and the Asad Regime

Introduction

While Syria consolidated its hegemony in Lebanon after the end of the civil war, it appears as an exaggeration to argue that

Syria fully orchestrated political, economic, social, military and diplomatic issues in Lebanon. In fact, although Prime Minister Hariri generally took Syrian interests into consideration and made concessions in order to carry forward his economic projects for Lebanon, he also attempted to use Syrians for his own ends. Hariri's actions and attitudes towards the Syrian regime over the political, economic, social, military and diplomatic issues are examined in this section.

Political Aspects

Before dealing with the political features of the relationship between Prime Minister Hariri and the Syrian regime, it is necessary to gain an understanding of the background of his nomination to the premiership. Two political and economic factors, both related to the legitimacy of Syrian presence on Lebanese soil, were decisive in the formation of his first cabinet.

First, Hariri's predecessors, Prime Ministers Karami and Rashid al-Sulh, failed to improve Lebanon's desperate economic condition caused by the 15-year civil war. Although Karami attempted to initiate reconstruction projects for Lebanon, the cabinet's failure to articulate a consistent and clear economic policy decreased the confidence of domestic and international investors and aid donors, leading to little economic recovery.[77] The deteriorating economic condition brought about a series of general strikes and mass demonstrations during the spring of 1992 that culminated in a riot on 6 May and finally led to Karami's resignation on that day.[78] Since the riot partly assumed the form of cross-sectarian opposition to the Karami cabinet as a surrogate of Damascus,[79] it forced Karami to resign in order to prevent further damage of Syrian policy and status in Lebanon.[80] However, after the subsequent cabinet led by Sulf was formed on 13 May 1992 with Syrian 'guidance',[81] its insistence that the Lebanese parliamentary elections be held in the summer of 1992 as scheduled despite the opposition of some Lebanese, especially the Maronites, prevented the cabinet from gaining the confidence of foreign investors necessary to boost the economy.[82]

Second, after Patriarch Sufayr criticized the Lebanese–Syrian Treaty of Brotherhood, Cooperation and Coordination,[83] which clearly favoured Syria and placed Lebanon in a rather disadvantageous position, he called for a boycott of the 1992 parliamentary elections until the Syrian army redeployed to the Biqa' area, which was stipulated by the Ta'if Agreement. Sufayr believed that the Syrian presence would obstruct the holding of 'fair elections' and thus most popular Christian, especially Maronite, political leaders indeed boycotted the elections in the summer of 1992.[84] Consequently, the failure of economic policy under the pro-Syrian Karami and Sulh cabinets, as well as the questioning of Lebanese electoral legitimacy by Western countries because of the Maronite boycott, forced the Asad regime to form a popular government that could increase the legitimacy of post-election politics in Lebanon. These circumstances relatively limited Damascus's scope of selection regarding the candidates for Lebanon's next premiership, resulting in the selection of Hariri, who was anticipated to bring about economic recovery in Lebanon because he enjoyed strong domestic and international support, especially that of the USA and Europe.

Hariri, a Sunni billionaire who enjoyed widespread domestic and international popularity, had potentially enormous power to form and perform government policies at will, one of which could have been counteracting the Syrian power in Lebanon. However, as Najem (1998) argued, 'the larger political and military issues in Lebanon, including the redeployment of Syrian troops and the disarming of [Hizbullah], were to be decided by Syria and its Lebanese allies.'[85] More importantly, Hariri's power was to be constrained by that of his opponents in his cabinets, mostly pro-Syrians, as well as his counterparts in Lebanon's governing body called the 'troika', i.e. those assuming the presidency and parliamentary speakership. On the one hand, President Hirawi was in the weakest position among the governing troika because of the institutionally decreased power of the presidency and his isolation within the Maronite community, most of which refused to admit the legitimacy of the Syrian-dominated post-Ta'if political process. On the other hand, the increase in the power of both the parliamentary speakership and the parliament, as well as the backing of Parliament Speaker Berri by Damascus as a reliable figure in Lebanon's Shi'a community, potentially provided him with enormous leverage over Hariri.

The 30 ministers of the first Hariri cabinet, which was formed on 31 October 1992,[86] included Faris Buwayz (Minister of Foreign and Expatriate Affairs), Muhsin Dallul (Minister of Defence) and Bishara Murhij (Minister of the Interior), all of whom were pro-Syrian,[87] as well as 12 experienced technocrats, most of whom were close allies of Hariri and were appointed to address economic issues.[88] While Hariri's sphere of influence concerning economic issues was sometimes curtailed (although he had theoretically been given free rein in economic affairs), he had the means to contain the pro-Syrian figures in the governing troika and his cabinet. Hariri had likely calculated that he was an indispensable government figure for President Asad, who needed to stabilize Lebanon to legitimize Syrian presence in the country and thereby attract foreign investment from Saudi Arabia and the West. With domestic and international backing, he used the tactic of either threatening to resign or actually resigning in order to make progress in his reconstruction-oriented policies.

While Hariri's first threat to resign in August 1993 was merely due to several ministers' criticism of his alleged monopolization of power,[89] his second threat to do so in May 1994 was due to a much more serious matter.[90] In that month, Hariri attempted to widen Christian representation in his cabinet,[91] and indeed 'accused certain ministers of being obstructive and of failing to perform their tasks adequately'.[92] After the cabinet reshuffle plan had been blocked by both Hirawi, who wanted his own Christian allies in the cabinet, and Berri, who demanded more Shi'a participation and the post of minister of finance in the cabinet,[93] Hariri decided to suspend his duties on 8 May.[94]

While the actions of these pro-Syrian figures were clearly backed by Damascus,[95] which especially feared the appointment of Christians in the cabinet who opposed Syrian hegemony in Lebanon, Hariri's 'strike' caused a serious economic crisis, including a drastic fall in the value of the Lebanese pound and a rush to buy dollars,[96] a situation that Syria could not ignore. Having succeeded in making the Asad regime realize how much Lebanon's stability depended on him, Hariri went to Syria on 14 May 1994,[97] where it was reported that the regime assured that his opponents would support him and perform their jobs properly.[98] Hariri might have calculated that wider Christian representation in his cabinet would enhance the credibility of his cabinet among foreign countries and thus contribute towards attracting more foreign investment. Even more importantly, Hariri's attempt at cabinet reshuffling was aimed at forcing Damascus to pressure its allies to stop their obstruction of his policies. In other words, Hariri exploited the idea of broadening Christian cabinet representation as a means of advancing his plan for economic revival in Lebanon, which was known as 'Horizon 2000'.[99]

After Hariri returned to office on 16 May 1994,[100] he soon found that his aim of implementing the reconstruction plan was not accommodated by his political opponents, especially Berri. To protest the refusal of the Lebanese parliament to attach the Horizon 2000 plan to the 1995 state budget in October 1994 and the refusal of Berri to support the plan, Hariri again announced his intention to resign on 2 December.[101] While Hariri eagerly pursued the timely passage of the reconstruction-related bills in parliament, Berri endeavoured to prevent his status as the parliamentary speaker and the role of the parliament from being neglected.[102] At the same time pro-Syrian ministers were accusing Hariri of corruption.[103]

Facing Hariri's threat to resign, Syria became more anxious than ever to prevent turmoil in Lebanon, especially as this situation coincided with its upcoming US-mediated peace talks with Israel.[104] Thus prompted to intervene to defuse the crisis as well as to prevent economic recession in Lebanon, Damascus summoned Hariri and Berri, both of whom met with Asad on 5 December 1994.[105] The result of the meeting was a compromise: while 'the link between the Horizon 2000 plan and the 1995 budget was to be broken, the draft legislation of some of the most important projects, worth over $2 billion, were to be passed by parliament' and 'other parts of the plan were to be dealt with in the first half of 1995'.[106] After the Syrian regime once again promised Hariri that it would order his critics (its supporters) to cooperate with him,[107] he decided to stay on as the premier.[108]

It appears that by repeatedly threatening to resign (in August 1993 and May and December 1994), Hariri forced Damascus to recognize his power, as well as his determination to make economic progress in Lebanon, and Damascus indeed pressured its Lebanese allies to support him. However, Hariri's attempt to reshuffle his cabinet to create a more cooperative one did not materialize due to objections from the Syrian regime and its Lebanese allies, particularly Berri. As a result, Hariri changed his tactics and actually handed in his cabinet's resignation to Hirawi on 19 May 1995, and the resignation was accepted.[109] By doing so, Hariri aimed to fulfil two objectives: to reshuffle the cabinet in his favour and to advance Hirawi's endeavour to amend the Lebanese constitution in order to give himself a second presidential term, which Hariri supported.[110] In terms of power calculations, Hariri wished to maintain a weaker figure in the presidency.

After Syrian interventions, especially the dispatch of President Asad's son, Bashar, to Beirut,[111] the second Hariri cabinet, which consisted of 30 members, was formed on 25 May 1995.[112] He had managed to expel two leading opponents in his first cabinet: Franjiya and Michel Samaha.[113] Although the ministerial posts of foreign and expatriate affairs, defence and interior were still occupied by pro-Syrian figures, Hariri succeeded in nominating two of his close associates: Fadl al-Shalak (Minister of Post and Telecommunications) and Farid Makari (Minister of Information).[114] Hariri also successfully refused Berri's demand for the ministerial post of finance to be occupied by the parliamentary speaker's close ally and kept the post for himself.[115]

On the other hand, the agreement between Hirawi and Hariri that any possible amendment of the Lebanese constitution regarding the presidential term would be postponed for six months was interpreted as Hariri's concession to both the Asad regime, which feared that disputes over the amendment could undermine Lebanon's internal stability, and Berri, who hoped to become a key figure in the process of electing a new president.[116] However, the dispute between Hariri and Berri over Hirawi's second term continued to deepen until the autumn of 1995,[117] when sufficient Syrian pressure brought the matter to a resolution. President Asad's focus on the peace process between Syria and Israel, regarding which he would not tolerate any disruption by unpredictable events in Syria and Lebanon, as well as his acknowledgement of Hirawi's loyalty and submission to Damascus,[118] resulted in the imposition of Syrian 'pressure' sufficient to force the vast majority of Lebanon's lawmakers (110 of 128) to endorse the constitutional amendment on 19 October. This in effect made it possible to extend Hirawi's term for three years, despite the objection of no small number of the Lebanese.[119] Berri's dependence on Damascus and his desire for a weak figure in the presidency, based on the same reason as that of Hariri, resulted in his temporary rapprochement with the premier.

Tensions among the governing troika further deteriorated after the parliamentary elections in 1996. After two weeks of disagreement, largely between Hariri and Berri, over the distribution of the next cabinet's posts,[120] the third Hariri cabinet was finally formed on 7 November.[121] After the formation, Berri complained that Hariri had not only retained the post of the finance minister, but also assumed that of the post and telecommunications minister. However, more important for Berri were the facts that instead of one of his allies, the post of the minister of information was occupied by Basim al-Sabah, a Shi'a with close ties to Hariri, and that at least 10 ministers among the 30 cabinet members were Hariri's close allies.[122] While Hariri might have been forced to include several vocal critics in his cabinet, i.e. Franjiya (Minister of Public Health) and Arslan (State Minister for Expatriates), his holding of the aforementioned two posts showed his strong determination to revive Lebanon as an economic centre in the Middle East.

Although Hariri's efforts for reconstruction had some positive impacts on Lebanon, the public became increasingly concerned over such challenges as the massive budget deficit and the failure to attract long-term private sector investment, for which Hariri's economic policy, intentionally or unintentionally, had been responsible. Hariri attempted to contain public criticism of his policy by monopolizing the mass media and imposing heavy restrictions against labour unions to prevent strikes and demonstrations.[123] However, the level of popular frustration became so high in 1998 that the post-Ta'if political process itself began to unravel. According to Najem (2000), at this point Damascus may have calculated that its strategy of maintaining the Hariri cabinet would undermine its legitimacy in Lebanon.[124]

As a result, when Hirawi's extended presidential term approached its expiration in October 1998, Damascus accordingly chose the commander of the Lebanese army, Lahoud, as his successor.[125] This decision was based on Syrian interests in breaking the continuous and long-term discord between Hariri and Berri, cleaning up corruption which had been widely criticized by the Lebanese public and, needless to say, shifting Lebanon's political discourse to a more pro-Syrian stance. On 13 October, the Lebanese parliament, under Syrian 'pressure', amended a clause in Article 49 of the Lebanese constitution requiring Grade 1 civil servants seeking the presidency to have retired from their posts at least two years before their participation in a presidential election.[126] Lahoud was then elected on 15 October with the support of the 118 members present (of the 128 members) in the Lebanese parliament.[127]

Although Lahoud's election was largely determined by the Asad regime, it also reflected the desires of a majority of the Lebanese. As Najem (2000) pointed out, Lahoud 'was popular with the Maronite community and also enjoyed considerable support across sectarian lines', because 'he had a strong reputation for being honest and was widely perceived as being incorruptible'.[128] In fact, a prominent, exiled anti-Syrian leader at that time, former President Jumayyil, even stated his support for Lahoud.[129]

After Lahoud's election, Hariri was concerned over the power balance vis-à-vis the new president and initially expressed his refusal to head a new cabinet,[130] an act that, as Leenders (1998) pointed out, was seen as a tactic 'to strengthen his position in further bargaining [with Damascus and its Lebanese allies] over the distribution of ministerial posts'.[131] However, Hariri appears to have miscalculated the impact of Lebanon's stalled economy, the strength of Lebanese public criticism of his alleged corruption and the antagonism within the governing troika related to his presence, all of which convinced the Syrian leadership that he was no longer indispensable to the stabilization of Lebanon. Furthermore, in 1998, Bashar al-Asad began to take over control of Lebanese affairs from Vice President Khaddam, a key ally of Hariri, and develop ties with Lahoud.[132] In short, Hariri's already soured relations with pro-Syrian Lebanese figures, especially Berri, the Syrian realization that his role as Lebanon's premier was no longer essential and the internal political changes in the Syrian regime paved the way towards his resignation in December 1998.

In a short while, a new cabinet was formed on 4 December 1998.[133] However, as Prime Minister Huss's attempts to bring about economic recovery in Lebanon by drawing on his experience as a competent technocrat failed, his policy soon began to be criticized.[134]

Under these circumstances, at the instigation of Damascus, President Lahoud met Hariri in August 1999, who still carried too much personal weight to be excluded.[135] It appears that Lahoud's demand for Hariri to cooperate in domestic economic affairs reflected Asad's concern that the continued split between the Lebanese government and Hariri-led business group would further depress the Lebanese economy, leading to increased questioning regarding Syrian presence and legitimacy in the country. However, Lahoud's attempt to win Hariri's cooperation failed,[136] and Hariri continued to be active both domestically and internationally, which became the foundation of his return to the premiership.[137]

Besides the enormous success of candidates aligned with Hariri in the 2000 parliamentary elections, several other factors convinced Damascus of the need to reinstate him. First, the election results indicated a decreased Lebanese support for the Huss cabinet because of his inability to deal effectively with the stalled economic situation. Second, despite Hariri's enormous spending, which had left Lebanon heavily in debt, the Syrian regime may have calculated that the international confidence that he continued to enjoy would allow him to draw the international aid and investment necessary for Lebanon's economic revival. Third, the risk of bringing Hariri back into the governing troika had been considerably reduced because of a change in the power balance. Because Lahoud had consolidated his power more strongly than had his predecessor, President Bashar al-Asad might have calculated that Hariri would not be able to exercise the same degree of influence as he had done before.

Among the 30 members of the fourth Hariri cabinet, which was formed on 26 October 2000,[138] were eight ministers considered his allies. These included Fouad al-Siniora (Minister of Finance), Basil Fulayhan (Minister of Economy and Trade), 'Abd al-Rahim Murad (Minister of Education and Higher Education), Ghazi al-'Aridi (Minister of Information) and Samir al-Jisr (Minister of

Justice).[139] In contrast, only three ministers were staunch allies of Damascus: Franjiya (Minister of Health), Najib Miqati (Minister of Public Works and Transport) and Karam Karam (Minister of Tourism).[140] However, Hariri's demand for full control over the economy-related ministerial posts and complete freedom in implementing his economic policy was not granted, forcing him to make several compromises with Lahoud and Berri. On the one hand, Jean Qurdahi (Minister of Telecommunications) was a close ally of Lahoud.[141] On the other hand, As'ad Diyab (Minister of Social Affairs), Muhammad 'Abd al-Hamid Baydun (Minister of Energy and Water) and 'Ali al-'Abd Allah (Minister of Agriculture) were close allies of Berri, and these posts were important for the Amal Movement in maintaining its patronage network in the Biqa' area and southern Lebanon.[142]

In spite of Hariri's 'forced' concessions to Lahoud and Berri regarding the economy-related ministerial posts, his cabinet's policy statement in November 2000 did not include a demand for redeployment of the Syrian army and defended the Syrian presence by describing it as temporarily necessary,[143] although Maronite Patriarch Sufayr had begun to make strong demands for the deployment. Hariri's attitude was based on the fact that he largely owed his nomination to the premiership to Lahoud, and his assumption 'that the Syrian leadership would support his efforts towards administrative reform and his plan for salvaging a deteriorating financial position'.[144] Later, when 'Awn's followers organized a political rally to protest the Syrian presence and commemorate their leader's 1989 Liberation War on 14 March 2001, the Lebanese government permitted only a sit-in and ordered its army to prevent demonstrations outside Syrian army centres in Beirut.[145] Also, Hariri reiterated that the Syrian presence was currently necessary,[146] a statement that was likely due to his fear that the situation might escalate out of control and further destabilize Lebanon. In return, Hariri managed to receive Lahoud's support, and probably that of Damascus, for budget cuts for the Lebanese army.[147]

Although Hariri had condemned their arrests in August 2001, when Lahoud, taking advantage of Hariri's visit to Pakistan, ordered Lebanon's security forces to crack down on supporters of the LF and 'Awn, leading to the detention of about 140 people,[148] he was forced to cooperate with Lahoud to make progress on his economic recovery plan, since it had been severely hampered by the arrests. Eventually, in March 2002, Hariri laid the blame for the lack of progress regarding his reconstruction efforts on the largely anti-Syrian Christian community in Lebanon.[149] By thus distancing himself from the anti-Syrian current, Hariri may have been expecting cooperation from Asad at the upcoming Arab League summit in Beirut.

As a result, despite Syrian concerns that the Beirut summit would be preoccupied with the ''Abdullah Proposal',[150] which inevitably could weaken its role in the Arab–Israel peace process, the summit was held and Hariri managed to obtain financial assistance from Saudi Arabia.[151]

However, Hariri's rivals in the governing troika and his opponents in the cabinet, directly or indirectly, continued to obstruct his reconstruction efforts, although he theoretically had a free hand in Lebanon's economic affairs. Under these disadvantageous conditions, Hariri could have threatened to resign or have actually resigned, as he had done before, with an aim of pressuring Damascus to force its Lebanese allies to support him. However, using either tactic became impractical for him after 2000. First, although Hariri still enjoyed international and domestic support, the expectation that he would bring about a 'miraculous' economic recovery had been dashed inside and outside Lebanon. Second, the Syrian regime's perception of Hariri's indispensability to the stabilization of Lebanon had changed. Asad did not have good relations with Hariri because of the premier's close connections with Khaddam, who was gradually sidelined in the Syrian regime after Asad's consolidation of power in 2000. Moreover, as Blanford (2006) reported, the Syrian regime attempted to oust Hariri in 2002 with the aim of installing in his position 'Prince

Walid bin Talal, a half-Saudi, half-Lebanese business tycoon, described as the world's sixth-richest man'.[152]

After the 'Paris II Conference' of 22 November 2002, at which donor states discussed the means of assisting Lebanon,[153] Hariri's efforts to privatize the telecommunication and electricity sectors made little progress, because Minister of Telecommunications Qurdahi (a close ally of Lahoud) and Minister of Energy and Water Baydun (a close ally of Berri) played key roles in stalling the privatization process.[154] As a result, Lebanon was criticized in late summer 2003 by the World Bank and the European Union and in early 2004 by French President Chirac, who had largely contributed to the holding of the conference, over the lack of progress regarding privatization.[155]

As the United States was preparing for a military operation in Iraq in early 2003, its relations with Syria became tense and even after the end of the operation, the US neoconservatives maintained hostile attitudes towards the Asad regime. Accordingly, Syria's alleged facilitation of militants in Iraq and its presence in Lebanon were seen as problems by the US administration. In this regional context, the Asad regime initiated a cabinet reshuffle which gave birth to an increasingly pro-Syrian cabinet excluding anti-Syrian Christian figures. In fact, the fifth Hariri cabinet, which was established on 17 April 2003 and had 30 ministers, included 'Asim Qansu (Minister of State), leader of the Lebanese branch of the Ba'th Party; As'ad Hardan (Minister of Labour), leader of the Syrian Social Nationalist Party; and Pakraduni (Minister of State for Administrative Reform), leader of the Kata'ib Party.[156] While Minister of Finance Siniora maintained his position, Minister of Telecommunications Qurdahi did so, and Minister of Energy and Water Resources Ayyub Humayd was a member of the Amal Movement.[157] In other words, Lebanon's telecom and resource sectors, the targets of Hariri's efforts at privatization, remained under the control of the figures close to Lahoud or Berri. According to Blanford (2006), '[Hariri] and his allies understood that the composition of the government not only strengthened Damascus's control over Lebanon at a time of heightened international pressure, but it also imposed further restraints on Hariri's ability to push his policies.'[158]

Damascus's influence on the cabinet formation and the international 'unfavourable wind' faced by the Asad regime led Hariri to begin efforts to counterbalance the Syrians. As expected, the allies of Lahoud and Berri in the cabinet obstructed Hariri's efforts to stimulate economic recovery through privatization in Lebanon, which resulted in the halting of the cabinet's regular meetings from May to June 2003.[159] As a consequence, Hariri did not initially support the amendment of the Lebanese constitution to renew Lahoud's presidential term, which was to expire in November 2004.[160] However, Asad's strong support of Lahoud remained unchanged, and Damascus allegedly hatched a plot to oust Hariri.[161] Additionally, at the end of 2003, Hariri was criticized by Syrian officials including Asad for 'conspiring' with the US and French authorities.[162] Although the Syrian allegation was based on Hariri's secret contact with a senior US State Department official in Beirut,[163] his close connection with Chirac might have also contributed to the Syrian suspicion.[164]

At the beginning of 2004, Lahoud continued to object to the privatization of Lebanon's telecom sector, a priority of Hariri,[165] and thus the promise of Paris II remained unfulfilled. Irritated by Lahoud, Hariri 'quietly pressed Western governments to pressure Asad into giving him a freer hand in managing economic policy'.[166] However, it appears that Asad did not pressure Lahoud to cooperate with Hariri regarding the economic issue, thus preserving their animosity within the governing troika.

Despite Hariri's balancing against Damascus and his objection to the extension of Lahoud's presidential term because of their mutual animosity that was largely due to the president's obstruction of his reform policies, his cabinet and parliamentary bloc finally endorsed the legal process regarding the extension from late August to early September 2004.[167] The vote for an extension of Lahoud's mandate in the parliamentary session on

3 September occurred within the context of allegedly strong pressure from the Syrian regime and Western opposition, especially from the United States and France. In fact, UN Security Council Resolution 1559, which was passed on 2 September, called for, at that time in particular, the halting of Damascus's intervention in Lebanon's presidential issue. Hariri's alignment with the Syrian regime over this issue was due not only to the exertion of its pressure, but also its assurance that it would restrain Lahoud in the formation of a new cabinet after 3 September.[168] However, the Syrian pledge did not materialize and resulted in Hariri's resignation in late October.

Even after the resignation, Hariri maintained his distance from the Bristol Gathering, whose first meeting was held on 22 September 2004 with the main participants of the PSP, the Qurnat Shahwan Gathering and the Democratic Renewal Movement, and which took a strong anti-Syrian stance.[169] Hariri's attitude appears to have resulted from his recognition of the need to form a broad coalition in order to win the forthcoming Lebanese parliamentary elections scheduled for May 2005. According to Blanford (2006), Hariri understood that 'if he proceeded too fast in embracing [the Qurnat Shawan Gathering] and other Christian groups sympathetic to Resolution 1559, he could lose the support of his Sunni constituency and hamper his attempts to bring on board the [Shi'as]'.[170]

However, after Hariri's assassination on 14 February 2005, the majority of the Lebanese Sunnis condemned the alleged Syrian involvement, an allegation that the Asad regime has categorically denied, and soon formed an anti-Syrian coalition (later referred to as the March 14 Coalition) with members of the PSP and the Qurnat Shahwan Gathering and other key Christian figures. Under mounting anti-Syrian current in Lebanon, Syria finally withdrew its military and intelligence forces completely on 26 April,[171] thus ending the era of its dominance in Lebanon.

In sum, Hariri had a strong commitment to overseeing the reconstruction of many war-torn neighbourhoods and regions of the country. Initially, with strong Lebanese and international support, Hariri had attempted to force Damascus to control his rivals in the governing troika, i.e. pro-Syrian Hirawi and Berri, and pro-Syrian ministers in his cabinet, because their cooperation was necessary for him to carry forward the Horizon 2000 plan. However, after the millennium, Hariri's level of indispensability to the Asad regime decreased, as did Lebanese enthusiasm for him. This led Hariri to refrain from challenging the Syrians until the US invasion of Iraq in 2003. Despite occasionally balancing against the Syrian regime after 2003, Hariri ultimately aligned himself with it over the extension of Lahoud's presidential mandate, for which he anticipated support for his formation of a new cabinet necessary to implement his economic policy.

Economic Aspects

As the Lebanese Civil War had largely destroyed the nation's infrastructure, Prime Minister Hariri, who had a strongly reconstruction-oriented mindset, prioritized the activities of Lebanon's construction sector. In order to achieve a smooth implementation of his economic policy, Hariri was required to consider the economic interests of not only his political rivals, but also Syrians, as by doing so he could gain the cooperation of his domestic opponents, most of whom were pro-Syrian. On the other hand, Lebanon benefited economically from further 'positive' aspects of its relations with Syria, including Syrian workers' presence in Lebanon, which was necessary for its reconstruction, and operations of Lebanese banks on Syrian soil, which had the potential to support the development of Lebanon's banking sector, a priority of Hariri. These Lebanese–Syrian economic relations, which largely contributed to Hariri's alignment with the Syrian regime, are examined here in detail.

First, many Syrian companies as well as Lebanese companies of Syrian origin became involved in Lebanon's reconstruction projects after the end of the civil war. For example, Shukri al-Shammas, originating from Homs, was involved in the construction of the village of Rabiyya in the suburb of Beirut, and al-Sharika al-Khumasiyya, a Syrian company, made large-scale investments in Lebanon's real estate sector.[172] While Abdul Rahman Huriyya, a contractor of Syrian origin, built most of the roads in Lebanon,[173] Hariri's political consideration towards the Syrian regime clearly manifested in a contract to build a coastal road from Beirut to southern Lebanon. One stretch of the road was to be built by Ittihad Contracting, a Lebanese company owned by Parliament Speaker Berri's wife Randa; and Mount Qassiun, a Syrian company controlled by Syrian Vice President Khaddam.[174] The remaining stretch was to be built by a Lebanese firm, Geneco, owned by Hariri's brother Shafiq.[175] The creation of such 'partnerships' between Lebanese and Syrian companies resulted from Hariri's consideration of not only the interests of his pro-Syrian political rivals, but also those of Syrians. In general, Hariri's primary aim by giving shares to Lebaese companies of Syrian origin and to Syrian companies was to secure the support of his rivals for the Horizon 2000 plan.

While Lebanon's reconstruction process needed and attracted Syrian workers, their actual number has remained a topic of great debate, as many flooded into the country immediately after the end of the civil war. While the Syrian–Lebanese Higher Council estimated the figure at 253,000,[176] the Lebanese newspaper *al-Nahar* reported in October 1994 that the Lebanese General Security Directorate had placed the number at 900,000 at least.[177] When these figures are considered along with other estimates, it appears that anti-Syrians in Lebanon have tended to overestimate the number to emphasize the 'occupation' of its labour market by Syrians, while pro-Syrians in Lebanon have tended to play down the number to lessen Lebanese criticism of the workers' presence.

The presence of Syrian workers in Lebanon has yielded several significant benefits for Syria, including a decrease in the unemployment rate and the collection of billions of dollars in remittances every year from Lebanon, the largest or second largest source of remittances for Syria. In contrast, the presence has yielded both benefits and drawbacks for Lebanon. On the one hand, Lebanon's business circle has enjoyed a supply of unskilled labourers willing to work at menial jobs generally scorned by the Lebanese for extremely low wages by native standards.[178] Furthermore, the Lebanese government has also benefited, as did Hariri, who shared the interests of the business community and considered Syrian workers' presence important for Lebanon's reconstruction. On the other hand, their presence has undoubtedly raised the unemployment rate in Lebanon and provided the Syrian regime with a pretext for intervention on behalf of the workers. Despite these drawbacks, the Lebanese government has not formally regulated the presence of Syrian workers because of the economic benefits for Lebanon.

Regarding Lebanese banks' operations in Syria, although the implementation of Syrian Law No. 10 in May 1991 aimed at stoking rapid economic growth by facilitating investment in Syria, it is necessary to note that potential investors were challenged by a lack of foreign banks with branches in Syria. This could have been an opportunity for Lebanon's well-respected banks; however, the state-owned Commercial Bank of Syria had been the only commercial bank authorized by the government to operate in the country until April 2000, when the Syrian regime finally passed a decree allowing international banks with at least US$11 million in equity to establish branches in the free zones.[179]

In December 2000, four Lebanese banks, i.e. Banque du Liban et d'Outre Mer, Banque Europeenne pour le Moyen–Orient, Fransabank and Societe Generale Europeenne–Libano de Banque, were granted licences to operate in Syria's free zones.[180] Granting such permission appears to have been influenced by the fact that Syrian citizens had long been using Lebanese banks, which had good knowledge of the Syrian market. In addition, the Lebanese government anticipated that once private banks were permitted to establish branches in Syria, as announced by the Ba'th Party Regional Command in late December 2000, Lebanese banks would contribute to the development of the private banking system in Syria.[181] As their expertise and proximity could appeal to international banks preparing for investment in Syria, Lebanese banks had the potential to increase the status of their country in the global financial community. Regarding this point, Najem (2000) emphasized that Hariri was struggling 'to return Beirut to its former role as the financial centre of the Middle East'.[182]

In sum, while remaining mindful of Syria's economic stakes in Lebanon in order to gain support of Damascus's Lebanese allies, Hariri progressed with his reconstruction efforts for Lebanon. The presence of Syrian workers in Lebanon and the operations of Lebanese banks in Syria, which have arguably benefited both countries in several respects, reflected the interests of Lebanon's business community that supported and had close connections with Hariri. These factors arguably increased his motivation to align himself with the Syrian regime.

Social Aspects

With the explicit or tacit understanding of Damascus, several restrictions were imposed on social freedoms in Lebanon on the pretext of maintaining its stability, a matter on which both the Lebanese and Syrian authorities placed priority. From this viewpoint, Lebanon's labour movement and the mass media are focused on here.

The general strike on 9 May 1992, which was called for by the General Labour Confederation (GLC) under the rather worsened economic situation in Lebanon, ultimately led Prime Minister Karami to resign (although bringing down the cabinet had not been the objective of the GLC leadership).[183] Since the anti-government protests were, as Najem (2000) pointed out, 'seen by many not just as a response to poor economic management [under Karami], but as a popular rebellion against the government in particular and the Syrian-dominated political order in general',[184] and since the subsequent Prime Minister Sulh also failed to halt the deteriorating situation of the Lebanese economy, President Asad may have felt the legitimacy of Syrian presence in Lebanon was further threatened. Under these circumstances, Prime Minister Hariri, Sulh's successor, continued to place priority on Lebanon's economic recovery, with a clear interest in preventing the labour movement from spreading and intensifying. As Syria had the dual goals of stabilizing Lebanon and containing criticism against its presence, both the Lebanese and Syrian authorities were motivated to engage in cooperation, which manifested in various forms.

First, the post of Lebanon's minister of labour had been occupied by pro-Syrian figures,[185] and Hariri appears to have been 'pressured' by the Syrian regime to install these figures in the post so as to prevent labour protests from escalating into anti-Syrian demonstrations. By doing so, Hariri not only furthered Syria's desire for social order, but also his own for economic progress in Lebanon.

In addition, the Asad regime interfered to restrict Lebanon's labour movement itself in a more direct manner. When the GLC called off a general strike planned for December 1993 after the formation of a Syrian-backed deal with the Lebanese government, many Lebanese believed that the Syrian leadership, particularly Vice-President Khaddam, had played an important role in reaching the compromise with the aim of averting the strike.[186] It is reasonable to conclude, considering the close relationship between Khaddam and Hariri and his priority given to Lebanon's social order necessary for its rapid economic recovery, that the premier tacitly supported the Syrian role. Later, when the GLC called for a general strike in July 1995 to compel the Lebanese government to remove the gasoline surcharge,[187] Hariri immediately banned all demonstrations and ordered the army and Internal Security Forces to enforce the ban.[188] This ban was clearly supported by the Syrians, as they had granted permission for the use of their security apparatus to Hariri, and thus Lebanese soldiers and policemen gained support from the Syrian army and were deployed in Beirut and other cities to crack down on protests.[189]

Faced with continuing confrontation between the Lebanese government and the GLC, Hariri and Parliament Speaker Berri in particular concluded that the leader, Ilyas Abu Rizq, should be replaced by a more cooperative figure.[190] As a result, a government-supported campaign to defeat Rizq in the GLC elections of April 1997 began with pro-Syrian Minister of Labour Hardan playing a leading role.[191] Berri also played an important role, as the recently licensed federations loyal to him had greatly contributed to the election of a pro-regime candidate, Ghanim Zughbi, in the second round of the elections.[192] When Rizq contested the electoral result,[193] according to Baroudi (1998), a large number of security officers attempted to prevent his supporters from entering GLC buildings.[194] Although the Asad regime was not directly involved in this case, it appears the regime's, as well as Hariri's, shared primary goal of containing social unrest in Lebanon was secured through its active allies such as Hardan and Berri.

As a result, it can be concluded that the Syrian regime generally sided with the Lebanese government on the basis of a common interest in maintaining social order and stability in Lebanon, which led Hariri generally to cooperate with and sometimes rely on the regime during his initial period as the premier. However, these relations later changed when the Lebanese government appeared to no longer need Syrian support after the GLC became 'moderate' despite Rizq's regaining of the top position in July 1998.[195] In fact, when the GLC held a general strike in May 2004, the Syrian army stationed in Lebanon appeared to do nothing.[196]

Regarding restrictions on the mass media in Lebanon, as Mallat (2000) pointed out, the country 'has long prided itself on its respect for free expression'.[197] However, as Hariri gave priority to economic recovery in Lebanon, and as the legitimacy of Syria's dominant position in the subordinate state largely relied on his government's efficiency, the premier and the Syrian leadership had a common interest in containing criticism of the Lebanese government in the name of maintaining Lebanon's social order. Although Damascus appears not to have been directly involved in issues concerning free expression in Lebanon, it is likely that considering the common interest, the Hariri cabinet's restrictions on the freedoms of Lebanon's mass media were tacitly supported by the Syrian regime.

Such instances of Lebanese and Syrian collaboration appeared in 1994 and 1996. In 1994, it manifested in the Lebanese government's attempt to introduce tough penalties on journalists and newspapers.[198] However, angry protests from journalists and parliamentary deputies in Lebanon forced the government to retreat and tone down the proposed penalties.[199] In 1996, Lebanese and Syrian collaboration manifested once again when 'the [Lebanese] government pronounced that only four television and eight radio stations (other than [official] Télé-Liban and Radio Liban) could use Lebanon's airwaves. It then licensed only those stations in which leading members of the political establishment had financial interests.'[200] The four licensed television stations were Future Television (Future TV), owned by Hariri; the National Broadcasting Network (NBN), owned by Berri; the Lebanese Broadcasting Corporation International (LBCI), with ties to President Hirawi; and Murr Television (MTV), with ties to Interior Minister (also Deputy Prime Minister) Michel al-Murr.[201] As the initial permission enabling Hizbullah to operate its Manar Television was soon cancelled,[202] it accused the government of dividing the spoils of the stations.[203] This change in the treatment of Hizbullah appeared to reflect the government's concern over the mass 'religious radicalization' of the Lebanese, which it appeared to share with the Syrian regime. While Hariri was required to bargain with his pro-Syrian political rivals, he secured a licence to operate Future TV, his own station.

In sum, Hariri had imposed restrictions on Lebanon's labour movement and the mass media, with either the explicit or implicit support of the Syrian regime. Although these constraints damaged Lebanon's status as a 'democratic state', they benefitted not only the Syrians, but also Hariri himself, as they had a shared interest in stabilizing the Lebanese state.

Military and Diplomatic Aspects

Although Lebanese sovereignty was restricted under Syria's indirect rule, Prime Minister Hariri wished to limit the military activities of Syrian-backed Hizbullah in southern Lebanon and proceed with the Middle East peace process in order to achieve his primary aim of acquiring international aid and investment necessary for economic recovery in Lebanon. However, Syria was interested in maintaining conflict in the south, specifically for the recovery of the Golan Heights. As a result, Hariri and the Syrian regime had clear differences over Hizbullah's militancy, which particularly manifested when Israel launched massive military operations against Lebanon and when Hariri struggled to obtain international donors' confidence. Their differences were also apparent over the peace process, in particular over the 'Lebanon first' option and the 'Abdullah Proposal.[204] This subsection thus discusses these issues in detail, focusing on their impact on Hariri's reconstruction efforts.

Regarding Hizbullah's military activities in southern Lebanon, the organization initiated a conflict with the Israeli army in the security zone in November 1991 after a lull in violence lasting two years in the region on account of its fierce battle with the Amal Movement.[205] Consequently, the value of the security zone decreased for Israel because its proxy, i.e. the SLA, for which it had recruited by a combination of material incentives and conscription, had little motivation to fight against Hizbullah.[206] Israel's response was carried out north of the zone with the aims of decreasing the capability of Hizbullah fighters and warning

Lebanese villagers not to support the group.[207] However, since Hizbullah members were mainly from southern villages and local support towards the group was strong due to its providing relief and rebuilding destroyed houses, Hizbullah militias managed to reach villages north of the zone and attack the Israeli army.[208]

When the Israeli army assassinated the then Secretary General of Hizbullah, 'Abbas Musawi, and his family in February 1992, Hizbullah reacted with rocket strikes into the security zone and northern Israel.[209] The continuous exchange of fire between Hizbullah and Israeli forces, and the additional Israeli deployment in the security zone raised the possibility of the army's full-scale invasion of Lebanon. Under these circumstances and facing pressure from Syria, Iran and Lebanon, Hizbullah pledged not to attack targets inside Israel and to confine itself to those in the security zone.[210]

After another lull in violence in the summer of 1992, conflict between Hizbullah and the Israeli army resurfaced, ultimately culminating in the summer of 1993. After Hizbullah continuously shelled northern Israel with rockets, Israel launched Operation Accountability, a large-scale military operation, on 25 July to test the Lebanese government's will.[211] The Israeli government hoped that complete disruption of Lebanon's civilian life caused by the heavy attack on southern Lebanon would generate enough pressure on the Lebanese and, by extension, the Syrian regime to curb Hizbullah activities.

However, instead of bowing to the Israeli pressure, the Lebanese government pursued several tactical policies. First, Hariri made diplomatic efforts, mainly in Europe, to end the conflict. Harik (1997) attributed the Hariri efforts to the fact that 'the United States persuaded Lebanon not to bring the issue to the Security Council, arguing that a bitter debate might prejudice Secretary of State Warren Christopher's forthcoming visit to the Middle East to try to restart the stalled peace negotiations'.[212] Second, the Lebanese government launched a programme to assist the displaced who had escaped from southern Lebanon.[213]

Third, while the Lebanese government did not try to restrict Hizbullah's military operations, it prohibited any demonstration showing solidarity with Hizbullah.[214]

Meanwhile, Syrian President Asad hoped for US mediation in stalled Israeli–Syrian negotiations at that time. Consequently, although Syria's military positions in Lebanon were attacked by the Israeli army, Asad not only maintained restraint, but also 'pressured [Hizbullah] into ending the rocket attacks on Israel, forced it to withdraw its heavy weapons and rockets to the [Biqa'] and cut off further supplies of rockets from Iran'.[215] In the ceasefire brokered by the United States with Syrian cooperation that Israel ultimately accepted on 31 July 1993, Israel agreed to refrain from attacking civilian targets north of the security zone while Hizbullah pledged to focus its activities on the zone, and a token number of Lebanese troops were to be deployed in southern Lebanon.[216] As the agreement gave Hariri some hope of being able to facilitate his reconstruction efforts by recovering, albeit nominally, Lebanese sovereignty over the south, he was probably satisfied with it.

However, Hariri's hope soon evaporated with the Lebanese army remaining inactive and stationed away from the security zone because of Damascus's demands for reductions in the size and role of the army. [217] This situation enabled Syria either to promote or to deactivate Hizbullah's military activities to suit its strategy and demonstrate to Israel that its security depended on its striking a peace accord with Syria.

For three years following the conclusion of Operation Accountability in July 1993, Hizbullah's military activities were generally confined to the security zone of southern Lebanon, because the Israeli government under the Labour Party focused on Syria's primary interest, i.e. recovery of the Golan Heights, in the Israeli–Syrian peace negotiations. However, a major breakthrough was not brought about, and tensions in southern Lebanon, which had been increasing since March 1996, finally led Israel to launch Operation Grapes of Wrath on 11 April.[218]

As Trendle (1996) analysed, Israel's massive assaults from land, sea and air on suspected Hizbullah targets in southern Lebanon and Beirut aimed at not only pressuring the Lebanese government into curbing Hizbullah, but also damaging investor confidence in Lebanon's stability and thus derailing its reconstruction process.[219]

The launch of Operation Grapes of Wrath posed a dilemma for Hariri, forcing him to choose between supporting Syrian-backed Hizbullah and pursing his current priority of economic revival in Lebanon. While Hariri remained active in securing international support to settle the conflict,[220] he firmly expressed solidarity with Hizbullah.[221] On the other hand, President Hirawi contacted the United Nations General Assembly with a demand to hold a special session.[222] Their actions were likely undertaken with Damascus's permission, as they had been in close contact with Asad since the outbreak of the Israeli operation.[223]

While the Lebanese government remained active on the international scene, which was backed by considerable cross-sectarian solidarity with Hizbullah in the country,[224] an Israeli attack on the UN base at Qana on 18 April 1996 marked a turning point in Lebanon's diplomatic manoeuvrability. After the Qana massacre, the United States recognized that to secure a ceasefire between Hizbullah and Israel required it to negotiate with Syria.[225] As a result, Asad, who only a month earlier had been isolated at the Sharm el-Sheikh anti-terrorism summit in Egypt, was provided with an opportunity to re-enter the centre stage of international diplomatic efforts to settle the conflict.[226] US Secretary of State Christopher was, by negotiating the ceasefire issue with Asad and without directly negotiating with Hariri,[227] clearly conveying that the United States had sidelined Lebanon.

However, Hariri appears to have viewed the outcome of the negotiations as reasonable, although French calls for the implementation of UN Security Council Resolution 425 were rejected.[228] The reaffirmation of the 1993 agreement was relatively advantageous to Hariri, as it confined Hizbullah's military activities to the security zone in southern Lebanon and, more importantly, granted Lebanon equal status as a member of the ceasefire monitoring committee, which included representatives of the United States, France, Syria and Israel.[229] Lebanon's position of equality on the committee could be interpreted as a result of Hariri's close relations with French President Chirac, which largely contributed to the recovery of Lebanon's status after it had been somewhat damaged by the US refusal to engage in direct negotiations with Lebanon.

Israel's retention of the Shabaa Farms even after the army's withdrawal from almost all parts of southern Lebanon on 24 May 2000 has given Hizbullah a pretext to retain its arms, which became a foremost concern for Hariri in terms of his priority given to economic revival in Lebanon. Hariri had little sympathy for Hizbullah's military operations, and his prediction that the exchange of fire between the Israeli army and Hizbullah fighters might undermine Lebanon's economic confidence was indeed realized. For example, Hizbullah's military operations in February 2001 came one day after Hariri reassured the attendees of the international donors' conference for Lebanon in Paris (the 'Paris I Conference') that Lebanon was now safe for investment and would not initiate any actions that would destabilize the region.[230] Anticipating Syrian containment of Hizbullah's military activities, he made a statement in March defending the dominant position in Lebanon.[231] However, Hizbullah launched another deadly attack in April, and the United States withheld $20 million of economic aid to Lebanon on the basis of its argument that Lebanon had refused to deploy its army to southern Lebanon to prevent the attack.[232]

In parallel with dealing directly with Hizbullah, Hariri attempted to regulate its military activities by diplomatic means. The 'Lebanon first' option, which had been vigorously proposed by Israeli Prime Minister Netanyahu and envisioned the possibility of a unilateral withdrawal of the Israeli army from southern Lebanon in exchange for security guarantees by the

Lebanese government for northern Israel, appears to have been inspired by Hariri's earlier action. In February 1993, Hariri had declared Lebanon's readiness to reach an agreement with Israel that would allow for the implementation of Resolution 425, although he denied that Lebanon was ready to sign a peace treaty with Israel.[233] Hariri might have been calculating that his statement would have some appeal for Israel as its peace negotiations with Syria were at a stalemate at that time.[234] Although Hariri cautiously denied the possibility of a peace agreement and only demanded Israeli withdrawal from southern Lebanon, his move had the potential to decrease the legitimacy of Syrian presence in Lebanon and Syrian-backed Hizbullah's military activities in the south, thus weakening Syria's negotiation position vis-à-vis Israel. In the end, his 'independent' action was soon contained, and by October, Lebanon's 'accord' with Syria regarding diplomatic affairs had been announced.[235]

As a result, when Netanyahu assumed the premiership in July 1996, he proposed the 'Lebanon first' option and hoped that the Israeli arrangement with Lebanon could provide the basis of its future negotiations with Syria.[236] The pressure from the Israeli army, which had been suspicious of maintaining its presence in the security zone of southern Lebanon, especially after Operation Grapes of Wrath, also prompted Netanyahu to propose the idea.[237] The backbone of the option was Israel's withdrawal from the security zone in return for Lebanon's provision of specific security arrangements, i.e. disarmament of Hizbullah and dispatch of the Lebanese army to the area.[238] According to Norton (1997), Israel was to gain several benefits from this proposal. First, its implementation might have relieved US pressure on Israel regarding other contentious aspects of the Middle East peace process, especially the West Bank. Second, by unilaterally withdrawing from southern Lebanon, Israel would have eliminated one of Syria's trump cards in the negotiations over the Golan Heights.[239]

Predictably, the Asad regime objected to the 'Lebanon first' option by stressing that Syria should maintain its central role in the peace process and arguing that Netanyahu was trying to separate the Syrian and Lebanese peace tracks.[240] As the realization of the Netanyahu proposal would likely not only to have stripped Syria of its influence in negotiations over the Golan Heights, but also led to the withdrawal of its army from Lebanon after the Israeli withdrawal, it was reported that 'Damascus signal[l]ed the Lebanese authorities to reject the Israeli proposal and instead repeat their insistence on unconditional Israeli withdrawal as demanded by UN Resolution 425 of 1978'.[241] Following Lebanese Foreign Minister Buwayz's assertion that the Israeli offer was unclear,[242] Hariri emphasized that Lebanon had not been officially notified of the 'Lebanon first' option and had only learned of its full scope from the mass media.[243]

Several factors may have been behind Hariri's unwillingness to make a more explicit statement regarding the 'Lebanon first' option. Facing fierce opposition to the proposal from not only the 'radical' Hizbullah, but also the 'moderate' Amal Movement,[244] Hariri appears, above all, to have been hoping to avoid causing turmoil in Lebanon, which scheduled the parliamentary elections in August and September 1996. In addition, Hariri might have calculated that if he explicitly dismissed the Israeli offer, Lebanon would not be able to attract foreign investment essential for his economic recovery efforts.

However, Hariri's ambiguous attitude towards the 'Lebanon first' option is likely to have dismayed the Asad regime. When Hariri visited Washington, DC in December 1996 with the aim of securing aid that had been promised as compensation for Operation Grapes of Wrath, the Syrian regime opposed his visit on the grounds that forming closer ties between the United States and Lebanon would decrease Syria's leverage in Lebanon.[245] Then, just before Hariri's visit to France in February 1997, Damascus stressed the inseparability of the Syrian and Lebanese peace tracks.[246] The Syrian leadership was indeed alarmed by the Israeli proposal that France would dispatch its army to southern Lebanon after the Israeli withdrawal,[247] a clear indication that Israel was contemplating a separate accord with Lebanon.

In January 1998, Israeli Defence Minister Yitzhaq Mordehay announced Israel's readiness to comply with Resolution 425 if Lebanon guaranteed security by sending its army to the Lebanese–Israeli border.[248] In response, Hariri, along with Hirawi, Berri and Buwayz, allegedly expressed to French Foreign Minister Hubert Vedrine Lebanon's willingness to deploy its army to southern Lebanon in the event of Israel's unilateral withdrawal from the south.[249] While such willingness demonstrated that even Damascus's allies in Lebanon's governing body supported Israel's unilateral withdrawal according to Resolution 425 along with several security requirements, the Asad regime, as expected, rejected this proposal. The Syrian leadership affirmed that Israeli withdrawal should be unconditional, as demanded by the resolution; however, it was concerned that the Israeli plan would diminish the legitimacy of Hizbullah, an important tool for Syria to exert pressure on Israel.[250] In other words, Syria needed Israel to stay in Lebanon until the final resolution of the Golan Heights conflict. In contrast, top Lebanese leaders might have calculated that deployment of the army would either diminish Hizbullah's popularity in southern Lebanon, which had largely overwhelmed that of the government, or would improve Lebanon's investment climate.

Although Lebanese political leaders were, more or less, interested in the 'Lebanon first' option, the Asad regime's consistent opposition prevented the option's realization. Nonetheless, after the two failed attempts to withdraw unilaterally from the security zone in southern Lebanon in July 1996 and January 1998, Israel finally withdrew its army from the zone in May 2000.

The Israeli withdrawal, however, did not precipitate peace in the region. After the eruption of the second Palestinian *intifada* in September 2000, relations between Israel on one side and the Arab states and the Palestinians on the other side became more strained, halting peace negotiations. Under these circumstances,

Saudi Crown Prince 'Abdullah presented his own peace proposal in mid-February 2002. The 'Abdullah Proposal was soon criticized by Syrian President Asad and Lebanese President Lahoud in a joint declaration on 3 March during Asad's visit to Beirut.[251] His objection was primarily on account of the proposal placing greater priority on Palestinian than Syrian and Lebanese peace tracks.[252] In addition, the Syrian leadership objected that the proposal did not explicitly mention the Golan Heights, although it did stipulate that only Israel's full withdrawal from all the Arab lands it had occupied since 1967 would lead to Arab states' recognition of Israel.[253] Moreover, Lebanon's core demand that Palestinian refugees be granted the right to return to their homeland, an especially important concern for the delicately balanced sectarian Lebanese state hosting around 400,000 refugees, was not mentioned in the proposal.[254] Thus, although Lebanon maintained a common stance with Syria, it did so to further its own interests.

However, Lahoud's stance ran the risk of worsening Lebanon's relations with Saudi Arabia and, by extension, the Western countries supporting the 'Abdullah Proposal, particularly as Hariri was struggling to revive the ailing Lebanese economy. Hariri thus appeared highly willing to hold the Arab League summit in Beirut, despite Asad's concern that the conference would be preoccupied with the proposal and could weaken Syria's role in the Arab–Israeli peace process. Under these circumstances, Hariri might have calculated that Syria would neither openly nor vehemently boycott the summit, since Asad was intent on improving its relations with Saudi Arabia and the West.

As a result, the Arab summit held on 27 and 28 March 2002 endorsed a revised form of the 'Abdullah Proposal in which permanent settlement of Palestinian refugees in Lebanon was rejected.[255] This rejection had merits for not only Hariri, since the presence of Palestinians remained a destabilizing factor in Lebanon, but also Christian leaders including Lahoud, as a permanent Palestinian settlement had the potential to change Lebanon's sectarian balance in favour of the Muslim community.

In sum, since Hizbullah's military activities initially in the security zone and later in the Shabaa Farms, as well as the evolution of the Middle East peace process, were firmly associated with Syria's national security, Hariri was forced to cooperate with Damascus on these issues. In other words, Hariri's 'independence' from the Syrian regime concerning Lebanon's diplomatic and security matters was generally restricted, despite its efforts to send the army to southern Lebanon as a means to demonstrate its recovery of full sovereignty and thereby receive financial aid. However, Hariri's cooperation with Damascus was not solely due to Syrian pressure, especially when massive Israeli attacks brought about widespread Lebanese support for Hizbullah. While Hariri was prevented by the Syrian regime from directly negotiating Lebanon's border issues with Israel, he might have expected that while Asad knew that the 'Abdullah Proposal would become a dominant issue, he would not oppose the 2002 Arab summit in Beirut.

Summary

Due to strong domestic and international support, Prime Minister Hariri was in a relatively stronger position in relation to Damascus, particularly between 1992 and 1996, when Lebanese and Western expectations regarding his ability to improve Lebanon's economic condition dramatically were especially high. This was also the case after 2003, when the hold of the United States became extremely strong in the Middle East after invading Iraq and when the US administration turned hostile towards the Asad regime. Indeed, considering himself indispensable to the Syrian regime, which calculated that perceptions of the legitimacy of its presence on Lebanese soil would be strengthened by economic improvement in Lebanon, Hariri used the tactic of either threatening to resign or actually resigning four times during the first and second cabinets from 1992 to 1996; specifically in August 1993, May and December 1994, and May 1995. After the formation of the fifth Hariri cabinet in 2003, he aligned with the US and French authorities, to pressure the Asad regime to grant him more authority to pursue his economic policy. By signalling the possibility that he could bring about a closer relationship for Lebanon with the United States and European countries or by actually strengthen its ties with the West, Hariri attempted to force Damascus to pressure its allies, particularly pro-Syrian ministers in his cabinet, pro-Syrian Presidents Hirawi and Lahoud, and Parliament Speaker Berri, to cooperate with him so that he could push through his Horizon 2000 plan.

On the other hand, with the aim of gaining the cooperation from these pro-Syrian figures, until 2003 Hariri had generally defended Syrian military presence in Lebanon against the demand for its withdrawal, which became rather powerful in the early 2000s. Later, in 2004, Hariri eventually complied with the Asad regime over the extension of Lahoud's presidential term (although he had initially opposed it). Hariri's consideration towards the interests of Syrian companies and Lebanese companies of Syrian origin also had the same aim, although he simultaneously pursed his own interests. A particular manifestation of his pursuit of these multiple interests was the creation of a contract to build a coastal road from Beirut to southern Lebanon.

In addition to taking into account Syria's political and economic interests, Hariri took a great care of its security and diplomatic interests in order to gain its control over the strong pro-Syrian non-governmental actor in Lebanon, i.e. Hizbullah. In other words, Hariri's power during his premiership was consistently and considerably restricted by not only the above-mentioned figures in Lebanon's governing body, but also by Hizbullah, since it launched military operations against the Israeli army in the security zone of southern Lebanon. Shortly after Israel launched massive operations against Lebanon as part of Operation Accountability in 1993 and Operation Grapes of Wrath in 1996,

Hariri engaged in diplomatic efforts, mainly in Europe, so as to minimize the damage to his economic reconstruction efforts while showing solidarity with Hizbullah and organizing compensation programmes for the displaced in southern Lebanon. While arguably demonstrating his interest in the possibility of unilateral Israeli withdrawal from the security zone, Hariri later opposed, albeit implicitly, the division of peace negotiations with Israel into the Lebanon–Israel and Syria–Israel tracks, which had been proposed by the Likud government under Israeli Prime Minister Netanyahu as the 'Lebanon first' option and inevitably opposed by Damascus.

While Hariri's alignment with the Syrian regime can largely be attributed to his aim of coping with the threats posed by pro-Syrian groups and figures in Lebanon, Lebanese and Syrian leaders' shared economic and political interests and their interdependency appeared to affect his actions and attitudes towards the Syrian leadership. Considering shared Lebanese and Syrian economic interests, Hariri accepted the presence of Syrian workers in Lebanon, which, on the one hand, decreased the unemployment rate in Syria and led to a considerable amount of remittances back into the country, and, on the other hand, provided Lebanon's business community, with which he had close connections, with the cheap labour force necessary for reconstruction projects. Hariri also matched a 2000 Syrian decree allowing foreign banks to operate in Syria's free zones, which had attracted several Lebanese banks, with efforts to recover Beirut's former status as the financial hub of the Middle East.

Considering shared Lebanese and Syrian political interests, both Hariri and the Syrian regime had prioritized Lebanon's political stability. While Hariri's primary motivation in achieving the stability was to create a favourable condition for foreign investment in Lebanon, Damascus's primary motivation was preventing the 'radicalization' of the Lebanese public, which could have led to the development of an opposition movement against Syrian presence. Thus, with tacit support from the Asad regime, Hariri restricted Lebanon's labour movement and the mass media. These restrictions led to various consequences over the years: in 1995, Hariri banned all demonstrations after the GLC called for a general strike; in 1996, he reduced the number of Lebanon's licensed television and radio stations allowed to operate (naturally, his own station, Future TV, was permitted to operate); and in 1997, he ousted the GLC's leader Rizq, who had consistently confronted the Lebanese government. The Syrian leadership, overtly or tacitly, supported Hariri's treatment against the GLC, because they had a common interest in preserving stability in Lebanon.

In conclusion, Hariri's alignment with the Syrian regime can be primarily attributed to his simultaneous pursuit of Lebanon's economic reconstruction and his own interests.

CHAPTER 4

LEBANON AFTER THE END OF SYRIAN HEGEMONY (SINCE 2005)

While Syrian hegemony in Lebanon ended with the withdrawal of the Syrian army and intelligence from Lebanon in 2005, Syria has maintained a pervasive influence on Lebanese soil to this day. Thus, whether Lebanon's top leaders formulate foreign or domestic policies, they must take Syrian power into consideration.

Syrian policy towards Lebanon has largely been a reflection of regional dynamics in the Middle East (as the theory of 'simple realism' predicts) and its trans-state ties with Lebanon's sectarian-based non-governmental actors have dominated over its official ties with the Lebanese government. Therefore, top leaders in the government have kept a close watch on both the regional and trans-state factors. This chapter first describes these factors and then examines in detail Lebanese–Syrian relations since 2005. Among top Lebanese leaders, Prime Minister Fouad al-Siniora, Prime Minister Sa'd al-Hariri and Prime Minister Najib Miqati are figures in focus, because the 1990 amendment of the Lebanese constitution increased the power of the country's premiership. Additionally, Siniora and Hariri in particular have attempted to maximize Lebanon's autonomy from Syria.

Middle East International Relations and the Impact on Syria and Lebanon

Introduction

The end of Syrian hegemony in Lebanon in April 2005 provided Saudi Arabia and Iran with opportunities to be more deeply involved in Lebanon. In August, the inauguration of Iranian President Mahmud Ahmadinejad greatly influenced the relationships between the three regional powers: Saudi Arabia, Syria and Iran. Since then, internationally isolated Syria and Iran have strengthened their alliance and pursued and implemented foreign policies which are often read by their antagonists (such as Saudi Arabia and the United States) as being provocative or even overtly confrontational. Consequently, Saudi Arabia's relations with both Syria and Iran have not been on good terms, and the country has, along with the United States, attempted to contain Iranian and Syrian power in the Middle East. Reflecting this regional rivalry, despite its recovery of sovereignty, Lebanon has predominantly become a focal point for regional power politics as its non-unitary state formation and the end of Syrian hegemony have allowed Saudi Arabia, Syria and Iran to play off against one another on Lebanese soil. These regional factors have influenced the actions and attitudes of Lebanon's premiers towards the Asad regime.

Impact of Hariri's Assassination on Regional Dynamics

Initially, the Asad regime was widely blamed for the assassination of former Prime Minister Rafiq al-Hariri (although Damascus has categorically denied the allegation up to the present) because he contributed to the formation of UN Security Council Resolution 1559, which primarily targeted the Syrian regime. The United States and Saudi Arabia, with whose top leaders Hariri had maintained close relationships, immediately recalled their ambassadors from Syria. Increased Lebanese, regional and international pressure on Syria, especially from the United States and France, forced President Bashar al-Asad to withdraw the Syrian army and intelligence from Lebanon, whose full withdrawal was announced on 27 April 2005.

However, the termination of Syrian hegemony in Lebanon did not improve the Asad regime's relations with the US administration under President George W. Bush, which was hesitant to have high-level contacts with the regime. Syria cooperated with Iraq over the latter state's efforts for internal stabilization by fortifying their common border to prevent terrorist movements. Syria also entered into indirect peace talks with Israel by Turkish mediation in May 2008 (although they were halted two months later) and established its diplomatic relations with Lebanon in October. Nevertheless, Syria's close relationships with 'terrorist organizations', specifically Hizbullah and Hamas, and its nuclear development programme prevented US–Syrian relations from improving.

On the other hand, after assuming the Iranian presidency, Ahmadinejad has pursued aggressive and provocative foreign policies while making progress in Iran's nuclear development programme. This has heightened international and regional concerns about Iran's 'true' intention regarding the programme. Saudi Arabia in particular, as the dominant player in the Gulf Cooperation Council (GCC), has contested Iran over regional influence. As a result, in 2005, relationships between the three regional powers were firmly established such that Saudi Arabia occupied a conflicting position with the joint powers of Iran and Syria, and this regional rivalry has been preserved up to the present.

Impact of the Regional Rivalry on Lebanon

Given the rivalry noted above, what are the intentions and interests of these regional powers towards Lebanon? Saudi Arabia has seen the power of Lebanon's Sunnis as a reflection of its influence in the Arab/Muslim world. On the other hand, Iran and Syria have seen the power of Lebanon's Shi'as as a reflection of their influence in the Middle East. All these powers have maintained trans-state ties with Lebanon's sectarian-based political organizations (as discussed in the next section of this chapter). As a result, while Saudi Arabia has supported the Sunni-based Future Movement with the aim of containing Iranian and Syrian power in the Middle East, Iran and Syria have strongly backed the Shi'a-based Amal Movement and Hizbullah (although the former party has been exclusively backed by Syria) with the aim of countering Saudi power in the region.

From 2005 to 2011, Lebanese Prime Minister Siniora and his successor Sa'd al-Hariri, both supported by the Future Movement, had aligned Lebanon with Saudi Arabia and, by extension, the United States following the increased international isolation of Iran and Syria. However, as their policy had especially alienated the Shi'as – Hizbullah and the Amal Movement – Lebanon's internal polarization reflecting the regional dynamics was further strengthened.

Although the US administration under President Barack Obama revealed its intention to improve its relationship with the Asad regime immediately after its inauguration in January 2009, it was soon clear that the realization would depend on the foreign policies of the Syrian regime. On this point, Syria's continued close relationships with Iran and the 'terrorist organizations', particularly Hizbullah, and its limited cooperation with the International Atomic Energy Agency (IAEA) over its nuclear development programme have not been endorsed by the United States. As Syrian behaviour has threatened the security of not only Saudi Arabia and other GCC countries, but also Israel, and as the Asad regime has continued its crackdown on anti-government forces calling for democratization since March 2011, the US perception of Syria has not dramatically changed and may have even worsened.

Under these circumstances, Prime Minister Miqati was elected in January 2011 with the support of Hizbullah, the

Amal Movement and other allies in the Lebanese parliament. Nevertheless, he has attempted to initiate 'balanced' or 'neutral' policies by accommodating opposite interests retained by Lebanese actors and their regional or international allies.

Brief Summary

With the end of Syrian hegemony in Lebanon, Saudi Arabia and Iran began to play more active roles in Lebanon. The establishment of the Ahmadinejad regime in Iran has dramatically worsened Saudi–Iranian relations and further consolidated the Iranian–Syrian alliance. The configuration of the relationship of the three regional powers – Saudi Arabia versus Iran and Syria – has influenced contemporary politics in Lebanon and contributed to its domestic polarization in particular.

Lebanese Non-Governmental Actors and Syria: Their Basic Interests and Relations

Introduction

Lebanon's sectarian-based non-governmental actors – the Maronites, Sunnis, Shi'as and Druzes[1] – have not only played an important role in domestic politics, but also maintained a variety of trans-state relations with Syria. These trans-state factors have influenced the actions and attitudes of Lebanon's premiers towards the Asad regime. As shown below, their differing extent of cooperation or antagonism has been mainly shaped by regional dynamics in the Middle East, Syria's stakes in Lebanon and the interests and identity of each sectarian group.

The Maronites and Syria

After the assassination of former Lebanese Prime Minister Rafiq al-Hariri in February 2005, Lebanese politics has been largely divided between the pro-Syrian March 8 Coalition, led by

Hizbullah's Secretary General Hasan Nasrallah, and the anti-Syrian March 14 Coalition, led by the Future Movement's leader Sa'd al-Hariri. The Maronites' traditional 'Lebanon-oriented' identity and bitter relationship with the Syrian regime as a whole during the period when Lebanon was under Syrian hegemony (1975–2005) have led most Maronite-based political parties/organizations to join the March 14 Coalition. These include the Kata'ib Party, led by former President Amin al-Jumayyil; the LF, led by Samir Ja'ja'; and the Qurnat Shahwan Gathering, led by Butrus Harb. Because of their anti-Syrian stance and traditional ties with the West, they have maintained close relationships with the United States and France in particular. In addition, as Hariri has strongly aligned himself with the Saudi monarchy, these Maronite parties/organizations have also constructed a relationship with Saudi Arabia.

On the other hand, the Marada Movement, led by a northern *za'im*, Sulayman Tony Franjiya, maintains its long-lasting ties with the Asad family. Michel 'Awn, leader of the Free National Current (FNC), initially maintained his hard-line stance on Syria. However, immediately after 'Awn returned to Lebanon from France in early May 2005, he disputed Hariri over strategies for Lebanon's parliamentary elections scheduled to start in late May. Thus, 'Awn started to distance himself from the March 14 Coalition and even issued a joint statement of understanding with Nasrallah in February 2006, proclaiming FNC support to Syrian-backed Hizbullah's arms resistance in southern Lebanon. Since then, 'Awn has become a key figure in the March 8 Coalition and even met Syrian President Asad in December 2008 to declare a 'new page' in relation to the regime.[2] 'Awn, along with Franjiya, has strongly backed the Asad regime in the face of the uprising since March 2011.

In addition to these leaders, President Emile Lahoud maintained his pro-Syrian stance until the end of his term in November 2007. On the other hand, current President Michel Sulayman, elected in May 2008 as the 'consensus figure' after the long dispute between the March 8 and March 14 Coalitions over Lahoud's successor,[3] has pursued 'neutral' policies towards Syria.

As for the Maronite religious establishment in Lebanon, Patriarch Nasr Allah Butrus Sufayr had maintained an anti-Syrian stance by the end of his term in March 2011 and is still an influential 'spiritual leader' for the March 14 Coalition. On the other hand, the succeeding Patriarch Bishara al-Ra'i has mended fences with Damascus after assuming the post. In September, Ra'i stated that the international community should give the 'open-minded' Asad more time to implement reform and resume dialogue with opposition forces. At the same time, Ra'i mentioned the necessity of keeping Hizbullah's arsenal until the full withdrawal of the Israeli army from all Lebanese territories,[4] a statement that soon triggered criticism from the March 14 Coalition.

The Sunnis and Syria

Among Sunni-based political organizations in Lebanon, the powerful Future Movement has led the March 14 Coalition and maintained close relations with 'moderate' Arab Gulf countries, particularly Saudi Arabia. This is largely because Rafiq al-Hariri, father of the movement's current leader Sa'd al-Hariri, had established deep connections with the Saudi royal family. In addition, the Future Movement has aligned itself with Western countries, especially the United States and France, which is also a 'legacy' of Rafiq al-Hariri. Under the international isolation of the Asad regime, Prime Minister Siniora (2005–2009) and his successor Sa'd al-Hariri (2009–2011), both strongly backed by the Future Movement, generally pursued anti-Syrian, pro-Western policies. These included their strong support for the Special Tribunal for Lebanon (STL), which the Asad regime has regarded as a means to weaken it. In addition, they persisted in demanding that Hizbullah disarm, which could surely reduce Syria's strategic bargaining power vis-à-vis Israel. Recently, Siniora and Hariri have not only focused on the issues of the STL and Hizbullah, but also criticized the Asad regime's harsh crackdown on the opposition forces in Syria since March 2011. Moreover, there is a rumour that the Future Movement has provided money and weapons with Sunni-dominated Syrian opposition forces, and in April an MP from the movement, Jamal Jarrah, was accused of involvement in the anti-regime activities, although he dismissed the allegation.[5]

On the other hand, Sunni leaders such as Salim al-Huss and Miqati have followed 'neutral' policies towards Damascus. Huss has stressed the importance of maintaining coordination between Lebanon and Syria as neighbouring countries, while recognizing the necessity of weapons held by Syrian-backed Hizbullah on the condition that Israel still occupies the 'Shabaa Farms'. Current Prime Minister Miqati, who also led the 'election management cabinet' from April to July 2005, has also not pursued provocative policies and prioritized dialogues between the March 8 and March 14 Coalitions, especially regarding the contentious issues such as the STL, the arsenal of Hizbullah and the Syrian uprising. While Miqati was elected in January 2011 with the support of the March 8 Coalition, he sometimes disregarded the coalition's preference, as manifested in his decision in late November to pay Lebanon's share of the annual funding for the STL.[6]

In the long run, most Lebanese Sunnis have shown not much sympathy with the Asad regime and Hizbullah. This attitude is based on their suspicion of the regime's and/or Hizbullah's involvement in the assassination of Rafiq al-Hariri. Their distrust also arises from the fact that Hizbullah's weapons, which have officially targeted Israeli forces, were actually used to attack its domestic foes in May 2008 (when Hizbullah militias assaulted Future Movement members in Beirut and other areas). However, 'Umar Karami, who was Lebanon's premier from December 1990 to May 1992 and later from October 2004 to April 2005, is one of the few Sunni politicians to have explicitly aligned themselves with the March 8 Coalition. Indeed, Karami has maintained his pro-Asad and pro-Hizbullah stance, which is based on his family's long-standing ties with the Asad family. Although the 'Alawi-dominated and secular-oriented Asad regime needed to establish good relations with the Sunnis in Lebanon because of Syrian Sunnis' suspicion of the regime, this has not taken place. Recently, the perception of the Asad regime by Lebanese Sunnis is worsening because of its crackdown on the Sunni-dominated anti-regime forces.

The Shi'as and Syria

The Shi'a community in Lebanon has two main political organizations: the Amal Movement, led by Parliament Speaker Nabih Berri, and Hizbullah, led by Nasrallah. Since Syria's Asad regime is 'Alawi-dominated, both organizations have maintained strong ties with it and are main pillars of the March 8 Coalition. On the other hand, the Amal Movement and Hizbullah have become more important tools than ever before for Syria to conduct its foreign policy towards Lebanon. This is because Syria withdrew its army and intelligence from Lebanon in 2005, and following its international isolation, the power of the anti-Syrian March 14 Coalition has been non-negligible at not just Lebanese, but also regional and international levels.

The Amal Movement has closer ties with Syria than has Hizbullah because Syria has been the only external patron for the movement. In addition, Hizbullah's popularity in Lebanon, owing to its provision of social services and its vanguard role in the resistance to Israel in southern Lebanon, has made the Amal Movement vulnerable within the Shi'a community. This is likely to have contributed to the Amal Movement's consistent alignment with Syria. Indeed, Berri has championed the Asad regime since the uprising in the country began in March 2011.

In contrast, Hizbullah has maintained strong ties not only with Syria, but also with Iran and although the organization has stressed its unitary structure, it was reported that its Secretary

General Nasrallah was pro-Syrian and Deputy Secretary General Na'im al-Qasim was pro-Iranian.[7] However, since the two internationally isolated countries have further strengthened their relations, the Iranian–Syrian power struggle within Hizbullah appears to have been, if anything, put aside for now.

Syria has been an important transit route for Iran's supply of money and arsenal to Hizbullah, and the Asad regime has allegedly provided the organization with military training. Nasrallah, thus, has vowed to support the Syrian regime in the face of the recent domestic uprising. Meanwhile, Syria has also needed Hizbullah's support for its Lebanese policy because the organization has incorporated the radicalized Shi'a lower class, unlike the Amal Movement. More importantly, Syria's need for a surrogate force to pressure Israel into withdrawing from the Golan Heights has not changed. In this context, the Syrian and Lebanese pretext, against international and Israeli claims, that the Shabaa Farms remains an Israeli-occupied Lebanese territory has enabled Hizbullah to retain its arms and start fighting against Israel. In spite of some Lebanese and international calls for Hizbullah to disarm, Syria has never pressured it to do so. This stance has reasonably contributed to the continued negative Western view of the Asad regime, especially by the United States and France.

The Druzes and Syria

Walid Junblat, the most prominent leader in Lebanon's Druze community and head of the PSP, was a central figure in the March 14 Coalition. Junblat, along with Hariri and Ja'ja', had maintained a strong anti-Syrian stance from 2005 to 2009.

However, after Lebanon's parliamentary elections in June 2009, Junblat began to distance himself from the March 14 Coalition and declared his 'centrist' position in August.[8] Furthermore, Junblat made public apologies about his previous, repeated insults to the Syrian regime and mended fences with President Asad at the end of March 2010.[9]

The PSP was part of the Siniora and Hariri cabinets, and the current Miqati cabinet also includes PSP ministers. Since the uprising started in Syria, Junblat has gradually increased his criticism against Damascus and demanded Asad to step down. Junblat has clearly become closer to the March 14 Coalition, as shown by not only his stance on the Syrian uprising, but also his April 2012 official visit to Saudi Arabia, which aimed to improve his relationship with the monarchy.[10] In September, Junblat visited Hariri's Paris residence, which was their first meeting after Junblat supported Miqati's assumption of the premiership in January 2011.[11]

Brief Summary

Overall, the Sunnis and Druzes have, in general, affiliated with the March 14 Coalition, while the Shi'as have led the March 8 Coalition. Although most Maronites initially aligned themselves with the March 14 Coalition, 'Awn's close relations with Hizbullah since 2006 and Patriarch Ra'i's recently adopted conciliatory stance towards the Asad regime and Hizbullah have torn the Maronite community between the two coalitions.

Prime Minister Fouad al-Siniora and the Asad Regime

Introduction

Under the reality of Syria's maintenance of power on Lebanese soil, especially by means of its close ties with non-governmental actors in Lebanon – Hizbullah and the Amal Movement – Prime Minister Siniora largely balanced against the Asad regime by exploiting Syria's international isolation. Siniora's relations with the Syrian regime were mainly developed on the issues of his cabinet formation, the international investigation of the assassination of former Prime Minister Rafiq al-Hariri and Hizbullah's military affairs.

Cabinet Formation

The parliamentary elections in Lebanon were held from May to June 2005. After the elections, Prime Minister Miqati, who formed his first cabinet in April with the aim of supervising the elections, tendered his resignation to President Lahoud on 21 June.[12] As the Future Movement, led by Sa'd al-Hariri, won the elections, it was widely believed that he would assume the premiership. However, Hariri's lack of political experience and his young age (35 at the time) led Siniora to run for the premiership. Siniora had assumed the ministerial post of finance under Rafiq al-Hariri and also had close ties with the Future Movement. On 30 June, Siniora was designated by Lahoud to the post with the support of 126 of the 128 deputies in the Lebanese parliament.[13]

The formation of a new cabinet took three weeks, as Lahoud rejected three line-ups presented by Siniora. After Lahoud named his three allies, and after Hizbullah and the Amal Movement accepted their share of the posts,[14] the first Siniora cabinet was finally established on 19 July. The faction led by 'Awn decided not to participate in the new cabinet following disputes over the posts. Thus, the 24-member cabinet had 15 anti-Syrian ministers, eight pro-Syrian ministers and one 'neutral' minister.[15]

The characteristics of Siniora's first cabinet are as follows. First, as an economist, Siniora gave priority to Lebanon's economic recovery, and thus posts of both the minister of finance and minister of economy and trade were occupied by figures experienced in economic affairs, not only those of Lebanon, but of international organizations as well. In fact, Minister of Finance Jihad Az'ur worked in the United Nations Development Programme and was an adviser for Siniora when he assumed the ministerial post of finance under Rafiq al-Hariri. Minister of Economy and Trade

Sami Haddad was a manager for Middle East and North Africa affairs at the International Monetary Fund and also a deputy governor at the Central Bank of Lebanon. Second, the following four ministers were pro-Syrian figures: Minister of Power and Water Resources Muhammad Funaysh, a member of Hizbullah; Justice Minister Sharl Rizk, a close ally of Lahoud and former Information Minister (although Siniora and Sa'd al-Hariri had attempted to install someone close to the Future Movement in the post); Defence Minister Iliyas al-Murr, Lahoud's son-in-law (although Murr narrowly escaped an attempt on his life in the middle of July);[16] and Foreign Minister Fawzi Sallukh, a Shi'a veteran diplomat supported by both the Amal Movement and Hizbullah.

To understand Siniora's relations with the Asad regime, it is necessary to examine the second characteristic. Given the unfavourable trend in Syria's international relations, Sinyura could have formed an explicitly anti-Syrian cabinet. However, he not only included a pro-Syrian Hizbullah member in his cabinet, but also installed the pro-Syrians in the ministerial posts for justice, defence and foreign affairs. Regarding this point, Siniora's election with overwhelming parliamentary support required him to form a national cabinet consisting of ministers from not only the March 14 Coalition, but also the March 8 Coalition. Furthermore, it appears that Siniora had his own reasons to show goodwill to the Asad regime by allocating the posts to the pro-Syrian figures that received strong interest from Syria in terms of its national security or the international investigation of Rafiq al-Hariri's assassination.

First, Siniora might have calculated that taking into consideration Syrian interests in Lebanon could win him support for his policies among pro-Syrian actors in Lebanon. Second, economic interdependency between Lebanon and Syria affected his way of cabinet formation. Strong US pressure had forced Damascus to tighten its border control with Lebanon under the pretext of preventing anti-US militias that were active in Iraq from moving freely in the neighbouring countries. Consequently, hundreds of Lebanese trucks carrying tonnes of perishable goods were delayed at the Lebanese–Syrian border, which badly affected the incomes of thousands of Lebanese families.[17] After Siniora met President Asad on 31 July 2005,[18] Lebanese trucks managed to cross the border.[19]

On 21 May 2008, the Doha Agreement was formed, which ended military clashes between the March 8 and March 14 Coalitions that had occurred earlier in the month.[20] Following the agreement, the newly-elected President Sulayman re-designated Siniora to the premiership on 28 May.[21] Although the agreement stipulated that the March 14 Coalition would have 16 cabinet seats, the March 8 Coalition would have 11 ministerial posts and another three would be nominated by Sulayman, the allocation of each post was not agreed upon. Thus, as the two coalitions competed over cabinet seats, it took more than one month for Siniora to form a 'national unity government', which was finally born on 11 July.[22]

With Defence Minister Murr and Foreign Minister Sallukh retaining their posts in the national unitary cabinet, its pro-Syrian tendency was maintained. It appears that Syria's preparation for the establishment of its diplomatic ties with Lebanon, which the March 14 Coalition had vigorously demanded, clearly affected Siniora's cabinet formation.[23] However, by showing Lebanon's will to ally with Syria over its military and diplomatic matters, Siniora once again might have anticipated cooperation from Lebanon's pro-Syrian actors (although when six pro-Syrian ministers, five of them Shi'as, resigned in November 2006 over the investigation of the Hariri assassination, the Asad regime did nothing).

International Investigation of the Hariri Assassination

Prime Minister Siniora consistently supported the international investigation of the assassination of former Prime Minister Rafiq al-Hariri, with whom he had enjoyed a close relationship. On the other hand, the Asad regime questioned the legitimacy of the International Independent Investigation Commission (IIIC), which was established in April 2005 by UN Security Council Resolution 1595 and began its work in June, as the IIIC initially blamed the regime for the murder. Thus, Syrian cooperation with the IIIC was the minimum, aimed only to avoid being sanctioned by the Security Council.

In late August 2005, the Lebanese authorities, at the recommendation of the IIIC, detained four top figures of the Lebanese security apparatus, all of them close to pro-Syrian President Lahoud, for involvement in the murder of Hariri. These were Major General Jamil al-Sayyid, former head of Sureté Générale; Major General 'Ali al-Hajj, former director general of the Internal Security Forces; Brigadier General Raymond Az'ar, former director general of military intelligence; and Brigadier General Mustafa Hamdan, commander of Lebanon's Presidential Guard.[24]

On 20 October 2005, Detlev Mehlis, head of the IIIC, submitted his first interim report to UN Secretary-General Kofi Annan. In the report, Mehlis accused the Syrian regime and Lebanese security apparatus of involvement in the Hariri murder. An unedited version of the report named the following figures in particular for planning the murder: Asif Shawkat, head of Syria's Military Intelligence Department and the brother-in-law of President Asad; Mahir al-Asad, an influential officer of Syria's Republican Guard and a younger brother of Asad; and Sayyid.[25] As Harris (2009) pointed out, UN Security Council Resolution 1636, which was adopted on 31 October, 'rebuked Damascus for stalling the holding of interviews with prominent Syrians and invoked Chapter VII of the UN charter, meaning that non-compliance could lead to military action'.[26]

In spite of the hostile international criticism against the Asad regime based on the IIIC report and Resolution 1636, Siniora coherently backed the commission's activities. Although Damascus immediately slammed the resolution as 'biased' and 'unfair',[27] Siniora asked the Syrian regime to cooperate with the IIIC, whose stance was shared by prominent figures in the March 14 Coalition such as Nasib Lahoud.[28] Opposing this, on 10 November 2005, President Asad lashed out at Siniora 'as a "slave" of his masters, in a thinly veiled reference to Western countries'.[29]

According to Harris (2009), since Asad's statement accused the March 14 Coalition of moving closer to Israel and conspiring against Syria, it was 'viewed in Beirut as death threats'.[30] Nevertheless, on 12 December 2005, the Siniora cabinet decided to ask the UN to form an 'international court' to try those accused for the assassination of Hariri.[31] Three days later, UN Security Council Resolution 1644 adopted the concept of 'a tribunal of an international character'.

From 2005 to 2006, Siniora continued to ask the Security Council to extend the IIIC mandate and relied on the US administration to force the Asad regime to comply with the council's resolutions regarding the investigation of Hariri. This stance definitely antagonized not only the Syrian regime, but also the March 8 Coalition, specifically the Amal Movement and Hizbullah. On 10 November 2006, Lebanon received the UN draft for a tribunal of an international character.[32] The next day, the Hariri-led March 14 Coalition's strong will to proceed to a swift cabinet vote for the draft approval triggered the resignation of five pro-Syrian Shi'a ministers, all of whom belonged to the March 8 Coalition.[33] However, Siniora did not accept their resignation. Despite the absence of the Shi'a ministers, who were members or sympathizers of the Amal Movement or Hizbullah, Siniora held the cabinet vote on 13 November.[34] On the other hand, President Lahoud and Hizbullah's chief, Nasrallah, insisted that the decision to hold the vote was illegal, arguing that a major sect, specifically the Shi'as, was not represented in the cabinet.[35] Later, on 12 December, the Siniora cabinet formally sent the UN draft to the Lebanese parliament,[36] where pro-Syrian Speaker Berri continued to block the session to vote the draft.

The United States, France and Saudi Arabia – the main international allies of the March 14 Coalition – supported the Siniora cabinet's approval of the Hariri tribunal. Although the Asad regime had consistently rejected the legitimacy of the UN-backed tribunal,[37] the Security Council accepted the cabinet decision and gave international endorsement to the establishment of the tribunal. The Hariri tribunal was finally approved by UN Security Council Resolution 1757 on 30 May 2007.

From 2007 to 2008, although the IIIC published several reports, they were obscure and did not mention Syrian regime figures as prime suspects. However, as Damascus still questioned the legitimacy of the IIIC, Siniora's periodic demand for the Security Council to extend the commission's mandate was still seen as a hostile diplomatic activity by the Asad regime. In addition, Siniora frequently met US and French senior officials to maintain their support for the IIIC.

On 26 November 2008, Secretary-General Ban Ki-moon announced that the STL could start its work on 1 March 2009.[38] Siniora soon showed his appreciation to Ban for the progress on the STL[39] and later made a statement to hail the commencement.[40] On the other hand, it was then reported that 'the majority of Syrian media, both public and private, electronic and print, did not cover or report the [STL]'.[41] Although the Syrian regime saw both the IIIC and STL as Western political tools to pressure it, Siniora consistently supported them and struggled to gain international support for his stance, particularly from Washington and Paris.

Hizbullah's Military Affairs

While Syria withdrew its army and intelligence from Lebanon in April 2005, its strategic interest in Hizbullah has not changed.[42] As Syria still needs Hizbullah's arms to pressure Israel into ending the occupation of the Golan Heights, the actions and attitudes taken by the Lebanese government towards Hizbullah could be a useful means to examine Lebanon's relations with Syria.

Prime Minister Siniora, who was strongly backed by the March 14 Coalition, followed mixed policies towards Hizbullah, especially in military matters. On the one hand, the policy statement of the first Sinyura cabinet, which was approved by the Lebanese parliament on 30 July 2005, voiced its support for Hizbullah's armed resistance against Israel under Hizbullah's first participation in the Lebanese government.[43] Later, the policy statement of the second Siniora cabinet, which was finally approved by the Lebanese parliament on 12 August 2008 after heated debates between the March 8 and March 14 Coalitions over Hizbullah's weapons, recognized the right of its armed resistance against Israel.[44] In this regard, it is non-negligible that the brief takeover of West Beirut by Hizbullah and its allies during the May confrontation forced Siniora and his cabinet members belonging to the March 14 Coalition to accept the March 8 Coalition's demand to give legitimacy to Hizbullah's weapons. At the same time, however, Siniora might have calculated that the consideration of Syria's important strategic asset would gain cooperation from the March 8 Coalition, particularly Hizbullah.

Additionally, since the Syrian withdrawal in 2005, a series of international resolutions have been issued to demarcate the Lebanese–Syrian border, and it is reported that there are 36 points of dispute along Lebanon's eastern border with Syria.[45] While Siniora received strong international, especially US and French, support for Lebanon's sovereignty, and while UN Security Council Resolution 1680 (adopted on 17 May 2006) urged Lebanon and Syria to demarcate their common border, he did not make vigorous efforts to do so following the Asad regime's strong objection to the resolution.[46] As a result, the permeability of the border has made it possible for Hizbullah to maintain an important supply route for its weaponry.[47] More specifically, the disputed area of the Shabaa Farms has given Hizbullah legitimacy to maintain its arms.

Although it is true that Siniora showed some understanding of Hizbullah's weapons and their strategic importance for

Syria with the aim of gaining cooperation from the March 8 Coalition, he generally attempted to strip Hizbullah of power on the basis of its arms possession. As this aim of Siniora was matched with the most important US interest in the Middle East – the protection of Israel – the Bush administration not only pressed the adoption of UN Security Council resolutions, but also issued dozens of statements about Lebanon, almost all of which condemned Hizbullah arms.

With strong US support, Siniora targeted Hizbullah on two occasions in particular: July 2006 and May 2008. Immediately after the outbreak of the 2006 Hizbullah–Israel Conflict, the Siniora cabinet reaffirmed on 13 July 2006 its commitment to implement all international resolutions regarding Lebanon. It also reaffirmed its commitment to expand the central government's authority to all Lebanese territory, including Hizbullah-dominated southern Lebanon, while respecting the 'Blue Line' along the Lebanon–Israel border.[48] In other words, on the basis of UN Security Council Resolutions 1559 and 1680, the Lebanese government showed a clear intention to disarm Hizbullah and establish sovereignty in the south. This policy intention was largely praised by not only the United States, but also the moderate Arab states, particularly, Saudi Arabia, Egypt and Jordan. The regional and international powers accused Hizbullah of harming Arab interests and taking 'adventurism'.

UN Security Council Resolution 1701, which was adopted on 11 August 2006 and was soon approved by both the Lebanese and Israeli governments, called for immediate cessation of hostilities; withdrawal of the Israeli army from Lebanon; expansion of the UNIFIL; deployment of the Lebanese army to the border area in southern Lebanon; and, most importantly, disarmament of Hizbullah. However, its widespread popularity among the Lebanese population prevented the Siniora cabinet from initiating definite moves against the resistance organization.

The international community, especially the United States and France, might have been irritated by the inaction of the

Lebanese government, and this may have led the UN Security Council's reiteration of its commitment to the disarmament of Hizbullah in mid-April 2008. Backed by international support, Siniora further antagonized Hizbullah in May, while their relations had been worsened by the resignation of the five Shi'a ministers in November 2006. In early May 2008, the Siniora cabinet decided to dismiss the head of security at the Rafiq al-Hariri International Airport in Beirut following the discovery that Hizbullah had installed surveillance cameras to monitor the movements of senior Lebanese and foreign officials. More importantly, the cabinet called for steps aiming to close down Hizbullah's secret, independent telecommunications network, which had been important for the organization to conduct intelligence and military operations beyond the control of the Lebanese government.

In response, Hizbullah issued a statement on 8 May 2008 declaring that the cabinet decisions were illegal and 'tantamount to a "declaration of war"' against it.[49] Hizbullah activists, along with those affiliated with other political organizations in the March 8 Coalition, attacked properties belonging to the March 14 Coalition, specifically the Future Movement, and took over West Beirut and the airport. About 100 Lebanese were killed during the clashes between the rival coalitions, and Siniora subsequently declared on 10 May his decision to hand over the two controversial issues taken by his cabinet to the Lebanese army, which then reversed the cabinet decisions.[50]

Because the Lebanese army's military weakness has given Hizbullah legitimacy to maintain its arms, the Siniora cabinet took measures to strengthen the army, mainly relying on US support. On 6 October 2008, Lebanon and the United States signed three military contracts worth $63 million in US grants to the Lebanese army, which aimed to provide the army with secure communications, ammunition and infantry weapons. On the same day, Lebanese Defence Minister Murr and US Assistant Secretary of Defence for International Security Affairs Mary Beth

Long agreed to establish a joint military commission in charge of their bilateral military relationship.[51]

On the other hand, Washington has provided its military assistance to the Lebanese army since 2006, and the amounts reached $410 million in 2008.[52] In addition, servicemen of the Lebanese army received training in the United States, which increased the necessary budget from 2006 to 2008.[53] The increased US involvement with the Lebanese army, as well as frequent visits by senior US defence officials to Lebanon, made the Syrian regime and the March 8 Coalition more suspicious of the Siniora cabinet, as the US support aimed at strengthening the Lebanese government led by the March 14 Coalition vis-à-vis Hizbullah.

In spite of Lebanon's main military partner, the United States was generally moving slowly to help increase the capabilities of the Lebanese army. More importantly, Washington had to take into account the Israeli concern that the heavy weapons provided to the Lebanese army by the USA might finally fall into Hizbullah's hands, and hence US assistance to the army was limited to the provision of light weapons. These situations definitely disappointed the Siniora cabinet, which sought other states to provide Lebanon with sufficient military equipment. Consequently, to strengthen its army, Lebanon contacted not only Germany,[54] but also Syria's main international ally – Russia, which agreed to give 10 MIG-29 fighter jets to Lebanon in December 2008.[55] Later, in January 2009, It was reported that Lebanon was receiving these warplanes.[56]

Summary

Although Prime Minister Siniora was strongly supported by the anti-Syrian March 14 Coalition, he had to take into account the strong identification of the March 8 Coalition, specifically Hizbullah, with the Asad regime. Siniora, therefore, sometimes followed conciliatory policies towards Damascus, especially through the formation of his two cabinets. Indeed, the first Siniora cabinet included not only Minister of Power and Water Resources Funaysh, but also Minister of Justice Rizk, Minister of Defence Murr and Minister of Foreign Affairs Sallukh (all pro-Syrian). This means that Siniora showed goodwill to the Asad regime, as it was especially concerned about who took Lebanon's ministerial posts regarding justice, defence and foreign affairs in terms of Syria's national security or the international investigation of the assassination of former Prime Minister Rafiq al-Hariri. Siniora's election to Lebanon's premiership with overwhelming parliamentary support demanded that he consider the March 8 Coalition's pro-Syrian stance. At the same time, Siniora's calculation that by counting Syrian interests in Lebanon, pro-Syrian Lebanese actors would support his policies, as well as the substantial degree of economic interdependency between Lebanon and Syria, largely affected his cabinet composition. Later, in the formation of his second cabinet, Siniora retained Murr and Sallukh on the basis of the same calculation.

However, Siniora strongly supported the IIIC's activities from its establishment and indeed asked the UN Security Council to extend the commission's mandate periodically. Siniora even asked the Asad regime to cooperate with the IIIC and further struggled to establish the STL with the help of Western powers, specifically the United States and France, following Syria's international isolation. As the Syrian regime questioned the legitimacy of both the IIIC and STL, recognizing them as Western political tools to put pressure on it, Siniora' cooperation with the IIIC and STL, as well as his close relationship with the West, was interpreted as hostile activities by Damascus.

While Siniora recognized Hizbullah's right to armed resistance and its strategic importance for Syria, with an aim to gain cooperation from the March 8 Coalition, he largely attempted to disarm Hizbullah or strip the organization of legitimacy to maintain its weapons. Although Siniora's attempts, which could enhance Israel's security, were praised by the United States, they were clearly contrary to Syria's interests, which has needed Hizbullah's weapons to pressure Israel into ending the occupation of the Golan Heights.

After the outbreak of the 2006 Hizbullah–Israel Conflict, Siniora intended to force Hizbullah to disarm, on the basis of UN Security Council Resolutions 1559 and 1680, as well as regional and international criticism of Hizbullah's military operation against Israel. Later, in May 2008, the Siniora cabinet decided to fire the head of security at Beirut's international airport for collaborating with Hizbullah and close down the organization's secret, independent telecommunications network.

In addition, the Siniora cabinet fostered Lebanon's military cooperation with the United States, which provided a variety of assistance to the army. Furthermore, as US provision of equipment to the army was confined to light weapons, the cabinet turned not only to the Germans, but also to the Russians in order to strengthen the army's capabilities.

Prime Minister Sa'd al-Hariri and the Asad Regime

Introduction

While Siniora's successor, Prime Minister Sa'd al-Hariri, was also backed by the March 14 Coalition, he had initially bandwagoned with the Asad regime, with the main aim of gaining Hizbullah's support for the STL. However, Hariri later balanced against Damascus, especially over the tribunal, which ultimately led to his ouster from the premiership. Hariri's relations with the Syrian regime were largely developed on the issues of his cabinet formation and the treatment of the STL.

Cabinet Formation

In Lebanon's parliamentary elections of June 2009, the March 14 Coalition won 71 seats and the March 8 Coalition won 57 seats.[57] Consulting with the newly-elected members of the parliament,

President Sulayman designated Hariri to the premiership on 27 June.[58] However, the victory of the March 14 Coalition was not so overwhelming, and it led Hariri to form a 'national unity government' with the March 8 Coalition. The Hariri cabinet, which was finally established on 9 November after the long disputes over ministerial posts, had the following composition: 15 ministers from the March 14 Coalition, 10 ministers from the March 8 Coalition and five ministers appointed by President Sulayman.[59]

In order to examine Hariri's relations with the Asad regime, it is important to note the fact that Minister of Foreign Affairs 'Ali Shami belonged to the Amal Movement, even though Minister of Defence Murr retained his post and Minister of Agriculture Husayn Hasan and Minister of State for Administrative Reform Funaysh were members of Hizbullah. Although it is widely believed that the Amal Movement's leader Berri convinced Hariri to appoint Shami to the post, Hariri might have anticipated that showing goodwill towards Damascus would result in the March 8 Coalition's cooperation with him, especially his support for the STL. The reason for this lay in Hizbullah's alleged involvement in the assassination of Rafiq al-Hariri, which had been reported since May 2009, after being first reported by the German magazine *Spiegel*.

Treatment of the Special Tribunal for Lebanon

After the formation of his cabinet in November 2009, Prime Minister Sa'd al-Hariri took into account Syria's strategic interest in Hizbullah and also began to improve his relations with President Asad. As far as the first issue is concerned, the policy statement of the Hariri cabinet, which was approved by the Lebanese parliament on 10 December, included a clause legitimating Hizbullah's possession of arms,[60] although it is difficult to deny the fact that the participation of the March 8 Coalition members in his cabinet strongly demanded cabinet approval for the weapons. Later, in April 2010, when Israel accused Syria of providing Scud missiles to Hizbullah, and when Syria denied the charge, Hariri stated that Israel was fabricating a story about the missiles.[61]

On the other hand, Hariri occasionally visited Syria to meet Asad, and it was reported that they agreed to coordinate their regional policies. In the case of their meeting on 31 May 2010, which was the third since December 2009, Hariri briefed Asad on his recent visit to Washington, DC, where he met US President Obama to discuss regional affairs.[62] Finally, Hariri admitted on 6 September 2010 that he had made an error in criticizing the Syrian regime for assassinating his father, Rafiq.[63]

Hariri's alignment with the Asad regime, first, could be explained by his expectation that it would pressure Hizbullah to cooperate with the STL. In addition, Lebanon and Syria had a common interest in preventing turmoil in Lebanon over the STL's upcoming indictment against members of Hizbullah, and this interest led Hariri–Asad relations to become closer than before. On 30 July 2010, Asad, along with Saudi King 'Abdullah, visited Lebanon and urged its political leaders to sustain internal stability under the increased tensions between the March 14 Coalition, specifically the Future Movement, and the March 8 Coalition, specifically Hizbullah, over reports of imminent indictment by the STL.[64]

In spite of Hariri's improved relations with Asad, Hizbullah continued to question the legitimacy of the STL and even take a hostile view of it. For example, on 9 August 2010, Nasrallah strongly accused the STL of being politicized and being part of an Israeli plot against Lebanon, in particular the resistance organization.[65] While Nasrallah repeatedly stated that Hizbullah would never cooperate with the STL, Damascus did nothing to change his insistence and instead attempted to force Hariri to terminate Lebanon's cooperation with the STL.

The uncooperative and hostile stance of the Asad regime and Hizbullah towards the STL angered Hariri and led him to seek international support for the tribunal with the aim of forcing Hizbullah to cooperate with it. On 30 November 2010, Hariri visited France to meet President Nicolas Sarkozy, who voiced French support for the STL.[66] Although Asad, in the middle of December, stated the acceptance of STL judgement on the basis of 'proofs',[67] he was consistently opposed to Hariri's cooperation with the tribunal and it was revealed in early January 2011 that even the Saudi monarchy was asking Hariri to refuse his cooperation.[68] Hariri then visited the United States and France to gain further Western support for the STL and himself. However, his anti-Syrian and anti-Hizbullah policies backed by the Western powers produced a backlash in Lebanon, where 10 ministers from the March 8 Coalition and one minister loyal to President Sulayman tendered their resignations on 12 January, leading to the collapse of the Hariri cabinet.[69]

Summary

While Prime Minister Hariri was also the leader of the anti-Syrian March 14 Coalition, he initially followed appeasing policies towards the Asad regime. First, the Hariri cabinet not only retained Defence Minister Murr, but also included two Hizbullah members, Minister of Agriculture Hasan and Minister of State for Administrative Reform Funyash, and an Amal Movement member, Minister of Foreign Affairs Shami. Second, the policy statement of the Hariri cabinet legitimized the possession of weapons by Hizbullah. Third, Hariri visited Syria three times between December 2009 and May 2010 to mend fences with President Asad, and finally apologized to him about accusing the Syrian regime of being responsible for the assassination of his father. While the strong identification of the March 8 Coalition with Damascus led Hariri to follow these policies, he might have expected that appeasing the Syrian regime would result in support from the coalition, specifically Hizbullah, for the STL. Furthermore, Lebanon and Syria had a common interest in warding off political unrest in Lebanon over the STL's imminent indictment against Hizbullah members, which led Hariri and Asad to coordinate their policies.

However, the Asad regime did not attempt to change Hizbullah's hostilities towards the STL and sought to force Hariri to abandon Lebanon's cooperation with the tribunal. As this was not acceptable to Hariri and the March 14 Coalition, he sought Western support, specifically US and French one, for the STL. Hariri's reliance on these two powers to force Hizbullah to cooperate with the STL ultimately led the March 8 Coalition to bring down his cabinet.

Prime Minister Najib Miqati and the Asad Regime

Introduction

Since Prime Minister Miqati assumed his post with the support of the March 8 Coalition, he has not, as such, adopted antagonistic policies towards the Asad regime. After his cabinet formation, Miqati's relations with Damascus have developed predominantly over the Syrian uprising issue.

Cabinet Formation

After the collapse of Hariri's cabinet on 12 January 2011, President Sulayman, on the basis of consultations with members of the Lebanese parliament, designated Miqati to the premiership on 25 January.[70] Since Hariri soon revealed that the March 14 Coalition would not participate in a new cabinet under Miqati,[71] he had to choose cabinet members largely from the March 8 Coalition, despite his initial intention to form a 'national unity government'. However, it took nearly five months for Miqati to form a new cabinet because of long-standing disputes over ministerial posts. The 30-member cabinet, which was finally established on 13 June, is composed of 18 ministers affiliated with the March 8 Coalition and 12 ministers associated closely with Miqati, Sulayman or Junblat (leader of the PSP).[72]

To analyse Miqati's relations with the Asad regime effectively, one must consider certain characteristics: Foreign Minister 'Adnan Mansur, a veteran Shi'a diplomat, is strongly supported by the Amal Movement; Defence Minister Fayiz Ghusn is a leading figure of the Marada Movement; and Justice Minister Shakib Qurtbawi is supported by the FNC. While the March 8 Coalition's support for Miqati required him to appoint these pro-Syrian figures to such key posts, to which Damascus also had to pay attention in terms of Syria's national security and the STL's activities, he might have calculated that showing goodwill towards the Asad regime would result in the March 8 Coalition's solid support for him.

Syrian Uprising

Prime Minister Miqati has officially stated Lebanon's 'disassociation policy' on the Syrian uprising.[73] However, the March 14 Coalition has criticized his stance because pursuing this policy has proved to be favourable for the Asad regime.

In the regional/international arena, as a non-permanent UN Security Council member, Lebanon decided to disassociate itself from the council's presidential statement condemning violence in Syria in August 2011.[74] Later, in November, Lebanon voted against the Arab League's decision to suspend Syria's membership and impose political and economic sanctions on it.[75] Although Lebanon's top officials and lawmakers have disputed over his stance, Miqati has defended Lebanon's disassociation from all Arab League decisions regarding Syria and did not recognize the Syrian National Council (SNC), while most Arab and Western states recognized the opposition body as 'a legitimate representative of Syrians seeking peaceful democratic change' in February 2012.[76]

In the domestic scene, the Syrian army's cross-border military operations, which have been conducted in the name of hunting 'terrorists', have not only resulted in the capture and killings of anti-regime figures fleeing from the country, but also damaged property in Lebanon and hurt the people. However, Miqati had initially tolerated the incursions of the Syrian army into Lebanese territory and hesitated to deploy the Lebanese army to the border area, which was strongly condemned by the March 14 Coalition. Indeed, after Interior Minister Marwan Charbil called for additional deployments of the Lebanese army to the Lebanese–Syrian border in January 2012,[77] the Miqati cabinet finally decided to boost the army presence in the border area in July, which was praised especially by the March 14 Coalition.[78] Additionally, in early September, Miqati informed the Syrian ambassador of the army's continuous shelling of Lebanese towns along the border.[79] On the other hand, the Miqati cabinet seems to have no intention of ceasing the deportation of Syrians to Damascus. In August, the cabinet decided to expel 14 Syrians (including the anti-regime figures); an action which soon evoked harsh criticism from the March 14 Coalition and concerns from the United States and European Union.[80]

The reason why Miqati has generally pursued accommodating policies towards the Asad regime can primarily be explained by the identification of one of his partners in the cabinet, i.e. the March 8 Coalition and in particular, Hizbullah, with the regime. However, it seems that a common political interest between Lebanon and Syria prompted Miqati initially to tolerate the incursions of the Syrian army into Lebanese territory. While the Syrian army aimed to capture the anti-regime figures, their inclusion of militant Islamists probably led Miqati to rely on the army's power to detain them to maintain Lebanon's stability.

Summary

As Prime Minister Miqati has been supported by the March 8 Coalition, its identification with Syria, especially the Asad regime, has largely shaped his policies towards the regime.

First, in his cabinet formation, Miqati considered Syria's interests by nominating Foreign Minister Mansur, Defence Minister Ghusn and Justice Minister Qurtbawi, who were supported by the March 8 Coalition. However, it seems difficult to ignore his calculations that an alignment with Damascus might foster the March 8 Coalition's support for him.

Lebanon's policies of disassociating itself from the Arab League and UN Security Council, its initial tolerance of the Syrian army's incursions into Lebanese territory and its decision to expel Syrians, including the anti-regime figures, can also be explained by the influence of the March 8 Coalition's sympathy with the Asad regime on Miqati's policymaking. Furthermore, a common interest between Lebanon and Syria regarding the latter's efforts to capture militant Islamists might have initially led Miqati to allow the Syrian army's incursions of Lebanese territory.

CHAPTER 5

CONCLUSION

The main aim of this chapter is to address the following question posed in the exordium of Chapter 1: Which theories of international relations are most relevant, or are best-suited, to explain Lebanon's relations – particularly its bandwagoning – with Syria since 1970? To answer this question, based on the summaries of Chapters 2, 3 and 4, the theoretical application is examined in the first section before extrapolating the lessons to more wide-ranging methodological issues in the second section.

Theoretical Application

Cases of Presidents Franjiya, Sarkis and Jumayyil

The already-described actions and attitudes of the Lebanese presidents towards the Asad regime from 1970 to 1988 can be partially explained by the application of the theory of 'complex realism'. As Harknett and Vandenberg (1997) explained, the existence of interrelated threats requires a state's leadership to cope with mutually reinforcing internal and external challenges. During the period, Lebanon's Maronite presidents were challenged by interrelated external and internal threats from Syria, because of Lebanon's disadvantageous balance of power with Syria and its maintenance of trans-state relations with non-governmental actors in Lebanon, particularly the Muslim and Palestinian communities (although Damascus occasionally opposed them), which were generally powerful and in opposition to the Lebanese authorities. Considering these circumstances, the theory of 'simple realism', which presumes a unitary state, cannot be applied to the Lebanese case except during the brief period after the 1982 Israeli invasion, which weakened the power of pro-Syrian Lebanese non-governmental actors.

By aligning Lebanon with the perceived less immediate external threat of Syria, President Sulayman Franjiya managed to contain the perceived greater internal threat of the strong coalition between the LNM and the PLO. President Ilyas Sarkis had initially attempted to contain Palestinian military activities by relying on Syrian power, although this resulted in failure mainly because of the fragmentation in the Arab world. The actions and attitudes taken by Franjiya and Sarkis, which complex realism would consider a form of 'bandwagon–balance', i.e. appeasing the Syrian regime as a perceived less immediate threat while resisting Syrian-backed Lebanese groups and figures as a perceived greater threat, resulted when both or either the LNM and/or the PLO violated Syria's spirit of tolerance by violating its national interests. President Amin al-Jumayyil had initially attempted, as deduced by simple realism, to be a rational actor defending Lebanese sovereignty by aligning Lebanon with the United States and Israel against Syria within the context of the weakness of non-governmental actors, specifically Arab-oriented Muslim forces, in Lebanon and the intensification of the Cold War in the Middle East. However, as Syrian-backed Lebanese groups and figures, particularly the NSF, soon recovered their power, one of the most important prerequisites on which simple realism is based, i.e. a unitary state, evaporated. In addition, the disastrous results for Lebanon, particularly the attacks against the MNF forces stationed in the country, led Jumayyil to improve his relationship with Damascus in order to win support from its Lebanese allies, particularly the Druze and Shi'a forces, which according to complex realism would be considered a form of 'double bandwagon', i.e. appeasing the Syrian regime in order to get support from Syrian-backed Lebanese groups and figures.

The reason why the Lebanese presidents were prepared to cooperate with the Syrian regime, either in the form of 'bandwagon–balance' or 'double bandwagon' according to complex realism, when facing interrelated external and internal threats can be partially explained by Syrian support for the domestic status quo in Lebanon. For example, granting the Christian community a disproportionate number of seats in the Lebanese parliament as stipulated by the Constitutional Document of February 1976, as well as the Syrian army supporting the Lebanese government when the poor Shi'a community revolted in August 1987, may have appealed to Franjiya and Jumayyil, respectively. The Asad regime had also occasionally taken action to appease the Lebanese presidents, such as the Syrian army's partial redeployment in January 1980, which may have softened Sarkis's perception of Damascus despite the strained Maronite–Syrian relations at that time.

On the other hand, as explained by the theory of constructivism, Lebanese identity also played a key role in determining the presidents' actions and attitudes towards the Asad regime. Theoretically, the presidents' Maronite identity led them to perceive Syria as a threat to Lebanese sovereignty. However, the Arab identity maintained by the majority of the Lebanese, particularly the Muslim community, and the relative power of the Arab-oriented groups and figures, along with each president's peculiar circumstances, constrained the presidents' possible strategies. Thus, the Lebanese presidents were caught between the identity of their own community and that of the Muslim community, whose interests, as the state leaders, they had to satisfy, consequently forcing them to consider Syrian interests to a great extent.

In the case of Franjiya, he appeared to balance his Maronite identity and the Arab identity of the majority of the Lebanese, which was championed by Damascus and its Lebanese allies, particularly the LNM–PLO coalition. Such an attempt at balancing was shown by his simultaneous preservation of Maronite prerogatives within the Syrian-initiated Constitutional Document and the nomination of Syrian-backed Rashid Karami to the premiership.

Regarding Sarkis, even after distancing himself from the Asad regime, he endeavoured not to further antagonize it, and worked with the Arab League in his attempts to pacify Lebanon. In other words, he avoided exclusive identification with a non-Arab notion of Maronite identity and, by appealing instead to the Arab identity of the majority of the Lebanese, attempted to appease both the Syrian regime and Muslim forces, although he was ultimately unsuccessful. He pursued the same aim with his consistent extension of the ADF's mandate, whose primary support came from Syria.

In the case of Jumayyil, his initial alignment with the US administration and Israel's Likud government had been influenced by the Maronite community's traditional perception of the West and Israel as its protectors. Even after his policies were strongly opposed by the Syrian-backed NSF forces, he attempted to gain US and Israeli support in containing the Lebanese allies backed by Damascus, but failed to do so. As Syria's hegemony in Lebanon was increasingly restored by the NSF military offensive, he recognized the importance of considering the Arab identity of the Lebanese Muslim community and began to improve his relationship with the Asad regime. These events demonstrate that the types of actions and attitudes presumed by complex realism, i.e. 'bandwagon–balance' and 'double bandwagon', both of which can explain Lebanese presidents' alignment with the Syrian regime, were not just a response to internal threats, but took into consideration the importance of identity. Indeed, as constructivism argues, 'threats' are not self-evident but, rather, shaped by the actor's identity.

In addition to the theories of complex realism and constructivism, the theory of complex interdependence can be applied to explain the actions and attitudes taken by the Lebanese presidents towards the Asad regime. First, it is possible to posit that the multiple relationships that had been forged between Lebanon and Syria through their mutual engagement in financial affairs, trade and smuggling had promoted their shared economic interests and thus influenced the policies of the Lebanese presidents. In fact, these multiple ties, along with the priority that Sarkis placed on maintaining good relations with the economic-oriented Sunni Prime Ministers Salim al-Huss and Shafiq al-Wazzan, can explain why Sarkis never attempted to sever the relationship with Damascus despite the strained Maronite–Syrian relations.

Second, Franjiya and the Asad regime had a common interest in holding his post until the official expiration of his presidential term. By exploiting the Syrian need for Franjiya's support to legitimize its Lebanese role, as well as his long-term personal relationship with the Asad family, Franjiya not only maintained his status and contained his rivals within the Maronite community, but also managed to defend Lebanese sovereignty. The actions and attitudes taken by Franjiya reflected his calculation that aligning with the Syrian regime would fulfil his interests better than promoting his identity as a member of the Maronite community.

Third, Jumayyil and the Asad regime appeared to have a shared interest in containing the revolt of the poor Lebanese Shi'a community in order to maintain stability in Lebanon. Hence, as explained by complex interdependence, the multiple transnational and interstate ties involving governmental and non-governmental actors in Lebanon and Syria, as well as their shared economic and political interests and interdependency, were important factors in shaping the Lebanese–Syrian relationships.

As discussed, the actions and attitudes taken by the Lebanese presidents towards the Asad regime can be predominantly explained by three theories of international relations: complex realism, constructivism and complex interdependence (although the less vulnerable party, the Syrian regime, had leverage over the more vulnerable figures, the Lebanese presidents).

Case of Prime Minister Rafiq al-Hariri

As explained by the theory of simple realism, the strong support that Prime Minister Rafiq al-Hariri enjoyed from not only Western governments, but also a wide range of the Lebanese population established a context within which he could behave as a rational actor defending Lebanese sovereignty by counterbalancing the power of Syria. During his first and second cabinet from 1992 to 1996, and after the formation of his fifth cabinet in 2003 in particular, Lebanon under Hariri occasionally either pressured Syria or attempted to negotiate with Israel by counting on the international and domestic support that he had acquired. Although it may initially appear that Lebanon's balancing acts against Syria could be explained by simple realism, Hariri's motivation for performing them was not based on his calculation of the power of external actors but, rather, his desire to both manipulate and appease Syrian-backed groups and figures in Lebanon. Specifically, Hariri's overall aim was either to regulate Hizbullah's military activities in southern Lebanon or to win the cooperation of Damascus's allies in Lebanon in order to create the conditions necessary for the success of his economic recovery plan.

Thus Hariri, as explained by the theory of complex realism, had to consider interrelated threats posed by Syria. That is, he was facing not only the powerful state as a neighbour, but also its close connections with Lebanese non-governmental actors, resulting from Lebanon's non-unitary state formation (in addition, as manifested in Lebanon's governing body called the 'troika', the government itself was not unitary). Under these circumstances, it is true that Hariri balanced against the Syrian regime on several occasions by explicitly or implicitly aligning himself with the Western authorities to contain Syrian-backed Lebanese groups and figures, such as Hizbullah, President Emile Lahoud and Parliament Speaker Nabih Berri ('double balance', i.e. resisting, by aligning with the authorities of Israel, the United States and/or France, the Syrian regime in order to contain Syrian-backed Lebanese groups and figures). However, Hariri generally bandwagoned with Damascus to gain the support of these pro-Syrian actors ('double bandwagon'), in spite of the restrictions imposed on Lebanese sovereignty. Specifically, he depended on Syria's capacity to control Hizbullah's military activities in southern Lebanon to prevent turmoil in Lebanon and attract foreign investment. He also recognized the need to take into account Syrian political and economic interests in Lebanon to gain support for his economic recovery plan among pro-Syrian actors while fulfilling their personal interests as well. Later, his ultimate alignment with the Asad regime regarding the extension of Lahoud's term intended to secure the president's cooperation in forming a new cabinet.

While Hariri's general tendency to align with the Syrian regime, applied to a type of actions and attitudes in the theory of complex realism, i.e. 'double bandwagon', can be partially explained by Damascus's occasional appeasement of him (by restricting Hizbullah's military activities in southern Lebanon and by taming its Lebanese allies), theoretical explanations based on such factors as identity (constructivism) and shared interests and interdependency (complex interdependence) can also explain his actions and attitudes towards the Syrians. First, although Hariri was a Sunni, he viewed the Syrian presence in Lebanon and Syrian-backed Hizbullah's military activities in the south as threats to his economic reconstruction efforts because they impeded Western aid and investment. In this respect, his economic interests appear to have overshadowed his Sunni identity.

However, as a politician from Sunni-dominated West Beirut, he needed to consider the Sunni community's Arab-oriented identity, particular its sympathy for Syria, and its support for the resistance to Israel. In consequence, he occasionally demonstrated support for Hizbullah, particularly when Lebanese sympathy for the group mounted after massive Israeli attacks, and ultimately abandoned his plan to pursue the 'Lebanon first' option, albeit also on account of strong Syrian opposition to it. Thus, as explained by the theory of constructivism, his recognition of the Arab-oriented identity of his supporters influenced his actions and attitudes towards the Syrian regime.

Second, while the Arab-oriented identity of his supporters led Hariri to take steps to appease Damascus, his consideration of shared Lebanese–Syrian economic and political interests and interdependency between them, according to the theory of complex interdependence, must certainly have influenced his decision to cooperate with the Syrian regime regarding certain issues. In particular, Lebanon's permission for Syrians to work in Lebanon and Syria's permission for Lebanese banks to operate in its free zones appeared to have benefited both states' leaders including Hariri and reinforced their economic interdependency. In addition, the Lebanese and Syrian leadership had a shared political interest in preventing Lebanon from becoming 'radicalized'. The Syrian regime feared that such 'radicalization' would develop into Lebanese mass opposition to its presence; Hariri feared that it would obstruct his economic reconstruction efforts, fortifying their political interdependency.

As discussed, Hariri's actions and attitudes towards the Syrian regime can be explained according to complex realism, constructivism and complex interdependence (although the less vulnerable party, the Syrian regime, had leverage over the more vulnerable figure, Hariri), three theories of international relations. On the other hand, Hariri's more explicit balancing against the Syrian leadership after 2003 than he had occasionally done between 1992 and 1996 (although he ultimately cooperated with it over the extension of Lahoud's presidential term in 2004) appears to have been influenced by the changed international dynamics of the Middle East where Lebanon found allies against Syria, i.e. the United States and France, the increasing anti-Syrian tendency among the Lebanese and the marginalization of his 'friends' in the Syrian regime such as 'Abd al-Halim Khaddam and Hikmat al-Shihabi, which decreased his interests in aligning himself with it. On this point, complex realism can presume both balancing and bandwagoning options for Lebanon's relations with Syria, constructivism can explain shifts in identity among the Lebanese and complex interdependence can explain shifts in Lebanese and Syrian leaders' shared interests, respectively. However, in order to examine why Hariri changed his actions and attitudes towards the Asad regime after 2003, an explanation deduced from simple realism, specifically neo-realism, that the systemic structure influences the Lebanese state's behaviour appears to supplement the above explanation based on complex realism, constructivism and complex interdependence (although it is necessary to keep in mind the characteristic of the non-unitary Lebanese state). Specifically, while heretofore no ally was available with which Lebanon might balance against Syria, once Paris and Washington were prepared to back Hariri against Damascus, the range of his options expanded.

Cases of Prime Ministers Siniora, Sa'd al-Hariri and Miqati

Although Prime Minister Fouad al-Siniora was backed by the anti-Syrian March 14 Coalition, he took up the post with the support of the pro-Syrian March 8 Coalition. Hence, as the theory of constructivism suggests, Siniora had to consider the identification of the March 8 Coalition, specifically Hizbullah, with the Asad regime and, indeed, followed conciliatory policies towards Damascus. Through the formation of his two cabinets, Siniora installed pro-Syrian figures in the ministerial posts of justice, defence and foreign affairs, as the Asad regime was especially concerned about who assumed these posts in terms of Syria's national security or the international investigation of Rafiq al-Hariri's assassination.

In addition, Siniora's goodwill policy towards the Asad regime could be explained by the theory of complex realism. This means that Siniora calculated taking account of Syrian interests in Lebanon by installing pro-Syrian figures in the posts that were politically important for Syria and the impetus for the March 8 Coalition's support of him, which applies to the strategy of 'double bandwagon'. Also, according to the theory of complex interdependence, the existence of economic interdependency between Lebanon and Syria could explain Siniora's consideration of Syrian interests in the formation of his first cabinet.

However, Siniora consistently supported the activities of the IIIC and the STL, defying the Asad regime, which saw the IIIC and the STL as Western political tools solely designed to exert pressure upon itself. While admitting that the theory of simple realism, specifically neo-realism, can explain how the international isolation of Syria initiated Siniora's policies, his domestic calculation that weakening Syria would adversely affect its Lebanese allies, particularly Hizbullah, played an important role under the non-unitary state formation in Lebanon. Thus, as deduced from the strategy of 'double balance' in complex realism, Siniora aligned with the US administration against the Syrian regime to contain Hizbullah, which was especially manifested in his commitments to UN Security Council Resolutions 1559 and 1680 and Lebanon's military cooperation with the United States.

The March 14 Coalition-backed Prime Minister Sa'd al-Hariri had initially appeased the Syrian leadership through his cabinet formation, the policy statement of his cabinet and his meetings with President Bashar al-Asad. As explained by constructivism, it is impossible to deny that the strong identification of the March 8 Coalition, which took part in the Hariri cabinet, with the Asad regime initiated the premier's conciliatory policies towards Damascus. However, at the same time, Hariri calculated that these policies would lead to Hizbullah's support for the STL, a strategy advocated by complex realism, i.e. 'double bandwagon'. Also, as deduced from complex interdependence, a shared interest between Lebanon and Syria to prevent turmoil in Lebanon over the treatment of the STL can explain Hariri's alignment with the Syrian regime.

However, despite Hariri's expectations, the Asad regime did nothing to change Hizbullah's hostilities towards the STL and, furthermore, pressured him into abandoning Lebanon's cooperation with the tribunal. Consequently, Hariri relied on the US and French authorities with the aim of forcing Hizbullah to cooperate with the STL, as explained by a strategy in complex realism, i.e. 'double balance'.

Unlike Siniora and Hariri, Prime Minister Najib Miqati has been supported by the March 8 Coalition. In effect, the coalition's identification with the Asad regime, as well as Miqati's calculation that aligning with the regime might result in the coalition's solid support of him, affected his cabinet formation, which could be explained by constructivism and complex realism (specifically, 'double bandwagon'), respectively.

As Lebanon's disassociation policies at regional and international levels, its initial tolerance of the Syrian army's incursions into Lebanese territory and its decision to expel Syrians (including the anti-regime figures) were largely affected by the March 8 Coalition's identification with the Asad regime, constructivism has an explanatory power for these cases. At the same time, as explained by complex interdependence, a shared political interest between Lebanon and Syria over the capture of militant Islamists seems to have also influenced Miqati's policymaking.

Extrapolating Lessons to More Wide-Ranging Methodological Issues

As discussed above, the actions and attitudes taken by Lebanese Presidents Franjiya, Sarkis and Jumayyil and Prime Ministers

Hariri (both Rafiq and Sa'd), Siniora and Miqati towards the Syrian regime can be, in almost all the cases, explained according to three theories of international relations, i.e. complex realism, constructivism and complex interdependence. By focusing on the key powerful figures directing the Lebanese state, this case study demonstrates that the relations of a penetrated weak state (in this case Lebanon) with a regional middle power (in this case Syria) cannot be, except in rare cases, explained by the state-to-state balance of power model, a major backbone of the theory of simple realism. Rather, it can only be understood by a combination of the following factors described by several theories, namely 'omnialignment' against interrelated external and internal threats described by complex realism, identity described by constructivism, and shared interests and interdependency described by complex interdependence.

Under the complexity of Lebanese–Syrian relations, simple realism is useful in understanding Syrian behaviour. By subordinating its domestic groups, Syria has largely freed its foreign policy from domestic constraints and thus can be considered a unitary rational actor. In effect, external factors, specifically regional dynamics in the Middle East, have chiefly shaped Syria's foreign policy, including its Lebanese policy and its placing of top priority on securing a national defence against Israel. In contrast, the Lebanese state cannot be considered a unitary actor because of the multitude of actors who have influenced its behaviour, which have included governmental (office-holding) and non-governmental groups and figures. Thus, while the regional dynamics have affected Lebanon's relations with Syria, they have been more strongly influenced by domestic factors in Lebanon. As explained by complex realism, when Lebanese government leaders were facing internal and external threats simultaneously, they generally called on the support of external actors posing a less immediate threat to help them resist and appease a greater threat posed by internal actors, namely non-governmental groups and figures, particularly those backed by Syria.

For Lebanon, unlike Syria, the term 'threat' has not automatically referred to a particular state, either Israel or Syria, even though both have been more powerful contiguous states and even though both, especially Syria, have threatened Lebanese sovereignty. In fact, Lebanese leaders have not necessarily considered the Syrian state as an unmitigated threat, because Lebanon is not a national state with a shared identity differentiated from that of Syria but rather a collection of sectarian communities, many of which have maintained trans-state ties with Syria. In consequence, irrespective of their own identity, Lebanon's top leaders have been forced to align themselves with the Syrian regime in order to secure their power and status, while the developments of their shared economic and political interests and interdependency between various Lebanese and Syrian actors have also led the Lebanese leaders to do so. On examining this Lebanese–Syrian case study, it appears possible to conclude that a state's perception of a 'threat' is strongly connected with and/or influenced by not only that state's identity, but also the interests and interdependency that it shares with other states. As such, and in contrast to neo-realism's assumption, the perception of a 'threat' is not configured *a priori* on the basis of a state's power relative to other states.

Although complex realism, constructivism and complex interdependence highlight different aspects of international relations, respectively, they share the assumption that states are not unitary and thus non-governmental actors exert much influence on their foreign relations. By offering a theoretical explanation for Lebanon's relations with Syria, combined consideration of these three theories is not only a means of grasping various dimensions of Lebanese–Syrian relations, but also essential, considering the formation of the non-unitary Lebanese state.

While simple realism can explain the behaviour of a consolidated or coherent state, such as Syria, only a combination of complex realism, constructivism and complex interdependence can explain that of a penetrated weak state, such as Lebanon.

Thus, the employment of a single analytical approach cannot provide a sufficient framework for examination of a complex case study, in this case Lebanese–Syrian relations since 1970. As this conclusion results from the examination of one specific case, the validity of its widespread application within the field of international relations must be verified by examining the cases of other penetrated weak states. Thus, this case study may provide a basis for constructing a novel and widely applicable theory for explaining the behaviour of penetrated weak states.

NOTES

Chapter 1. Introduction: The Analytical Framework

1. Hinnebusch (1998), p. 142.
2. Hitti (1989), p. 3.
3. Salem (1994), p. 69.
4. Referring to the Iranian and Syrian case, Ehteshami and Hinnebusch define the concept of regional middle powers as states which play key roles in their regional arena, but which should be treated as middle powers on the global scene, and list their characteristics as follows. First, while regional middle powers' behavioural pattern is similar to that of great powers, their goals and spheres of influence are more limited than those of great powers and thus they mainly focus on regional affairs. Second, regional middle powers, in general, have leaders who enjoy extra-regional influence and aspiration. Third, while these powers are dependent on great powers, especially for economic and technological assistance, they hope to maximize autonomy by diversifying their economic links and by balancing the regional impact of great powers. Fourth, regional middle powers need to possess enough resources as the basis of their power. For details, see Ehteshami and Hinnebusch (1997), pp. 6–9.
5. For the concept of authoritarian rule and the Syrian case, see Hinnebusch (1990).
6. Hinnebusch (2002b), p. 153.
7. Ibid. In this regard, except for President Reagan and President George W. Bush, President Richard M. Nixon, President Jimmy Carter, President George H. W. Bush and President Bill Clinton were willing to engage with the Asad regime, and this allowed Syria to enlist the United States in

trying to resolve the issues regarding the Israeli occupation of the occupied Arab territories.

8. Ehteshami and Hinnebusch (1997), p. 11.
9. The area roughly encompasses the territorial expanse of present-day Syria, Lebanon, Jordan and Israel.
10. For details on the concept, see Evron (1987).
11. David (1991), p. 237.
12. Harknett and Vandenberg (1997), p. 119.
13. Ibid.
14. Ibid., pp. 121–123.
15. Ibid., p. 123.
16. For details on these strategies proposed by Harknett and Vandenberg, i.e. 'double balance', 'balance–bandwagon', 'bandwagon–balance' and 'double bandwagon', see Harknett and Vandenberg (1997), pp. 124–128.
17. Walt (1987), p. 47.
18. Ibid., p. 48.
19. Ibid.
20. Ibid.
21. Based on the 'National Pact' in 1943, which was formed as a 'gentlemen's agreement' between Maronite President Bishara al-Khuri and Sunni Prime Minister Riyd al-Sulh and has nevertheless been the backbone of Lebanese politics and foreign policies until today, the presidency has been reserved for the Maronites, the premiership for the Sunnis and the parliament speakership for the Shi'as. For details on the pact, see Solh (2004) and Zisser (2000).
22. Hinnebusch (2002a), p. 2.
23. Gause (1997), p. 201.
24. Hinnebusch (2002a), p. 7.
25. Ibid., pp. 9–10.
26. Gause (1992), p. 466.
27. Wendt (1999), pp. 336–337.
28. Although the complex interdependence theory originally focuses on economic ties between 'equal states', in this study the theory is applied to explain not only economic, but also political ties under asymmetrical Lebanese–Syrian relations since 1970.
29. Keohane and Nye (2001), pp. 21–24.
30. Ibid., pp. 10–17.
31. Lawson (1996), p. 95.

Chapter 2. Disruption of the Lebanese State and Syrian Intervention (1970–1988)

1. For details on the concept of consociational democracy, see Lijphart (1969) and Lijphart (1977).
2. According to Hottinger, the three main criteria identified in delimiting the category of *za'im* are as follows: 'local limitation of the group; tendency towards heredity of function; [and] exchange of economic support given to the clients against political loyalty coming from the clients'. See Hottinger (1966), p. 104.
3. Thompson (2002), p. 75.
4. Hinnebusch (2001), p. 147.
5. For the concept of 'presidential monarchy', see Hinnebusch (2001), pp. 67–69.
6. Hinnebusch (2002b), p. 148.
7. Taylor (1982), pp. 51–52.
8. Ibid.
9. Hinnebusch (2001), p. 154. For details on Sinai I, see Seale (1988), pp. 235–237.
10. Taylor (1982), p. 66.
11. Ibid., p. 68. For details on Sinai II, see Seale (1988), pp. 255–261.
12. Weinberger (1986), p. 271.
13. By 1972, Kamal Junblat had formed the LNM with the aim of destroying Lebanon's discriminative and pro-Christian consociational system, since it did not reflect the increased power of the ideological movements. The LNM was mainly composed of Junblat's Progressive Socialist Party (PSP), the Independent Nasserist Movement (led by Ibrahim Qulailat), the Lebanese Communist Party (led by Fu'ad Shamali) and the Syrian Socialist Nationalist Party (led by In'am Ra'd). For details, see Deeb (1980), pp. xiii, 60–69.
14. For further details on the 'Red Line Agreement', see Seale (1988), pp. 278–280.
15. Sela (1998), p. 181.
16. Taylor (1982), p. 68.
17. Ibid., pp. 68–69.
18. Pogany (1987), pp. 74, 108–109.
19. Thompson (2002), p. 76.
20. Ibid.
21. Ibid.
22. Pogany (1987), p. 109.

23. Zamir (1999), pp. 121–122.
24. Sela (1998), p. 195.
25. Zamir (1999), p. 120.
26. Brynen (1990), p. 147.
27. Ibid.
28. Rabinovich (1984), p. 56.
29. Brynen (1990), p. 148.
30. Ibid.
31. *Middle East International*, 23 November 1979, p. 14.
32. Brynen (1990), p. 148.
33. Haddad (1985), p. 68.
34. Ibid., pp. 68–69.
35. Taylor (1982), pp. 81–88.
36. Ibid., pp. 89–92.
37. Ranstorp (1997), p. 116.
38. Ibid., p. 117.
39. Hinnebusch (1998), pp. 145–147.
40. Ehteshami and Hinnebusch, (1997), p. 134.
41. Salem (1992), p. 20.
42. Ibid.
43. Seale (1988), pp. 406–409.
44. Salem (1995), pp. 92–93.
45. Thompson (2002), p. 78. In this regard, '[t]he agreement itself did not demand as a condition for Israel's departure the simultaneous departure of Syrian forces. But in a separate United States–Israel exchange of "letters of understanding" the United States agreed that Israeli troops should remain in Lebanon as long as did Syrian and PLO forces'; Petran (1987), p. 310.
46. Hinnebusch (1998), p. 143.
47. Thompson (2002), p. 78.
48. Petran (1987), p. 311.
49. Haddad (1985), pp. 93–95.
50. Ibid.
51. Ibid., p. 95.
52. Ibid.
53. Ibid., pp. 95–96.
54. For details on the war, see Seale (1988), pp. 413–418.
55. Hinnebusch (1998), p. 144.
56. Seale (1988), p. 414.
57. Seale (1997), pp. 70–72.

58. Seale (1988), pp. 406–417.
59. Haddad (1985), p. 120.
60. Salem (1994), p. 75.
61. For details on this process, see Hinnebusch (1998), pp. 145–150.
62. Ehteshami and Hinnebusch (1997), pp. 129–133.
63. See Abukhalil (1994), pp. 128–130.
64. Rabinovich (1984), p. 60.
65. Ibid., p. 64. Franjiya's good relations with Asad dated back to 1957, when he fled to Syria and was provided with home protection after clashing with the Duwayhi clan over his influence in Zgharta, northern Lebanon; Harris (1996), p. 112.
66. Deeb (1980), p. 39.
67. Ibid., p. 42; and Rabinovich (1984), pp. 70–71.
68. Rabinovich (1984), pp. 72–74.
69. Zamir (1999), p. 119.
70. Ibid., p. 120.
71. Ibid., pp. 120–121.
72. 'Relations between Phalangists and Syria Said to Be Improving', *The Arab World Weekly* (in English), 26 April 1980, pp. 14–17 in *Foreign Broadcast Information Service*, no. 2140, 26 June 1980, pp. 51–55.
73. Ibid.
74. Ibid.
75. Petran (1987), p. 313.
76. Salem (1995), p. 176. For details on activities of Hubayqa and Ja'ja' during the civil war in Lebanon, see Charbel (2011), pp. 23–264.
77. Petran (1987), pp. 358–359.
78. Ibid., p. 359.
79. Ibid.
80. Harris (1996), p. 193.
81. Ibid., pp. 192–193.
82. Hanf (1993), pp. 307–309.
83. Harris (1996), pp. 200–201; and Petran (1987), pp. 368–369.
84. Johnson (1986), p. 210.
85. Ibid., pp. 204–205.
86. Ibid., p. 210.
87. Ibid., pp. 198, 210–211.
88. Petran (1987), pp. 352–353.
89. For the organizations' details, see Deeb (1988). Both groups are still main pillars of Lebanon's Shi'a community.
90. Ajami (1986), p. 174.

91. Rabinovich (1984), p. 37.
92. Abukhalil (1990), p. 11.
93. Ibid., p. 10.
94. Ibid.
95. Ibid., p. 11.
96. Deeb (1988), p. 687.
97. Abukhalil (1990), p. 11.
98. Ibid., pp. 11–12.
99. Ibid., p. 12.
100. Ehteshami and Hinnebusch (1997), pp. 120–122.
101. Ibid., p. 122.
102. Norton (1998), p. 151.
103. Ibid.
104. Abukhalil (1990), p. 13.
105. For Hizbullah's 'extreme' activities, see Ranstorp (1997).
106. Ehteshami and Hinnebusch (1997), p. 131.
107. Ibid.
108. Ibid., pp. 132–133.
109. Abukhalil (1990), p. 15.
110. Ehteshami and Hinnebusch (1997), p. 133. Ranstorp pointed out that a series of Syrian attacks by using its proxy, the Amal Movement, was 'to advance its design in Lebanon by demonstrating to the American administration that it was firmly committed to confronting [Shi'a] extremism in the form of [Hizbullah] abductions of foreigners and uncontrolled attacks against Israel'; Ranstorp (1997), pp. 124–125.
111. Ehteshami and Hinnebusch (1997), p. 134.
112. Ibid.
113. Mohtashemi was indeed ousted from Iran's interior minister post in 1989; Ranstorp (1997), pp. 126–127.
114. Ehteshami and Hinnebusch (1997), p. 134. Also see Muir (1989).
115. The newly formed cabinet led by Salam after the 1972 parliamentary elections in Lebanon ousted Junblat because of worsening relations between them; Khazen (2000a), p. 203. It appears that Salam feared Junblat's increasing popularity among the Muslims.
116. Goria (1985), pp. 106–107.
117. Rabinovich (1984), p. 77.
118. Ibid., pp. 76–77.
119. Ma'oz and Yaniv (1986), p. 198.
120. Rabinovich (1984), p. 77.

121. Ibid., pp. 77–78. Also see Seale (1988), pp. 288–289.
122. Petran (1987), p. 319.
123. Ibid., p. 362.
124. Ibid.
125. Harris (1996), pp. 215–216.
126. Ibid., p. 216.
127. Ibid., p. 217.
128. Ma'oz and Yaniv (1986), pp. 195–196.
129. Khazen (2000a), p. 214.
130. Ibid., p. 223.
131. Rabinovich (1984), pp. 49–50.
132. As Junblat, the LNM's leader, explained in his memoir, the main reason for 'Arafat's aligning with the LNM under pressure from Asad to choose between himself and Junblat was that Junblat generally respected the freedom of Palestinian activities in Lebanon; Joumblatt (1982), pp. 64–69. As for Asad's expression of complaint about 'Arafat's alignment with Junblat, see Ma'oz (1988), p. 129.
133. Brynen (1990), pp. 183–184.
134. Ibid., p. 184.
135. McLaurin (1989), p. 19.
136. For details on the Palestinian withdrawal, see Ménargues (2004), pp. 389–413.
137. Hinnebusch (1986), p. 14.
138. Hinnebusch (1998), p. 144.
139. Hinnebusch (1986), p. 17.
140. Ibid., p. 15.
141. Brynen (1990), pp. 187–191.
142. Ibid., p. 61.
143. Ibid.
144. Harris (1996), p. 157.
145. Ibid.
146. Salibi (1976), p. 68.
147. Harris (1996), p. 157; and Khazen (2000a), p. 206.
148. Khazen (2000a), p. 206. Also see Salibi (1976), p. 68. For the Syrian stance, see 'Syrian Statement on Resumption of Fighting in Lebanon', in *Summary of World Broadcasts*, 9 May 1973, ME/4290/A/11.
149. Brynen (1990), p. 62.
150. Ibid. Also see Salibi (1976), p. 68.
151. Goria (1985), p. 144.
152. Harris (1996), p. 158

153. Although the Milkart Agreement was more comprehensive and detailed than the Cairo Agreement, the backbone of its contents was that while Lebanon acknowledged the PLO's supremacy in the refugee camps, the Palestinians should respect Lebanese sovereignty and accommodate their activities not to violate it. For details, see Brynen (1990), pp. 50–51; Harris (1996), pp. 153–154; and Khazen (2000a), pp. 208–211.
154. Goria (1985), p. 160.
155. Ibid., p. 171. Also see 'Lebanese Request for Arms from Arab States', in *Summary of World Broadcasts*, 19 December 1974, ME/4785/A/5–6.
156. Haddad (1985), p. 47.
157. Ibid.
158. *L'Orient Le Jour*, 16 May 1975.
159. Ibid., 24 May 1975. Also see Kassir (1994), p. 109.
160. Haddad (1985), p. 47.
161. Salibi (1976), p. 106.
162. Petran (1987), pp. 167–168. Also see Gordon (1983), p. 108.
163. Weinberger (1986), p. 153.
164. Salibi (1976), p. 108.
165. Seale (1988), p. 270. These three figures became key figures in Syrian policy towards Lebanon and Khaddam played a dominant role.
166. Deeb (1980), p. 124.
167. Dawisha (1980), pp. 87–88; and Weinberger (1986), p. 155.
168. Dawisha (1980), p. 88; and Khazen (2000a), p. 296.
169. Khazan (2000a), p. 296.
170. Ibid.
171. Dawisha (1980), p. 88; and Khazen (2000a), p. 295.
172. Khazen (2000a), pp. 295–296.
173. Weinberger (1986), p. 156.
174. Khazen (2000a), p. 296.
175. Ibid.
176. Petran (1987), p. 168.
177. Deeb (1980), p. 124.
178. Ibid.
179. Ibid.
180. Ibid., p. 3.
181. Ibid.
182. Khazen (2000a), p. 316.
183. Ibid., pp. 316–317.
184. Deeb (1980), p. 4.

185. Petran (1987), p. 180.
186. Ibid.
187 Deeb (1980), p. 4. On the other hand, the Franjiya–Karami rapprochement understandably worsened relations between Karami and the Junblat-led LNM.
188. For details, see Salibi (1976), pp. 149–159.
189. Hinnebusch (1986), p. 5; and Hinnebusch (1998), p. 140.
190. Ravinovich (1984), p. 49.
191. Ibid., pp. 49–50.
192. Khazen (2000a), p. 327.
193. Deeb (1980), p. 125. Also see Petran (1987), p. 182.
194. Khazen (2000a), p. 327.
195. Ibid.
196. Ibid.
197. For details, see Deeb (1980), p. 6; and Khazen (2000a), p. 329.
198. Khazen (2000a), p. 328.
199. Ibid., pp. 330–331.
200. For example, 66 deputies in the Lebanese parliament (two-thirds of the deputies) signed a petition for Franjiya's resignation; Khazen (2000a), p. 340.
201. Khazen (2000a), p. 340.
202. Ibid.
203. Khazen (2000a), pp. 340–341; Petran (1987), p. 196; and Weinberger (1986), p. 201.
204. Weinberger (1986), p. 202.
205. Petran (1987), pp. 196–197.
206. Weinberger (1986), p. 202. Also see Petran (1987), p. 197.
207. Weinberger (1986), p. 202.
208. Odeh (1985), p. 168.
209. Deeb (1980), p. 130.
210. Petran (1987), p. 197.
211. Ibid.
212. Khazen (2000a), p. 344.
213. Weinberger (1986), p. 204.
214. Petran (1987), p. 212. According to Petran, while 67 deputies attended the ceremony, Iddi, Junblat, Karami and their supporters boycotted it. Although Petran mentioned Karami as one of the main figures who boycotted the ceremony, it appears correct that Weinberger mentioned Salam instead of Karami. This is because Karami supported Sarkis during the electoral process and Salam had been generally on bad terms

with the Syrians before the outbreak of the civil war; see Weinberger (1986), p. 224.

215. In this point, 'Sarkis, in his speech after the [inauguration] ceremony, tried to depict his role as that of a middle-of-the-road statesman'; Deeb (1980), p. 15.
216. Kassir (1994), p. 257.
217. Rabinovich (1984), p. 56.
218. Hoss (1984), p. 20.
219. The author's conversation with a former prime minister, 10 July 2001.
220. Kassir (1994), pp. 433–434.
221. *Middle East International*, 25 May, 1979, p. 14; 6 July 1979, p. 13; and 20 July 1979, p. 14.
222. For the process, see ibid., 15 August 1980, pp. 9–10; Pakradouni (1984), p. 218; and Rabinovich (1984), p. 96.
223. Pogany (1987), pp. 123–124.
224. Hinnebusch (1986), p. 8.
225. Avi-Ran (1991), p. 75.
226. Ibid., pp. 75–76.
227. Ma'oz and Yaniv (1986), p. 200.
228. Brynen (1990), p. 116.
229. Ibid.
230. Avi-Ran (1991), p. 101.
231. Petran (1987), p. 243.
232. Ibid.
233. Pakradouni (1984), pp. 146–147.
234. Hanf (1993), p. 239.
235. For example, Sham'un stated that since the Syrian army abandoned its original peacekeeping role and was engaged in the Lebanese conflict as a party, it could not stay in Lebanon permanently; Hanf (1993), p. 234. Also, Sham'un maintained that the Maronites would continue the fighting until the last Syrian soldiers could be expelled from Lebanon; Cobban (1978), p. 15.
236. Pogany (1987), p. 133.
237. Haddad (1985), p. 61; and Petran (1987), p. 249.
238. Pogany (1987), p. 134.
239. Petran (1987), p. 249.
240. Pogany (1987), p. 137.
241. Ibid.
242. Thompson (2002), p. 76.
243. Haddad (1985), p. 69.

244. Pogany (1987), p. 145; and Thompson (2002), p. 77.
245. Ibid.
246. Pakradouni (1984), p. 231. For details on the crisis, see Seale (1988), pp. 368–373.
247. Hanf (1993), p. 251.
248. Salem (1982), p. 12; Pogany (1987), pp. 145–146; and Thompson (2002), p. 77.
249. Thompson (2002), p. 78.
250. Picard (2000), p. 293.
251. Ibid., pp. 293–300.
252. Lawson (1996), p. 95.
253. *Middle East Economic Digest*, 4 August 1978, p. 33; and 10 April 1981, p. 32.
254. Ibid., 10 April 1981, p. 32.
255. Ibid. 16 April 1982, p. 2.
256. Ibid., 23 April 1982, p. 38.
257. Ibid., 4 June 1982, p. 29.
258. Starr (1984), p. 76.
259. Haddad (1985), pp. 83–84.
260. Seale (1988), p. 392.
261. Haddad (1985), p. 84.
262. Petran (1987), p. 295.
263. Hanf (1993), p. 270.
264. Hudson (1988), p. 217.
265. Ibid., pp. 217–218.
266. Haddad (1985), pp. 100–101.
267. Petran (1987), p. 295. Also see McLaurin (1984), pp. 101–102.
268. Petran (1987), p. 296.
269. Ibid.
270. Ibid.
271. McLaurin (1984), p. 102.
272. Haddad (1985), p. 101.
273. Ibid., pp. 102–103. Also see McLaurin (1984), p. 103.
274. Haddad (1985), p. 103.
275. McLaurin (1984), p. 103.
276. Haddad (1985), pp. 108–111.
277. Jureidini and McLaurin (1984), p. 25.
278. Haddad (1985), pp. 113–114; and *Middle East International*, 11 November 1983, p. 8.
279. Haddad (1985), pp. 113–114.

280. *Middle East International*, 11 November 1983, p. 8.
281. Ibid.
282. Haddad (1985), p. 117.
283. Gerges (1997), p. 98.
284. For details on Lebanon's conflict situation leading to the MNF withdrawal in February 1984, see *Middle East International*, 25 November 1983, pp. 5–6; 10 February 1984, pp. 5–6; and 24 February 1984, pp. 3–4.
285. Seale (1988), p. 417.
286. *Middle East International*, 9 March 1984, p. 3.
287. Ibid.
288. Haddad (1985), p. 121.
289. For details on their antagonism, see Seale (1988), pp. 421–440.
290. *Middle East International*, 23 March 1984, p. 3.
291. Ibid.
292. Petran suspects the Syria regime's real intention on Franjiya's demand, given his close relations with President Asad; see Petran (1987), p. 356. However, the Syrian regime monitored the conference and feared the failure of the conference and the resulting fierce internecine fighting, 'Syria Closely Watches Lausanne Conference', *Al-Mustaqbal* (in Arabic), 24 March 1984, p. 14 in *Foreign Broadcast Information Service*, no. 81, 21 May 1984, pp. 8–9. It appears that while carefully observing the developments of the conference, the Syrian regime did not manage to put pressure on Franjiya, because of its preoccupation with the inner power struggle.
293. *Middle East International*, 4 May 1984, p. 8.
294. Ibid., 15 June 1984, p. 5.
295. Ibid.
296. Salem (1995), p. 176.
297. Ibid., p. 193.
298. The Israeli army withdrew to the 'security zone' in June 1985 and maintained its proxy forces: the SLA, which was created in 1978 after the Litani Operation and was led by Antoine Lahad after the death of the first leader Sa'd Haddad in 1984.
299. Rabinovich (1987), p. 63.
300. For details on the agreement, see *Middle East International*, 10 January 1986, pp. 10–11; and Thompson (2002), pp. 78–79.
301. Hanf (1993), p. 309.
302. For details on the process, see Harris (1996), pp. 200–201; *Middle East International*, 24 January 1986, pp. 3–4; and Petran (1987), pp. 368–369.

303. Hinnebusch (1998), pp. 145–148.
304. Salem (1992), p. 32. Also see 'Syria Sets Conditions for Reconciliation with al-Jumayyil', *al-Qabas* (in Arabic), 15 October 1986, p. 20 in *Foreign Broadcast Information Service*, no. 87, 9 January 1987, pp. 89–90.
305. Devlin (1988), p. 90.
306. Charbel (2011), p. 371.
307. See *Middle East International*, 10 January 1986, pp. 10–11; and Petran (1987), p. 368.
308. Harris (1988), p. 96.
309. *Middle East International*, 27 June 1986, p. 8.
310. Ibid., 11 July 1986, p. 5.
311. Chami (1992), p. 325.
312. *Middle East Economic Digest*, 13 September 1986, p. 16.
313. Ibid., 11 October 1986, p. 24; and 18 October 1986, p. 23.
314. Ibid., 5 September 1987, p. 46.
315. Ibid., 26 September 1987, p. 29.

Chapter 3. Lebanon from 'Anarchy' to 'Indirect Rule' under Syria (1988–2005)

1. See Abul-Husn (1998), pp. 107–108; and Salem (1991), p. 66.
2. For details on the Ta'if Agreement, see Hamdan (1997), pp. 216–226; and Norton (1991), pp. 460–465. For an English version of the full text, see the homepage of the Middle East Research Institute of Japan. http://www.mideastinfo.com/documents/taif.htm (accessed on 14 April 2012).
3. Nasrallah (1993), pp. 106–107. Also see Harris (1996), pp. 264–266.
4. Norton (1991), p. 466.
5. Laurent (1991), pp. 97–98.
6. Norton (1991), p. 466.
7. Ibid., pp. 466–467.
8. Zisser (2001), p. 141.
9. Harris (1996), p. 274.
10. Zisser (2001), p. 141.
11. Ehteshami and Hinnebusch (1997), pp. 136–137; and Hinnebusch (1998), p. 149.
12. Zisser (2001), p. 141. For details on the military operation by the Syrian army, see Harris (1996), pp. 277–278.
13. Hinnebusch (1996), p. 48.

14. Ibid.
15. Zisser (2001), p. 105.
16. Hinnebusch (1996), pp. 51–52.
17. Ibid., p. 52.
18. Ehteshami and Hinnebusch (1997), p. 166.
19. Hinnebusch (1996), pp. 52–53.
20. Norton (1997), p. 10. Also see Hinnebusch (1998), p. 157.
21. Ehteshami and Hinnebusch (1997), p. 172.
22. Ibid.
23. Hinnebusch (1996), p. 54.
24. Hajjar (1999), p. 113.
25. Ibid., pp. 122–123.
26. Norton (1997), p. 12. Also see Zisser (2001), p. 146.
27. Norton (1997), p. 12.
28. Ibid. Also see Hinnebusch (1998), p. 157.
29. Hajjar (1999), p. 124; and Zisser (2001), p. 146.
30. Hajjar (1999), p. 124.
31. Zisser (2001), p. 146.
32. Ibid., pp. 124–125.
33. Ibid., p. 125.
34. Ghadbian (2001), p. 628.
35. For details, see Ghadbian (2001), p. 628; and Perthes (2001), p. 38.
36. For details on 'Abdullah's plan and its analysis, see Montagu (2002).
37. *The Daily Star*, 4 March 2002. In addition, Asad's visit was also aimed at softening Maronite opposition to the Syrian presence in Lebanon.
38. Ehteshami and Hinnebusch (2002), p. 348.
39. *Middle East International*, 12 October 2001, p. 22.
40. Ibid., 26 October 2001, p. 19.
41. Hinnebusch (2006), pp. 130–131.
42. Ibid., p. 136.
43. On 11 May 2004, the Bush administration actually imposed sanctions against Syria, which 'banned American exports to Syria, except for food and medicine, and barred Syrian air carriers from landing in or taking off from the United States'. Also, additional sanctions not included in the SALSRA, such as 'freezing the assets of certain individuals and government entities and severing business with the [C]ommercial [B]ank of Syria', were imposed; Rabil (2006), pp. 158–159.
44. Hinnebusch (2006), p. 137.
45. *Middle East International*, 10 September 2004, pp. 7–8.
46. For details on the attacks, see *Middle East International*, 21 January 2005, pp. 10–11.

47. The main reason why the case of the Palestinians is not dealt with here is that their power in Lebanon was weakened by the 1982 Israeli invasion in Lebanon and the 'Camps War' in the late 1980s. In consequence, Syria did not need to take the Palestinian presence in Lebanon into consideration overly in implementing its Lebanese policy. For details on the Palestinian situation in Lebanon after the end of the civil war, see Peteet (1996).
48. Hinnebusch (1998), p. 148.
49. Ibid., pp. 148–149.
50. For details, see Harris (1996), p. 300; and *Middle East Mirror*, 24 March 1994, pp. 19–24.
51. Harris (1996), p. 300.
52. Ibid. Ja'ja' has categorically denied the charges in both cases.
53. *Middle East International*, 4 March 1994, p. 10.
54. Khazen (2001), p. 46.
55. Phares (1995), p. 212.
56. Harris (1996), p. 299.
57. For details on the formation, see *The Daily Star*, 1 May 2001 and 2 May 2001; and *Middle East International*, 15 June 2001, pp. 11–12.
58. Phares (1995), pp. 218–219.
59. Gambill (2001b).
60. Ibid.
61. For details on the power struggles and the process of Pakraduni's election to the party president, see Gambill (2001b).
62. *The Daily Star*, 25 January 2002. Although there are some possible explanations for his assassination such as Israeli or Syrian plots, as shown by Gambill and Endrawos (2002), there still remains no confirmation about this.
63. Hinnebusch (1998), p. 152.
64. Harris (1996), p. 305.
65. Hinnebusch (1998), p. 154.
66. See Pölling (1994), p. 22.
67. For each statement, see *The Daily Star*, 15 November 2000 and 17 May 2001.
68. Hinnebusch (1998), p. 152.
69. Picard (2000), p. 315.
70. Zisser (2001), pp. 139–140.
71. Hinnebusch (1998), p. 148.
72. Ibid., p. 152.
73. For the restarted military operations by Hizbullah, see *Middle East International*, 12 October 2001, p. 22.

74. For details, see *Middle East International*, 21 January 2005, pp. 10–11.
75. Harris (1996), p. 308.
76. For details, see Gambill and Aoun (2000).
77. Najem (2000), pp. 29–32.
78. For the escalation process, see Najem (2000), p. 33; and Trendle (1992), p. 3.
79. Trendle (1992), p. 4.
80. See 'Lebanese Prime Minister Resigns; Blames External Pressures for Crisis', in *Summary of World Broadcasts*, 8 May 1992, ME/1375 A/1–3.
81. For the formation process, see *Middle East International*, 29 May 1992, p. 7.
82. Najem (2000), pp. 37–41.
83. Sufayr charged that the treaty was 'an unequal and imposed treaty'; Muir (1991), p. 3.
84. For Christian, especially Maronite, attitudes towards the elections, see Baaklini, Denoeux and Springborg (1999), pp. 98–99; Harik (1998), pp. 140–141; Khazen (1998), pp. 35–40; and Norton and Schwedler (1994), pp. 53–54. Regarding a Maronite view which emphasized a characteristic of the Syrian-imposed Lebanese parliamentary elections in 1992, 1996 and 2000, see Khazen (2000b).
85. Najem (1998), p. 26.
86. For details, see 'Decree Names Members of New Government', in *Summary of World Broadcasts*, 2 November 1992, ME/1527 A/6.
87. Najem (2000), p. 48.
88. Ibid. Also see *Middle East International*, 6 November 1992, p. 12.
89. Najem (2000), p. 218.
90. Indeed, it was analysed that the May 1994 case 'threatened to trigger the most serious political crisis in the country since he was appointed prime minister in October 1992'; *Middle East Mirror*, 9 May 1994, p. 13.
91. *Middle East Mirror*, 9 May 1994, p. 13.
92. *Middle East International*, 27 May 1994, p. 11.
93. Najem (2000), p. 218.
94. '"Cabinet Crisis" as Hariri Stays at Home', in *Summary of World Broadcasts*, 10 May 1994, ME/1993 MED/17.
95. *Middle East International*, 27 May 1994, p. 11.
96. For details, see *Middle East Mirror*, 10 May 1994, pp. 14–15; and 13 May 1994, pp. 15–16.
97. 'Prime Minister Meets Asad in Damascus, Calls Extraordinary Cabinet Meeting', in *Summary of World Broadcasts*, 17 May 1994, ME/1999 MED/11–12.

98. See *Middle East International*, 27 May 1994, p. 12.
99. For details on the revival plan, see Najem (2000), pp. 57–101.
100. *Middle East International*, 27 May 1994, p. 11; and *Middle East Mirror*, 16 May 1994, p. 11.
101. *Middle East International*, 16 December 1994, p. 11; and *Middle East Mirror*, 2 December 1994, p. 18.
102. *Middle East International*, 16 December 1994, p. 11
103. Najem (2000), p. 218.
104. In fact, US Secretary of State Warren Christopher was scheduled to visit Syria on 6 December 1994; see *Middle East Mirror*, 5 December 1994, p. 9.
105. *Middle East Mirror*, 5 December 1994, p. 9.
106. Najem (2000), p. 219.
107. See *Middle East Mirror*, 7 December 1994, p. 12.
108. 'Prime Minister Hariri Reportedly Calls off Resignation after Talks with Asad', in *Summary of World Broadcasts*, 7 December 1994, ME/2172 MED/8.
109. 'Prime Minister Hariri Resigns, Asked to Stay on to Head Caretaker Government', in *Summary of World Broadcasts*, 20 May 1995, ME/2308 MED/8. Also see *Middle East International*, 26 May 1995, p. 12.
110. *Middle East International*, 26 May 1995, p.12.
111. *Middle East Mirror*, 22 May 1995, p. 14.
112. Ibid., 25 May 1995, p. 16. For the cabinet line-up, see Najem (2000), p. 220.
113. *Middle East Mirror*, 25 May 1995, p. 16; and Najem (2000), pp. 219–220.
114. Najem (2000), p. 220.
115. Ibid.
116. *Middle East International*, 26 May 1995, p. 12.
117. For details on this process, see *Middle East Mirror*, 14 July 1995, pp. 11–13; 30 August 1995, pp. 11–12; 5 September 1995, pp. 13–14; 26 September 1995, pp. 17–18; 28 September 1995, p. 19; and 29 September 1995, pp. 16–17.
118. *Middle East International*, 3 November 1995, p. 13.
119. As for details on the process of the constitutional amendment, see *Middle East Mirror*, 2 October 1995, pp. 15–17; 11 October 1995, pp. 19–20; 16 October 1995, pp. 11–15; 17 October 1995, pp. 15–17; and 19 October 1995, pp. 13–16.
120. *Middle East International*, 22 November 1996, p. 14.
121. 'President Issues Decree Appointing New Government', in *Summary of World Broadcasts*, 9 November 1996, ME/2765 MED/13.
122. *Middle East International*, 22 November 1996, p. 14.

123. For details, see the next two subsections of this section.
124. Najem (2000), pp. 230–231.
125. For details on Emile Lahoud's career, see Venter (1998).
126. For the amendment process, see *Middle East Mirror*, 15 October 1998, p. 19; *Middle East International*, 16 October 1998, pp. 12–13; Najem (2000), p. 232; and Zisser (2001), p. 142.
127. *Middle East Mirror*, 15 October 1998, p. 19.
128. Najem (2000), p. 231.
129. For the Jumayyil statement, see *Middle East Mirror*, 28 October 1998, pp. 17–18.
130. *Middle East Mirror*, 30 November 1998, pp. 20–22.
131. Leenders (1998), p. 4.
132. For the Syrian situation, see Blanford (1999), p. 11; *Middle East Mirror*, 1 February 1999, pp. 17–18; and Zisser (2001), p. 145.
133. For the composition, see 'Prime Minister Names New Government', in *Summary of World Broadcasts*, 7 December 1998, ME/3403 MED/12.
134. *Middle East International*, 7 May 1999, pp. 16–17.
135. Ibid., 20 August 1999, p. 15.
136. Ibid, pp. 15–16.
137. After the Huss cabinet was established, Hariri indeed waited for the time ripe for his coming back to the post, with criticising Huss's economic policy; see *Middle East Mirror*, 29 March 1999, pp. 20–23.
138. For the cabinet line-up, see *The Daily Star*, 27 October 2000; and 'New Government Announced', in *Summary of World Broadcasts*, 30 October 2000, ME/3984 MED/8–9.
139. *Middle East International*, 10 November 2000, p. 11. See also *The Daily Star*, 27 October 2000.
140. *Middle East International*, 10 November 2000, p. 11.
141. Ibid.
142. Ibid. See also *The Daily Star*, 27 October 2000.
143. 'Prime Minister Tells Parliament about New Government's Policy Outlines', in *Summary of World Broadcasts*, 4 November 2000, ME/3989 MED/12–15.
144. Iskandar (2006), p. 107.
145. For details on the process of 14 March 2001, see *Middle East International*, 23 March 2001, pp. 12–13; and 'Army Deploys in Beirut to Prevent anti-Syria Demonstrations', in *Summary of World Broadcasts*, 15 March 2001, ME/4095 MED/6–7.
146. 'Prime Minister Says Syrian Presence Necessary "at Present"', in *Summary of World Broadcasts*, 30 March 2001, ME/4108 MED/13–14.

147. For details on the budget cut, see *Middle East International*, 6 April 2001, pp. 16–17.
148. For details, see *Middle East International*, 31 August 2001, pp. 11–13.
149. *Middle East International*, 22 March 2002, pp. 21–23.
150. For details on the proposal, see pp. 144–145.
151. In fact, the Saudi Fund for Development granted US$38 million in loans to the Council for Development and Reconstruction (CDR) for four road projects and a drinking water project; *Middle East International*, 5 April 2002, p. 9.
152. Blanford (2006), p. 85.
153. For details on the conference, see Iskandar (2006), pp. 118–124.
154. Ibid., p. 125.
155. Ibid.
156. See Blandford (2006), p. 87; and *Middle East International*, 2 May 2003, pp. 22–23.
157. *Middle East International*, 2 May 2003, p. 22.
158. Blanford (2006), p. 87.
159. Ibid., p. 90.
160. *Middle East International*, 10 October 2003, p. 25.
161. Gambill (2003). Also see *Middle East International*, 10 October 2003, p. 24.
162. Blanford (2006), p. 92.
163. Ibid.
164. In this respect, Hariri met Chirac in the autumn of 2003; *Middle East International*, 10 October 2003, p. 24.
165. *Middle East International*, 23 January 2004, pp. 19–20.
166. Abdelnour (2004).
167. *The Daily Star*, 30 August 2004 and 4 September 2004.
168. Blanford (2006), pp. 106–108.
169. For details on the formation and composition of the Bristol Gathering, see Blanford (2006), p. 116–117; *The Daily Star*, 23 September 2004; and Harris (2006), p. 301. For the Democratic Renewal Movement, Nasib Lahoud founded it in mid-July 2001. For details, see *The Daily Star*, 16 July 2001; and *Middle East International*, 10 August 2001, p. 14.
170. Blanford (2006), p. 117.
171. For details on the process leading to the withdrawal, see Quilty (2005), pp. 4–7. Also see *The Daily Star*, 27 April 2005.
172. Nasrallah (1994), p. 138.
173. Ibid.
174. Najem (2000), p. 146. Also see *EIU Country Report: Lebanon*, 3rd quarter, 1996, p. 20.

175. Ibid.
176. For the data by the council, see Saidi (1999), p. 363.
177. For the *al-Nahar* report, see Tinaoui (1994), p. 108.
178. Tinaoui mentioned Syrian workers' average earnings per month at home as about $50, compared to some $200 per month in Lebanon; see Tinaoui (1994), p. 109.
179. For details on the process, see *Middle East Economic Digest*, 7 July 2000, p. 10; and 21 July 2000, p. 9.
180. *The Daily Star*, 5 December 2000.
181. *EIU Country Report: Lebanon*, January 2001, p. 28.
182. Najem (2000), p. 181.
183. Baroudi (1998), pp. 534–535.
184. Najem (2000), p. 35.
185. For details, see Gambill (2001a).
186. *Middle East Mirror*, 15 December 1993, pp. 22–23.
187. Baroudi (1998), p. 538.
188. 'Cabinet Restates Ban on Demonstrations', in *Summary of World Broadcasts*, 19 July 1995, ME/2359 MED/14.
189. *Middle East Mirror*, 20 July 1995, pp. 10–13.
190. For details on the process leading to the conclusion, see Baroudi (1998), pp. 538–543.
191. For details, see Gambill (2001a).
192. Baroudi (1998), p. 543.
193. 'New Labour Federation Head Elected; Outgoing Head Rejects Results', in *Summary of World Broadcasts*, 26 April 1997, ME/2903 MED/6–7.
194. Baroudi (1998), p. 544.
195. See Young (1998), p. 6.
196. For details on the event, see *Middle East International*, 11 June 2004, pp. 19–21. Needless to say, the other and more persuasive reason behind the non-intervention by the Syrian army was the mounting Lebanese criticism against its presence in those days.
197. Mallat (2000), p. 159.
198. *Middle East Mirror*, 29 March 1994, pp. 11–13; and 7 April 1994, pp. 18–20.
199. *Middle East Mirror*, 8 April 1994, pp. 14–16; and 12 April 1994, pp. 12–14.
200. Young (1998), p. 6.
201. See Hudson (1999), pp. 31–32; and 'New Licences for Political and News Programs', in *Summary of World Broadcasts*, 19 September 1996, ME/2721 MED/18. Although the NBN was still in preparation for its operation at that time, it was granted a licence; Young (1998), p. 6.

202. 'Cabinet Revokes Exception Given to Hezbollah Radio, TV over Licences', in *Summary of World Broadcasts*, 20 September 1996, ME/2722 MED/11.
203. 'Hezbollah Criticizes Cabinet's "Pompous" Decisions on News Broadcasts', in *Summary of World Broadcasts*, 21 September 1996, ME/2723 MED/3.
204. This statement does not deny that both Lebanon and Syria had common interests, such as Israel's full withdrawal from southern Lebanon.
205. Harris (1996), p. 315.
206. Ehteshami and Hinnebusch (1997), p. 148.
207. Hinnebusch (1998), p. 156.
208. Ehteshami and Hinnebusch (1997), p. 148.
209. Muir (1992), pp. 3–4.
210. Ehteshami and Hinnebusch (1997), p. 149.
211. Harik (1997), p. 255.
212. Ibid.
213. Muir (1993), p. 3.
214. Harik (1997), p. 255.
215. Ehteshami and Hinnebusch (1997), p. 150.
216. Ibid.
217. *Middle East International,* 28 August 1993, p. 5.
218. For a chronology about the escalation process, see *Middle East International*, 26 April 1996, p. 4.
219. Trendle (1996), p. 5.
220. For details on Hariri's international activities, see 'Lebanese PM in London Says Major "Understands the Lebanese Point of View"', in *Summary of World Broadcasts*, 18 April 1996, ME/2589 MED/9; 'Lebanese PM Says Saudi Leaders Making Efforts to Stop Israeli Attack', in *Summary of World Broadcasts*, 18 April 1996, ME/2589 MED/9–10; and 'Saudi Defence Minister on Talks with Visiting Lebanese PM', in *Summary of World Broadcasts*, 18 April 1996, ME/2589 MED/10.
221. *Middle East International*, 10 May 1996, p. 6.
222. Salem (1996), p. 76.
223. Hariri, along with Foreign Minister Buwayz, met Asad on 13 April 1996; 'Syrian President Holds Talks with Lebanese Prime Minister on Israeli Action', in *Summary of World Broadcasts*, 15 April 1996, ME/2586 MED/4. In addition, Hirawi received a telephone call from Asad on 11 April; 'Lebanese, Syrian Presidents Confer on How to React to Israeli Raids', in *Summary of World Broadcasts*, 13 April 1996, ME/2585 MED/15.
224. For Lebanese solidarity, see *Middle East International*, 26 April 1996, pp. 4–5; and Salem (1996), pp. 76–77.
225. Jaber (1997), p. 194.

226. Ibid., p. 193.
227. *Middle East International*, 26 April 1996, p. 7.
228. Ibid., 10 May 1996, p. 6.
229. Harik (1997), p. 261.
230. For the Hariri assurance, see Blanford (2001), p. 9.
231. For the statement by Hariri, see 'Prime Minister Says Syrian Presence Necessary "at Present"', in *Summary of World Broadcasts*, 30 March 2001, ME/4108 MED/13–14.
232. *Middle East International*, 20 April 2001, p. 11. In February 2001, US ambassador to Lebanon David Satterfield had already warned Hariri that Hizbullah's further cross-border attacks would badly affect the Lebanese economy and the perception of potential investors; see *Middle East International*, 23 February 2001, p. 14.
233. 'Lebanese Prime Minister Denies He Said He Was Ready for Peace Treaty with Israel', in *Summary of World Broadcasts*, 13 February 1993, ME/1612 A/6.
234. In fact, Israeli Foreign Minister Peres asked US Secretary of State Christopher to persuade Asad into reactivating the peace process; see 'Peres Reportedly Asks US Secretary of State to "Pressure" Syria on Peace Process', in *Summary of World Broadcasts*, 18 February 1993, ME/1616/A1.
235. Norton (1997), p. 10.
236. Zisser (2001), p. 146.
237. Norton (1997), p. 12.
238. Ibid.
239. Ibid.
240. For the Syrian criticism, see 'Syrian Press Says Israel Trying to Separate Syrian and Lebanese Tracks', in *Summary of World Broadcasts*, 29 July 1996, ME/2676 MED/7–8; 'Syrian Radio Commentary Stresses Syria's Central Role in Peace Process', in *Summary of World Broadcasts*, 26 July 1996, ME/2676 MED/8; 'Syrian Radio Criticizes Netanyahu's "Lebanon First" Proposal', in *Summary of World Broadcasts*, 30 July 1996, ME/2677 MED/12–13; and 'Syrian Press Says Netanyahu Trying to Set a "Deadly Trap" with Lebanon First Proposal', in *Summary of World Broadcasts*, ME/2677 MED/13.
241. Malik (1997), pp. 94–95.
242. 'Lebanese Foreign Minister Says Israeli Withdrawal Offer "Vague"', in *Summary of World Broadcasts*, 29 July 1996, ME/2676 MED/6.
243. 'Lebanese PM Meets US Coordinator in Brussels, Says Not Told of "Lebanon First" Proposal', in *Summary of World Broadcasts*, 3 August 1996, ME/2681 MED/7.

244. In fact, Berri objected to the separation of Lebanese and Syrian peace tracks; 'Lebanese Speaker Birri Comments on Israeli Withdrawal Offer', in *Summary of World Broadcasts*, 30 July 1996, ME/2677 MED/12. Nasrallah, leader of Hizbullah, rejected not only the proposal, but also any accords between Lebanon and Israel; 'Hezbollah Leader Rules out any Arrangements with Israel', in *Summary of World Broadcasts*, 31 July 1996, ME/2678 MED/8.
245. Najem (2000), p. 225. For details on the visit, see *Middle East Mirror*, 16 December 1996, pp. 15–17; and 17 December 1996, pp. 15–19.
246. For the Syrian attitude, see 'Radio Stresses Syrian and Lebanese Tracks Cannot Be Separated', in *Summary of World Broadcasts*, 11 February 1997, ME/2840 MED/4–5.
247. For the French statement, see 'Prime Minister Denies France to Send Troops to Lebanon', in *Summary of World Broadcasts*, 13 February 1997, ME/2842 MED/7.
248. *Middle East International*, 16 January 1998, p. 8.
249. 'Lebanon Leaders Reportedly Vow to Deploy Army if Israel Withdraws Forces', in *Summary of World Broadcasts*, 17 January 1998, ME/3127 MED/13.
250. Hajjar (1999), p. 124.
251. *Middle East International*, 8 March 2002, pp. 14–15.
252. Ibid., p. 15.
253. Ibid.
254. Ibid.
255. Ibid., 5 April 2002, pp. 7–8.

Chapter 4. Lebanon after the End of Syrian Hegemony (since 2005)

1. Although there has been no official census in Lebanon except the one conducted in 1932 during the French mandate, the population as of 2005 was estimated to be 4.2 million, and proportions of the four major sects were estimated as follows: Maronites, 24 per cent; Sunnis, 21 per cent; Shi'as, 32 per cent; and Druzes, 7 per cent. For details, see *Le Monde*, 27/28 February 2005.
2. *The Daily Star*, 4 December 2008.
3. Sulayman was elected when almost all of the Lebanese parliament members at the time, i.e. 118 of 127, voted for him; *Al-Nahar*, 26 May 2008.
4. *The Daily Star*, 9 September 2011.
5. Ibid., 14 April 2011.

6. Ibid., 1 December 2011.
7. For details, see *Al-Sharq Al-Awsat*, 13 December 2007.
8. *The Daily Star*, 8 August 2009.
9. Ibid., 1 April 2010.
10. Ibid., 23 April 2012 and 25 April 2012.
11. Ibid., 5 September 2012.
12. Ibid., 22 June 2005.
13. Ibid., 1 July 2005.
14. Harris (2006), p. 307.
15. For details on the cabinet line-up, see *The Daily Star*, 20 July 2005.
16. For the assassination attempt, see *The Daily Star*, 13 July 2005.
17. 'The Lebanese Syndicate of Agriculture estimate[d] that losses could reach $1.5 million ($300,000 per day) worth of agricultural goods since Syrian customs officials began security inspections of Lebanese trucks more than two weeks ago'; *The Daily Star*, 12 July 2005.
18. *The Daily Star*, 1 August 2005.
19. Ibid., 2 August 2005.
20. Ibid., 22 May 2008.
21. Ibid., 29 May 2008.
22. For details on the cabinet line-up, see *Al-Nahar*, 12 July 2008.
23. It was not until 12 July 2008 that Lebanon and Syria formally agreed to establish diplomatic ties; *The Daily Star*, 14 July 2008. Three months later, on 15 October, a joint statement on the establishment of Syrian–Lebanese diplomatic ties was signed; *The Daily Star*, 16 October 2008.
24. See *The Daily Star*, 31 August 2005; Harris (2006), p. 309; and Harris (2009), p. 68. Later, in April 2009, the four generals were released on the ground of insufficient evidence; *The Daily Star*, 30 April 2009.
25. Harris (2006), pp. 310–311.
26. Harris (2009), p. 68.
27. *The Daily Star*, 1 November 2005.
28. Ibid., 2 November 2005.
29. Ibid., 11 November 2005.
30. Harris (2009), p. 68.
31. *The Daily Star*, 13 December 2005.
32. Ibid., 11 November 2006.
33. Ibid., 13 November 2006.
34. Ibid., 14 November 2006.
35. Harris (2009), p. 76.
36. *The Daily Star*, 13 December 2006.
37. For one of the statements by the Syrian regime, see *The Daily Star*, 11 May 2007.

38. *The Daily Star*, 28 November 2008.
39. Ibid., 1 December 2008.
40. Ibid., 2 March 2009.
41. *Al-Sharq Al-Awsat*, 2 March 2009.
42. Regarding this point, '[t]he Russians later indicated that Syrian officers transferred Russian missiles to [Hizbullah] during the April 2005 Syrian withdrawal from Lebanon'; Harris (2009), p. 71.
43. For details, see *The Daily Star*, 29 July 2005 and 1 August 2005.
44. For the contents of the policy statement and the process of its approval, see *The Daily Star*, 5 August 2008 and 13 August 2008.
45. For details, see a report published in *The Daily Star*, 14 January 2012.
46. For details on the Syrian attitude, see Ziadeh (2011), pp. 112–114.
47. UN Secretary-General Ban told on 7 May 2007 that weapons regularly reached Hizbullah across the Lebanese–Syrian border; *The Daily Star*, 9 May 2007.
48. For details on the cabinet position, see *The Daily Star*, 14 July 2006.
49. *The Daily Star*, 9 May 2008.
50. Ibid., 12 May 2008.
51. For details on the deals between the United States and Lebanon on 6 October 2008, see *The Daily Star*, 7 October 2008 and 8 October 2008.
52. Schenker (2009), p. 227.
53. Ibid., p. 228.
54. When Siniora met German Chancellor Angela Merkel on 5 September 2007, he asked for German assistance to help arm and train the Lebanese army; *The Daily Star*, 6 September 2007.
55. *The Daily Star*, 18 December 2008.
56. *Al-Sharq Al-Awsat*, 21 January 2009.
57. For details on the elections result, see *The Daily Star*, 9 June 2009; *Al-Nahar*, 9 June 2009; *L' Orient Le Jour*, 9 June 2009; and *Al-Safir*, 9 June 2009.
58. *L' Orient Le Jour*, 27/28 June 2009; and *The Daily Star*, 29 June 2009.
59. For details on the cabinet line-up, see *The Daily Star*, 10 November 2009; and *L' Orient Le Jour*, 10 November 2009.
60. *L' Orient Le Jour*, 11 December 2009.
61. *The Daily Star*, 21 April 2010.
62. Ibid., 1 June 2010.
63. Ibid., 7 September 2010.
64. Ibid., 31 July 2010.
65. *Al-Safir*, 10 August 2010.
66. *The Daily Star*, 1 December 2010.

67. *L' Orient Le Jour*, 11/12 December 2010.
68. Hizbullah's fierce hostility towards the STL might have modified the Saudi stance on the tribunal in terms of stability in Lebanon.
69. *L' Orient Le Jour*, 13 January 2011.
70. *The Daily Star*, 26 January 2011.
71. Ibid., 27 January 2011.
72. For details on the cabinet line-up, see *The Daily Star* 14 June 2011; *L' Orient Le Jour*, 14 June 2011; and *Al-Safir*, 14 June 2011.
73. It is worthwhile to note that a report in early September 2012 analyses Prime Minister Miqati and President Sulayman's decision to distance themselves from Damascus; *The Daily Star*, 4 September 2012.
74. *The Daily Star*, 5 August 2011.
75. Ibid., 14 November 2011; and *L' Orient Le Jour*, 14 November 2011.
76. *The Daily Star*, 27 February 2012.
77. Ibid., 13 January 2012.
78. For details on the cabinet's decision, the army's deployment and Lebanese reactions, see *The Daily Star*, 10 July 2012; 11 July 2012; and 16 July 2012.
79. *The Daily Star*, 4 September 2012.
80. Ibid., 4 August 2012.

BIBLIOGRAPHY

Books and Articles

Abdelnour, Ziad K. (2004), 'Syria and the Presidential Succession in Lebanon', *Middle East Intelligence Bulletin* (www.meib.org, accessed on 18 October 2004), February–March.

Abukhalil, As'ad (1990), 'Syria and the Shiites: Al-Asad's Policy in Lebanon', *Third World Quarterly*, 12:2, April, 1–20.

Abukhalil, As'ad (1994), 'Determinants and Characteristics of Syrian Policy in Lebanon', in Deirdre Collings, ed., *Peace for Lebanon?: From War to Reconstruction*, Boulder, CO and London, Lynne Rienner Publishers, 123–135.

Abul-Husn, Latif (1998), *The Lebanese Conflict: Looking Inward*, Boulder, CO and London, Lynne Rienner Publishers.

Ajami, Fouad (1986), *The Vanished Imam: Musa al Sadr and the Shia of Lebanon*, London, I.B.Tauris Publishers.

Avi-Ran, Reuven (1991), *The Syrian Involvement in Lebanon since 1975*, Boulder, CO, San Francisco and Oxford, Westview Press.

Baaklini, Abdo, Guilian Denoeux and Robert Springborg (1999), *Legislative Politics in the Arab World: The Resurgence of Democratic Institutions*, Boulder, CO and London, Lynne Rienner Publishers.

Baroudi, Sami E. (1998), 'Economic Conflict in Postwar Lebanon: State–Labor Relations between 1992 and 1997', *The Middle East Journal*, 52:4, Autumn, 531–550.

Blanford, Nicholas (1999), 'All Change in Lebanon', *The Middle East*, February, 11–12.

Blanford, Nicholas (2001), 'Shebaa Farms and Beyond', *Middle East Insight*, September–October, 7–10 and 80.

Blanford, Nicholas (2006), *Killing Mr Lebanon: The Assassination of Rafik Hariri and its Impact on the Middle East*, London and New York, I.B.Tauris Publishers.

Brynen, Rex (1990), *Sanctuary and Survival: The PLO in Lebanon*, Boulder, CO and San Francisco, Westview Press and London, Pinter Publishers.

Chalala, Elie (1985), 'Syrian Policy in Lebanon, 1976–1984: Moderate Goals and Pragmatic Means', *Journal of Arab Affairs*, 4:1, Spring, 67–87.

Chami, Saade N. (1992), 'Economic Performance in a War-Economy: The Case of Lebanon', *The Canadian Journal of Development Studies*, 13:3, 325–336.

Charbel, Ghassan (2011), *Aina Kunta fi al-Harbi? (Where were you during the war?)*, Beirut, Riad El-Bayyes Books S.A.R.L.

Cobban, Helena (1978), 'Lebanon: The Tangled Wreck', *Middle East International*, November, 15–16.

David, Steven R. (1991), 'Explaining Third World Alignment', *World Politics*, 43:2, January, 233–256.

Dawisha, Adeed I. (1980), *Syria and the Lebanese Crisis*, London and Basingstoke, The Macmillan Press.

Dawisha, Adeed (1984), 'The Motives of Syria's Involvement in Lebanon', *The Middle East Journal*, 38:2, Spring, 228–236.

Deeb, Marius (1980), *The Lebanese Civil War*, New York, Praeger Publishers.

Deeb, Marius (1988), 'Shia Movements in Lebanon: Their Formation, Ideology, Social Basis, and Links with Iran and Syria', *Third World Quarterly*, 10:2, April, 683–698.

Deeb, Marius (1989), 'The External Dimension of the Conflict in Lebanon: The Role of Syria', *Journal of South Asian and Middle Eastern Studies*, 12:3, Spring, 37–52.

Dessouki, Ali Hillal (1988), 'Security in a Fractured State', in *Prospects for Security in the Mediterranean*, Adelphi Papers, 230, London, International Institute for Strategic Studies, 14–20.

Devlin, John F. (1988), 'Syria and Lebanon', *Current History*, February, 77–80, 90 and 96.

Ehteshami, Anoushiravan and Raymond A. Hinnebusch (1997), *Syria and Iran: Middle Powers in a Penetrated Regional System*, London and New York, Routledge.

Ehteshami, Anoushiravan and Raymond Hinnebusch (2002), 'Conclusion: Patterns of Policy', in Anoushiravan Ehteshami and Raymond Hinnebusch, eds, *The Foreign Policies of Middle East States*, Boulder, CO and London, Lynne Rienner Publishers, 335–350.

Ellis, Kail C. (2002), 'The Regional Struggle for Lebanon', in Kail C. Ellis, ed., *Lebanon's Second Republic: Prospects for the Twenty-first Century*, Gainesville, FL, University Press of Florida, 25–51.

Evron, Yair (1987), *War and Intervention in Lebanon: The Israeli–Syrian Deterrence Dialogue*, London and Sydney, Croom Helm.

Faksh, Mahmud A. (1992), 'Syria's Role and Objectives in Lebanon', *Mediterranean Quarterly*, Spring, 81–95.

Gambill, Gary C. (2001a), 'Syrian Workers in Lebanon: The Other Occupation', *Middle East Intelligence Bulletin* (www.meib.org, accessed on 1 November 2001), February.

Gambill, Gary C. (2001b), 'Damascus Co-opts the Phalange', *Middle East Intelligence Bulletin* (www.meib.org, accessed on 1 November 2001), October.

Gambill, Gary C. (2003), 'Hariri's Dilemma', *Middle East Intelligence Bulletin*, (www.meib.org, accessed on 18 October 2004), November.

Gambill, Gary C. and Bassam Endrawos (2002), 'The Assassination of Elie Hobeika', *Middle East Intelligence Bulletin* (www.meib.org, accessed on 11 February 2002), January.

Gambill, Gary C. and Elie Abou Aoun (2000), 'Special Report: How Syria Orchestrates Lebanon's Elections?', *Middle East Intelligence Bulletin* (www.meib.org, accessed on 17 August 2000), August.

Gause, F. Gregory III (1992), 'Sovereignty, Statecraft and Stability in the Middle East', *The Journal of International Affairs*, 45:2, Winter, 441–469.

Gause, F. Gregory III (1997), 'Sovereignty and its Challengers: War in Middle Eastern Inter-State Politics', in Paul Salem, ed., *Conflict Resolution in the Arab World: Selected Essays*, Beirut, The American University of Beirut, 197–215.

Gerges, Fawaz A. (1997), 'Lebanon', in Yezid Sayigh and Avi Shlaim, eds, *The Cold War and the Middle East*, Oxford, Clarendon Press and New York, Oxford University Press, 77–101.

Ghadbian, Najib (2001), 'The New Asad: Dynamics of Continuity and Change in Syria', *The Middle East Journal*, 55:4, Autumn, 624–641.

Gordon, David C. (1983), *The Republic of Lebanon: Nation in Jeopardy*, Boulder, CO, Westview Press, and London and Canberra, Croom Helm.

Goria, Wade R. (1985), *Sovereignty and Leadership in Lebanon 1943–1976*, London, Ithaca Press.

Haddad, Wadi D. (1985), *Lebanon: The Politics of Revolving Doors*, New York, Praeger Publishers.

Hajjar, Sami G. (1999), 'The Israel–Syria Track', *Middle East Policy*, 6:3, 112–130.

Hamdan, Kamal (1997), *Le Conflit Libanais: Communautés Religieuses, Classes Sociales et Identité Nationale*, Éditions Garnet France.

Hanf, Theodor (1993), *Coexistence in Wartime Lebanon: Decline of a State and Rise of a Nation*, London, The Centre for Lebanese Studies and I.B.Tauris Publishers.

Harik, Judith Palmer (1997), 'Syrian Foreign Policy and State/Resistance Dynamics in Lebanon', *Studies in Conflict and Terrorism*, 20:3, 249–265.

Harik, Judith Palmer (1998), 'Democracy (Again) Derailed: Lebanon's Ta'if Paradox', in Bahgat Korany, Rex Brynen and Paul Noble, *Political Liberalization and Democratization in the Arab World*, Boulder, CO and London, Lynne Rienner Publishers, 127–155.

Harknett, Richard J. and Jeffrey A. Vandenberg (1997), 'Alignment Theory and Interrelated Threats: Jordan and the Persian Gulf Crisis', *Security Studies*, 6:3, Spring, 112–153.

Harris, William (1985), 'Syria in Lebanon', *Middle East Report*, 15:6, July–August, 9–14.

Harris, William (1988), 'Syria in Lebanon', *Third World Affairs*, 90–106.

Harris, William (1996), *Faces of Lebanon: Sects, Wars, and Global Extensions*, Princeton, NJ, Markus Wiener Publishers.

Harris, William (2006), *The New Face of Lebanon: History's Revenge*, Princeton, NJ, Markus Wiener Publishers.

Harris, William (2009), 'Lebanon's Roller Coaster Ride', in Barry Rubin, ed., *Lebanon: Liberation, Conflict, and Crisis*, New York, Palgrave Macmillan, 63–82.

Hinnebusch, Raymond A. (1986), 'Syrian Policy in Lebanon and the Palestinians', *Arab Studies Quarterly*, 8:1, 1–20.

Hinnebusch, Raymond A. (1990), *Authoritarian Power and State Formation in Ba'thist Syria: Army, Party and Peasant*, Boulder, CO, San Francisco and Oxford, Westview Press.

Hinnebusch, Raymond A. (1996), 'Does Syria Want Peace?: Syrian Policy in the Syrian–Israeli Negotiations', *Journal of Palestinian Studies*, 26:1, Autumn, 42–57.

Hinnebusch, Raymond (1998), 'Pax-Syriana?: The Origins, Causes and Consequences of Syria's Role in Lebanon', *Mediterranean Politics*, 3:1, Summer, 137–160.

Hinnebusch, Raymond (2001), *Syria: Revolution From Above*, London and New York, Routledge.

Hinnebusch, Raymond (2002a), 'Introduction: The Analytical Framework', in Anoushiravan Ehteshami and Raymond Hinnebusch, eds, *The Foreign Policies of Middle East States*, Boulder, CO and London, Lynne Rienner Publishers, 1–27.

Hinnebusch, Raymond (2002b), 'The Foreign Policy of Syria', in Anoushiravan Ehteshami and Raymond Hinnebusch, eds, *The Foreign Policies of Middle East States*, Boulder, CO and London, Lynne Rienner Publishers, 141–165.

Hinnebusch, Raymond (2006), 'Syria: Defying the Hegemon', in Rick Fawn and Raymond Hinnebusch, eds, *The Iraq War: Causes and Consequences*, Boulder, CO and London, Lynne Rienner Publishers, 129–142.

Hitti, Nassif (1989), *The Foreign Policy of Lebanon: Lessons and Prospects for the Forgotten Dimension*, Papers on Lebanon, 9, Oxford, Centre for the Lebanese Studies.

Hoss, Salim (1984), *Lebanon: Agony and Peace*, Beirut, Islamic Center for Information and Development.

Hottinger, Arnold (1966), 'Zu'ama in Historical Perspective', in Leonard Binder, ed., *Politics in Lebanon*, New York, London and Sydney, John Wiley, 85–105.

Hudson, Michael C. (1988), 'The United States' Involvement in Lebanon', in Halim Barakat, ed., *Toward a Viable Lebanon*, London and Sydney, Croom Helm, 210–231.

Hudson, Michael C. (1999), 'Lebanon after Ta'if: Another Reform Opportunity Lost?', *Arab Studies Quarterly*, 21:1, Winter, 27–40.

Iskandar, Marwan (2006), *Rafiq Hariri and the Fate of Lebanon*, London and San Francisco, Saqi Books.

Jaber, Hala (1997), *Hezbollah: Born with a Vengeance*, New York, Columbia University Press.

Johnson, Michael (1986), *Class & Client in Beirut: The Sunni Muslim Community and the Lebanese State 1840–1985*, London and Atlantic Highlands, NJ, Ithaca Press.

Joumblatt, Kamal (1982), *I Speak for Lebanon*, London, Zed Press.

Jureidini, Paul A. and R. D. McLaurin (1984), 'Lebanon after the War of 1982', in Edward E. Azar *et al.*, *The Emergence of New Lebanon: Fantasy or Reality?*, New York, Praeger Publishers, 3–35.

Kassir, Samir (1994), *La Guerre du Liban: De la Dissension Nationale au Conflit Régional*, 2nd edition, Paris, Karthala and Beirut, Cermoc.

Keohane, Robert O. and Joseph S. Nye (2001), *Power and Interdependence*, 3rd edition, New York, San Francisco and Boston, Longman.

Khazen, Farid El (1998), *Lebanon's First Postwar Parliamentary Election, 1992: An Imposed Choice*, Prospects for Lebanon, 8, Oxford, Centre for Lebanese Studies.

Khazen, Farid El (2000a), *The Breakdown of the State in Lebanon: 1967–1976*, London and New York, I.B.Tauris Publishers.

Khazen, Farid El (2000b), *Ịntihābāt Lubnān mā baada al-Harbi, 1992, 1996, 2000: Dimqrātīya bilā Khiyāri (Lebanese Elections after the War, 1992, 1996 and 2000: Democracy without Choice)*, Beirut, Dār al-Nahār.

Khazen, Farid El (2001), 'Lebanon: Independent No More', *The Middle East Quarterly*, 8:1, 43–50.

Koury, Enver M. (1976), *The Crisis in the Lebanese System: Confessionalism and Chaos*, Washington DC, American Enterprise Institute for Public Policy Research.

Laurent, Annie (1991), 'A War between Brothers: The Army–Lebanese Forces Showdown in East Beirut', *The Beirut Review*, 1, Spring, 88–101.

Lawson, Fred H. (1996), *Why Syria Goes to War: Thirty Years of Confrontation*, Ithaca and London, Cornell University Press.

Leenders, Reinoud (1998), 'Lebanon's Democratic Coup', *Middle East International*, 11 December 1998, 4–6.

Lijphart, Arend (1969), 'Consociational Democracy', *World Politics*, 21:2, January, 207–225.

Lijphart, Arend (1977), *Democracy in Plural Societies: A Comparative Exploration*, New Haven and London, Yale University Press.

Malik, Habib C. (1997), *Between Damascus and Jerusalem: Lebanon and Middle East Peace*, Washington DC, The Washington Institute for Near East Policy.

Mallat, Chibli (2000), 'Trouble with the Neighbours', *Index on Censorship*, 5, 158–160.

Ma'oz, Moshe (1988), *Asad: The Sphinx of Damascus*, London, George Weidenfeld & Nicolson.

Ma'oz, Moshe and Avner Yaniv (1986), 'On a Short Leash: Syria and the PLO', in Moshe Ma'oz and Avner Yaniv, eds, *Syria under Assad: Domestic Constraints and Regional Risks*, London and Sydney, Croom Helm, 191–205.

McLaurin, R. D. (1984), 'Lebanon and its Army: Past, Present, and Future', in Edward E. Azar *et al.*, *The Emergence of New Lebanon: Fantasy or Reality?*, New York, Praeger Publishers, 79–113.

McLaurin, R. D. (1989), 'The PLO and the Arab Fertile Crescent', in Augustus Richard Norton and Martin H. Greenberg, eds, *The International Relations of the Palestine Liberation Organization*, Carbondale and Edwardsville, Southern Illinois University Press, 12–58.

Ménargues, Alain (2004), *Les Secrets de la Guerre du Liban: Du Coup d'État de Bachir Gémayel aux Massacres des Camps Palestiniens*, Paris, Éditions Albin Michel.

Montagu, Caroline (2002), 'A Peace in the Offing?', *Middle East International*, 8 March, 20–21.

Morgenthau, Hans (1948), *Politics among Nations: The Struggle for Power and Peace*, New York, Alfred Knopf.

Muir, Jim (1989), 'Lebanon's Shi'ites Forced to Call a Truce', *Middle East International*, 3 February, 3–4.

Muir, Jim (1991), 'The Syrian–Lebanese Treaty: Grounds for Concern or Hope?', *Middle East International*, 31 May, 3–4.

Muir, Jim (1992), 'The Slaying of Abbas Musawi Portends a Spiral of Violence', *Middle East International*, 21 February, 3–4.

Muir, Jim (1993), 'Rabin's Revenge Exacts an Appalling Toll', *Middle East International*, 6 August, 3–4.

Najem, Tom (1998), *The Collapse and Reconstruction of Lebanon*, Durham Middle East Paper, 59, Durham, The University of Durham, The Centre for Middle Eastern and Islamic Studies.

Najem, Tom Pierre (2000), *Lebanon's Renaissance: The Political Economy of Reconstruction*, Reading, Ithaca Press.

Nasrallah, Fida (1993), 'The Treaty of Brotherhood, Cooperation and Coordination: An Assessment', in Youssef M. Choueiri, ed., *State and Society in Syria and Lebanon*, Exeter, University of Exeter Press, 103–111.

Nasrallah, Fida (1994), 'Syria after Ta'if: Lebanon and the Lebanese in Syrian Politics', in Eberhard Kienle, ed., *Contemporary Syria: Liberalization between Cold War and Cold Peace*, London, British Academic Press, 132–138.

Nizameddin, Talal (2006), 'The Political Economy of Lebanon under Rafiq Hariri', *The Middle East Journal*, 60:1, Winter, 95–114.

Norton, Augustus Richard (1991), 'Lebanon after Ta'if: Is the Civil War Over?, *The Middle East Journal*, 45:3, 457–473.

Norton, Augustus Richard (1997), 'Lebanon: With Friends Like These…', *Current History*, January, 6–12.

Norton, Augustus Richard (1998), 'Hizballah: From Radicalism to Pragmatism?', *Middle East Policy*, 5:4, January, 147–158.

Norton, Augustus Richard (1999), 'Lebanon's Conundrum', *Arab Studies Quarterly*, 21:1, Winter, 41–53.

Norton, Augustus Richard and Jillian Schwedler (1994), 'Swiss Soldiers, Ta'if Clocks, and Early Elections: Toward a Happy Ending?', in Deirdre Collings, ed., *Peace for Lebanon?: From War to Reconstruction*, Boulder, CO and London, Lynne Rienner Publishers, 45–65.

Odeh, B. J. (1985), *Lebanon: Dynamics of Conflict*, London, Zed Books.

Pakradouni, Karim (1984), *La Paix Manquée: Le Mandat d'Elias Sarkis (1976–1982)*, Éditions Fiches du Monde Arabe.

Perthes, Volker (2001), 'Syrian Regional Policy under Bashar al-Asad: Realignment or Economic Rationalization?', *Middle East Report*, 220, Fall, 36–41.

Peteet, Julie (1996), 'From Refugees to Minority: Palestinians in Post-War Lebanon', *Middle East Report*, 200, July–September, 27–30.

Petran, Tabitha (1987), *The Struggle over Lebanon*, New York, Monthly Review Press.

Phares, Walid (1995), *Lebanese Christian Nationalism: The Rise and Fall of an Ethnic Resistance*, Boulder, CO and London, Lynne Rienner Publishers.

Picard, Elizabeth (2000), 'The Political Economy of Civil War in Lebanon', in Steven Heydemann, ed., *War, Institution, and Social Change in the Middle East*, Berkeley and Los Angeles, CA and London, University of California Press, 292–322.

Pipes, Daniel (1990), *Greater Syria: The History of an Ambition*, New York and Oxford, Oxford University Press.

Pogany, Istvan (1987), *The Arab League and Peacekeeping in the Lebanon*, Aldershot, Avebury.

Pölling, Sylvia (1994), 'Investment Law No. 10: Which Future for the Private Sector?', in Eberhard Kienle, ed., *Contemporary Syria: Liberalization between Cold War and Cold Peace*, London, British Academic Press, 14–25.

Quilty, Jim (2005), 'Lebanon's Interregnum', *Middle East International*, 29 April, 4–7.

Rabil, Robert G. (2006), *Syria, the United States, and the War on Terror in the Middle East*, Westport, CT and London, Praeger Security International.

Rabinovich, Itamar (1984), *The War for Lebanon*, Ithaca, NY and London, Cornell University Press.

Rabinovich, Itamar (1987), 'Syria and Lebanon', *Current History*, February, 61–64 and 89.

Ranstorp, Magnus (1997), *Hizb'allah in Lebanon: The Politics of the Western Hostage Crisis*, Basingstoke and London, Macmillan Press and New York, St. Martin's Press.

Saidi, Nasser H. (1999), *Growth, Destruction and the Challenges of Reconstruction: Macroeconomic Essays on Lebanon*, Beirut, The Lebanese Center for Policy Studies.

Salem, Elie A. (1992), 'A Decade of Challenges: Lebanon 1982–1992', *The Beirut Review*, 3, Spring, 17–37.

Salem, Elie A. (1995), *Violence and Diplomacy in Lebanon: The Troubled Years, 1982–1988*, London and New York, I.B.Tauris Publishers.

Salem, Mohammed Anis (1982), 'Peace Signals from Fez', *Middle East International*, 17 September, 12–13.

Salem, Paul E. (1991), 'Two Years of Living Dangerously: General Awn and the Precarious Rise of Lebanon's Second Republic', *The Beirut Review*, 1, Spring, 62–87.

Salem, Paul (1994), 'Reflections on Lebanon's Foreign Policy', in Deirdre Collings, ed., *Peace for Lebanon? From War to Reconstruction*, Boulder, CO and London, Lynne Rienner Publishers, 69–82.

Salem, Paul (1996), 'In the Wake of "Grapes of Wrath": Meeting the Challenge', in Rosemary Hollis and Nadim Shehadi, eds, *Lebanon on Hold: Implications for Middle East Peace*, London, The Royal Institute of International Affairs, 75–78.

Salibi, Kamal S. (1976), *Crossroads to Civil War: Lebanon 1958–1976*, Delmar, NY, Caravan Books.

Schenker, David (2009), 'America and the Lebanon Issue', in Barry Rubin, ed., *Lebanon: Liberation, Conflict, and Crisis*, New York, Palgrave Macmillan, 213–237.

Seale, Patrick (1988), *Asad: The Struggle for the Middle East*, Berkeley, Los Angeles and London, University of California Press.

Seale, Patrick (1997), 'Syria', in Yezid Sayigh and Avi Shlaim, eds, *The Cold War and the Middle East*, Oxford, Clarendon Press and New York, Oxford University Press, 48–76.

Sela, Avraham (1998), *The Decline of the Arab–Israeli Conflict: Middle East Politics and the Quest for Regional Order*, Albany, NY, State University of New York Press.

Sirreiyeh, Hussein (1989), *Lebanon: Dimensions of Conflict*, Adelphi Papers, 243, London, The International Institute for Strategic Studies.

Solh, Raghid El (2004), *Lebanon and Arabism: National Identity and State Formation*, London and New York, I.B.Tauris Publishers.

Starr, Joyce R. (1984), 'Lebanon's Economy: The Costs of Protracted Violence', in Edward E. Azar *et al.*, *The Emergence of a New Lebanon: Fantasy or Reality?*, New York, Praeger Publishers, 69–78.

Taylor, Alan R. (1982), *The Arab Balance of Power*, Syracuse, NY, Syracuse University Press.

Thompson, Eric V. (2002), 'Will Syria Have to Withdraw from Lebanon?', *The Middle East Journal*, 56:1, Winter, 72–93.

Tinaoui, Simon Ghazi (1994), 'An Analysis of the Syrian–Lebanese Economic Cooperation Agreements', *The Beirut Review*, 8, Fall, 97–112.

Trendle, Giles (1992), 'Popular Fury Brings down Lebanon's Government', *Middle East International*, 15 May, 3–4.

Trendle, Giles (1996), 'Lebanon's Heavy Price of Allegiance', *The Middle East*, June, 5–7.

Venter, Al J. (1998), 'President Lahoud's Rise to Power', *Middle East Policy*, 6:2, October, 174–182.

Walt, Stephen (1987), *The Origins of Alliances*, Ithaca, NY and London, Cornell University Press.

Waltz, Kenneth N. (1979), *Theory of International Politics*, Reading, MA, Addison–Wesley.

Weinberger, Naomi J. (1986), *Syrian Intervention in Lebanon: The 1975–76 Civil War*, New York and Oxford, Oxford University Press.

Wendt, Alexander (1999), *Social Theory of International Politics*, Cambridge, Cambridge University Press.

Young, Michael (1998), 'Two Faces of Janus: Post-War Lebanon and its Reconstruction', *Middle East Report*, Winter, 4–7 and 44.

Zamir, Meir (1999), 'From Hegemony to Marginalism: The Maronites in Lebanon', in Ofra Bengio and Gabriel Ben-Dor, eds, *Minorities and the State in the Arab World*, Boulder, CO and London, Lynne Rienner Publishers, 111–128.

Ziadeh, Radwan (2011), *Power and Policy in Syria: Intelligence Services, Foreign Relations and Democracy in the Modern Middle East*, London and New York, I.B.Tauris Publishers.

Zisser, Eyal (2000), *Lebanon: The Challenge of Independence*, London and New York, I.B.Tauris Publishers.

Zisser, Eyal (2001), *Asad's Legacy: Syria in Transition*, London, Hurst & Company.

Periodicals

EIU Country Report: Lebanon (London)
The Daily Star (Beirut)
Middle East Economic Digest (London)
Middle East International (London)
Middle East Mirror (London)
Le Monde (Paris)
Al-Nahar (Beirut)

L' Orient Le Jour (Beirut)
Al-Safir (Beirut)
Al-Sharq Al-Awsat (Riyadh)

Information Services

Foreign Broadcast Information Service
BBC Summary of World Broadcasts

INDEX